DIONYSIUS
OF HALICARNASSUS:
ON THUCYDIDES

DIONYSIUS
OF HALICARNASSUS:
ON THUCYDIDES

English translation,
based on the Greek text of Usener-Radermacher

With commentary

by W. KENDRICK PRITCHETT

UNIVERSITY OF CALIFORNIA PRESS

Berkeley / Los Angeles / London

University of California Press
Berkeley and Los Angeles, California

University of California Press, Ltd.
London, England

Copyright © 1975, by
The Regents of the University of California

ISBN 0-520-02922-4
Library of Congress Catalog Card Number: 74-27296
Printed in the United States of America

Ὦ φίλος, εἰ σοφὸς εἶ, λάβε μ᾽ ἐς χέρας· εἰ δέ γε πάμπαν
  νῆϊς ἔφυς Μουσέων, ῥῖψον ἃ μὴ νοέῃς.
εἰμὶ γὰρ οὐ πάντεσσι βατός· παῦροι δ᾽ ἀγάσαντο
  Θουκυδίδην Ὀλόρου, Κεκροπίδην τὸ γένος.

AP 9.583

Ὦ ξένε, εἰ μύθων πολυδαίδαλα ψεύδεα δίζῃ,
  τῶνδ᾽ ἐγὼ οὐδὲν ἔχω· ἐς χέρα μή με λάβε.
Εἰ μαλακοῖς φθόγγοισι τεαὶ χαίρουσιν ἀκουαί,
  οὐδὲν ἐμοὶ καὶ σοί· ἐς χέρα μή με λάβε.
Σύντομον εἰ ῥῆσιν στυγέεις, ξένε, καινοπρερῆ τε,
  πᾶν τε τὸ δυσξύνετον, ἐς χέρα μή με λάβε.
Εἰ δέ σε ἱστορίης παναληθέος ἵμερος αἱρεῖ,
  γράμμα τὸ Θουκυδίδου ἐς χέρα, ξεῖνε, λάβε.
Εἰ σὺ βαρυφθόγγου τέρπῃ σάλπιγγος ἀϋτῇ,
  σαλπίζοντι ἔοικ᾽· ἐς χέρα, ξεῖνε, λάβε.
Σύντομον εἰ φιλέεις λόγου ἀτραπὸν ἠδ᾽ ἀπάτητον,
  κἄν που ἔῃ χαλεπή, ἐς χέρα, ξεῖνε, λάβε.

Epigram of H. Stephanus

CONTENTS

BIBLIOGRAPHY OF SHORT TITLES

Bibliography of the *De Thucydide* is given at the end of the volume, in a separate appendix. References to the two-volume edition of the rhetorical works of Dionysius (*Dionysii Halicarnassei quae exstant*, vols. 5 [Leipzig 1899] and 6 [1904], reprinted in 1965) by H. Usener and L. Radermacher are given by chapters, pages and lines of the separate treatises. References to periodicals follow the system of Marouzeau. Abbreviations of titles of ancient works are those of Liddell and Scott.

Bonner, *LTDH*	S.F. Bonner, *The Literary Treatises of Dionysius of Halicarnassus* (Cambridge 1939).
Ernesti, *Lexicon*	J.C.T. Ernesti, *Lexicon Technologiae Graecorum Rhetoricae* (Leipzig 1795, reprinted 1962).
Jacoby, *FGH*	F. Jacoby, *Die Fragmente der griechischen Historiker* (Berlin 1923-1930, Leiden 1940–).
Geigenmüller *Quaestiones*	P. Geigenmüller, *Quaestiones Dionysianae de vocabulis artis criticae* (Diss. Leipzig 1908).
Grube, *GCDS*	G.M.A. Grube, *A Greek Critic: Demetrius on Style* (Toronto 1961).
——, *GRC*	*The Greek and Roman Critics* (London 1965).
HCT	A.W. Gomme, A. Andrewes, and K.J. Dover, *A Historical Commentary on Thucydides*, vols. 1-4 (Oxford 1945-1970).
Luschnat, *Thukydides*	Pauly-Wissowa, *Real-Encyclopädie*, Supplement-Band 12 (1970), cols. 1085-1354.
Roberts, *DHLC*	W.R. Roberts, *Dionysius of Halicarnassus on Literary Composition* (London 1910).
——, *DHTLL*	*Dionysius of Halicarnassus, The Three Literary Letters* (Cambridge 1901).
——, *DS*	*Demetrius on Style* (Cambridge 1902).
——, *LS*	*Longinus on the Sublime* (Cambridge 1899).
RE	*Real-Encyclopädie der classischen Altertumswissenschaft.*

Ros, *Metabole*   J.G.A. Ros, *Die Metabole (Variatio) als Stilprinzip des Thukydides* (Paderborn 1938, reprinted Amsterdam 1969).

Russell, *ALC*   D.A. Russell and M. Winterbottom, *Ancient Literary Criticism* (Oxford 1972).

van Hook, *Terminology*   L. van Hook, *The Metaphorical Terminology of Greek Rhetoric and Literary Criticism* (Diss. Chicago 1905).

von Fritz, *DGG*   K. von Fritz, *Die griechische Geschichtsschreibung* vol. 1, Text- und Anmerkungsband (Berlin 1967).

INTRODUCTION

INTRODUCTION

In teaching courses in Thucydides for over twenty-five years, I have found that students benefited greatly by being schooled in Dionysius' observations on the syntax and style of Thucydides. In the commentary, accordingly, I have presented an inventory of modern scholarship on Dionysius' comments, adding appropriate illustrations from the Thucydidean text. One may recall a truism, "He who does not know the syntax of Thukydides does not know the mind of Thukydides" (B.L. Gildersleeve, *AJP* 28 [1907] 356). Or in the dictum of Buffon, "Le style est l'homme même." I fancy that I might do some slight service by attempting to document Dionysius' criticisms and elucidations of the *History of the Peloponnesian War*.

In the early part of his Preface to *The History of Sicily* 1 (Oxford 1891), E.A. Freeman says:

From the most obscure *Abhandlung* or *Programm* or *Dissertation* we are sure to learn something. There is sure to be some fact, some reference, some way of putting something, which one is glad to come across. The pity is that there is no way of marking outside on which page the precious morsel is to be found. And no man can undertake to find out every pamphlet and every article. And, when one has found what is wanted, it is sometimes forbidden to buy the number that one wants, unless one chooses to buy a whole volume that one does not want. Yet the Englishman is sure to be found fault with if he misses the smallest scrap of the whole "Litteratur" of any matter. In this our High-Dutch friends are sometimes a little unreasonable.

Unreasonable or not, an imperative obligation in this bibliography-mad learned world when sending out an edition of an ancient classic is to attempt to refer to all that has been written. Now the literature on Dionysius is very scattered. Moreover, modern Καρίωνες (κλεπτίστατοι: Aristophanes *Plutus* 27) have made such raids on university libraries that some volumes are quite unprocurable. I have tried to give references to all studies which illuminate Dionysius' treatment of Thucydides. The result may seem like a clothes-tree on which are hung syntactical analyses and stylistic disquisitions; but the reader can help himself to those studies he wishes to pursue. I doubt that the men who used Greek as their native tongue were guilty of all the subtleties attributed to them; but the trouble is that what is illuminating to one is not illuminating to another. Of many dissertations I have made brief abstracts. In a few cases, suggestions have been offered for new lines of research. Of course the ideal of reading everything ever written on a subject is a vain one. Nine centuries ago, when the happy Benedict of Clusa could boast in 1028, "I have two large houses filled with books...There is not in the whole earth a book that I have not read", such an ambition was feasible; today it is often fantastic, tomorrow it will become even more so.

The coincidence of two translations into English of a work hitherto

never translated was not anticipated. The announcement of S. Usher's
Loeb edition appeared after this manuscript had been completed and had
been typed for photographic reproduction.

METAPHORICAL VOCABULARY OF DIONYSIUS

The translation of Dionysius is no light task. The terminology of the
antique rhetoricians presents the student with a formidable array of problems, as may be gathered from the four valuable glossaries which W. Rhys
Roberts has appended to his volumes on Dionysius, Demetrius, and [Longi-
nus]. To a single term, applied to the participle, the σχῆμα περιβλητικόν,
B.L. Gildersleeve (*AJP* 9 [1888] 143-146) devoted several perceptive pages
to show that none of the common equivalents (ausführlich, full, copious,
detailed) answered perfectly.[1] W.G. Rutherford declined to translate ὕψος
by "sublimity" or "elevation" and simply transliterated it, hypsos. When
Dionysius (*De Comp.* 25.133.5-6) speaks of Plato τοὺς ἑαυτοῦ διαλόγους
κτενίζων καὶ βοστρυχίζων, "combing and curling his dialogues," indicating
the elaborate care and attention given them, or when Plutarch (*Mor.* 350d)
refers to Isocrates κολαπτῆρσι καὶ ξυστῆρσι τὰς περιόδους ἀπολεαίνων,
"smoothing down his periods with chisel and file," or Ben Jonson, imitating
the Roman critics, speaks of a "bony and sinewy" style, there is no difficulty in the recognition of such figures. On the other hand, weak and
vague figures are far more numerous, for any expressive word may have
been used with varying shades of meaning before it was employed in literary
criticism. Some of the rhetorical terminology can be traced to the dis-
courses of Isocrates, or, on the philosophical side, to Plato (*Gorgias* and
Phaedrus), to Aristotle (*Rhetoric* and *Poetics*), or to the *Ars Rhetorica ad
Alexandrum* commonly attributed to the rhetor Anaximenes and probably
later than Aristotle. From this point to Dionysius, in the first century B.C.,
we possess little Greek literary criticism.[2] In his works we meet for the
first time a wealth of rhetorical terminology.[3] Figures of speech and comparisons abound. Metaphors are drawn from nature (water, heat and cold,
light and darkness, flowers, weight and size) and human life (man's physical
condition, his participation in war and athletics, youth and sex, social status, the theater, and, in particular, the trades and arts, from which general

---

[1]Cf. the same scholar's comments (*AJP* 30 [1909] 231-232) on the difficulty of
rendering ψυχρότης and ψυχρόν.

[2]The works of four great critics are lost: Demetrius of Phalerum, Hegesius,
Hermagoras, and Caecilius.

[3]L. Radermacher (*RM* 54 [1899] 373) writes that Dionysius "schreibt aber kein
attisches Griechisch." Photius (*Bibl.* 83 p. 65A) describes him as τὴν φράσιν καὶ λέξιν
καινοπρεπής. M. Egger (*Denys D'Halicarnasse* [Paris 1902] 245) says that his dialect is
the κοινή. J.F. Lockwood (*CQ* 31 [1937] 192 n. 5) reported that there are one hundred words appearing first in the rhetorical works of Dionysius and about fifty found
only in him.

field probably the largest number of comparisons are borrowed). The more obvious and conscious metaphorical terminology has been studied in a valuable Chicago dissertation by Larue van Hook, *The Metaphorical Terminology of Greek Rhetoric and Literary Criticism* (1905). For reasons of economy, my practice has been to place in parenthesis in transliterated form many of the Greek words, and then in the notes to give references to the glossaries of W. Rhys Roberts and to the work of van Hook. I have always had at hand the solid and informative book, J.C.T. Ernesti's *Lexicon Technologiae Graecorum Rhetoricae* (Leipzig 1795, reprinted by Olms in 1962), a work which has not been superseded by R. Volkmann, H. Lausberg, or J. Martin. The notes of A. Greilich (*Dionysius Halicarnassensis quibus potissimum vocabulis ex artibus metaphorice ductis in scriptis rhetoricis usus est* [Diss. Breslau 1886]) and P. Geigenmüller (*Quaestiones Dionysianae de vocabulis artis criticae* [Diss. Leipzig 1908]) on the vocabulary of Dionysius have been consulted; but the problem of translation from the Latin or German is an added hurdle. Indeed, W.G. Rutherford (*CR* 17 [1908] 61-67) directed severe criticism at Roberts' translations because he thought that they were colored too much by Latin equivalents. The promise of J.F. Lockwood (*CQ* 31 [1937] 192 n. 5) to publish a complete lexicon of the vocabulary of ancient criticism has to the best of my knowledge never been fulfilled.

That translation must always be ultimately unsatisfactory is obvious. In a translation are involved such difficult points as those of taste, of ambiguities in the original, and the inadequacy of all attempts to render those words which are meant to be significant and informing to Greeks alone. Dionysius included long passages from Thucydides. Modern translations of this difficult author pass the steamroller over the rough places so thoroughly as to remove all traces of their original ruggedness. Since this work is written for the "studious youth," not the rhetorical specialist, I have adopted a practice which I find from my long teaching of Thucydides that students appreciate the most, the practice of K.J. Dover in his school editions of Books VI and VII, with a literal translation and the use of angular brackets to supply words or phrases necessary to complete the meaning.

TEXT OF DIONYSIUS' *DE THUCYDIDE*

Usener-Radermacher collated two fifteenth-century manuscripts containing the text of the *De Thuc.*: (1) M = Ambrosianus D119 and (2) P = Vatic. Palatinus gr. 58.[1] Usener in his introduction to the Teubner text regards these MSS. as derived from a rhetorical *Sylloge* (S) now lost. M is said to have scholia to which reference is occasionally made in Krüger's 1823 edition, and even more infrequently in the apparatus of Usener-Radermacher.

---

[1] H. Schenkl (*RM* 2 [1880] 26) lists eight other MSS., dating from the late fifteenth through the seventeenth centuries, which apparently have no independent value. Variant readings for the text of *De Thuc.* are collected in L. Sadée, *De Dionysii Halicarnassensis scriptis rhetoricis quaestiones criticae* (Diss. Strassburg 1878) 123-171.

Nine folia (nos. 66-74) were left blank in the interval between 365.6 and 365.7 of chap. 25, according to the Us.-Rad. pagination. This gap was in the archetype of MP. The Vatican codex is reported by Usener as written by a very negligent hand presumably on the dictation of a person who was not Greek. The text is in unusual disorder: a passage containing the text of 328.24-330.22 was placed after 332.19, and another passage with 340.14-342.16 after 344.21. According to the text of the Teubner editors, there are fourteen major lacunae, all of which have been recognized since the edition of Krüger. Some, as in chap. 13, must be of considerable length. In other cases, one suspects that words have dropped out.[1] The words *hiatum indicavi* or *lacunam indicavi* are a constantly recurring feature of the Teubner critical notes. Misspellings, incorrect declensions and parts of speech, wrong case-endings, etc., are common. Iota subscript was almost never written. Words omitted in one of the MSS. are sometimes found in the other.

In the *De Thuc.* sixty-nine passages are quoted from Thucydides. The majority come from speeches, and this fact may help to explain the absence of any quotation from Book VIII. Books I (14 citations), II (16), and V (14) are the most frequently quoted, although the passage which receives by far the most detailed treatment is Thucydides' account of stasis at Corcyra in III.81-83. Serious discrepancies between the text of Thucydidean passages as given by Dionysius and as found in our manu-scripts of Thucydides have been indicated in the commentary. The MSS. of Dionysius were of course subject to the same types of corruption as those of Thucydides. Or, as A.W. Gomme (*HCT* 2.133) succinctly puts it, "the MSS. of Dionysios are no better evidence of what he wrote than those of Thucydides for him." The passage in Thucydides VII.20.2 is a case in point. Both E and the MSS. of Dionysius (chap. 26) insert a καί after δέ, whereas J.E. Powell (*CR* 52 [1938] 4) has shown that they have no other affinity. Byzantine scribes, Powell explains, have a tendency to insert καί in such places. Moreover, by comparing passages which are twice quoted by Dionysius, it can be established that Dionysius sometimes cited hastily and from memory.[2] That Dionysius was lax in quotation can be shown by

---

[1] For lost leaves from the codex of the treatise *On the Sublime*, see D.A. Russell, *'Longinus' on the Sublime* (Oxford 1964) xlix-l.

[2] As to the common practice of quotation from memory, E.M. Cope (*Rhetoric of Aristotle* 3 [Cambridge 1877] 48 n. 1) has written about Aristotle a statement which has general application: "I think that nothing more can fairly be inferred from cases like this than that Aristotle has misquoted the *words* of our present version: all the sub-stance is there. As we have already so many times had occasion to notice, Ar. has here quoted from memory; and like all other men of very extensive reading and very reten-tive memory, Bacon for example, and Walter Scott, has trusted too much to his memo-ry, not referred to his author, and consequently misquoted. And I think that is all that can be reasonably said about it." H.V. Appel (*Literary Quotation and Allusion* [Diss. Columbia 1935]) observes that Demetrius often quoted the same passage of Thucydides with slightly differing words (p. 36) and that the ancient practice was to quote from memory (p. 109) when strict accuracy was unnecessary.

comparing his extracts in chap. 26 of the *De Thuc.* with the same passages
in the *Ep. II ad Amm.* 2-6. In both cases he professes to be reproducing
word for word (κατὰ λέξιν). Textual reproduction did not preclude occasional omissions and additions, as well as minute variations in word order.[1]
The inconvenience in consulting papyrus rolls may account for part of the
difficulty. It is noteworthy that in the lengthy quotations, Dionysius' text
usually agrees exactly with the text established by modern editors from the
Thucydidean manuscripts.[2] The difficulties arise in the quotations of words
and phrases.[3] This disparity between the long and short quotations suggests
that Dionysius consulted his text of Thucydides for the lengthy passages,
but otherwise relied on his memory.

H. Stuart Jones in the introduction to the Oxford edition of Thucydides enunciated the critical principle which he applied to the quotations of
Dionysius as follows: *"Testimonia scriptorum antiquorum, et praecipue
Dionysii Halicarnassensis, ut in codicum varietate aliquantum ponderis
habent, ita raro contra codicum auctoritatem valent."* Even so W.R.
Roberts ("Dionysius of Halicarnassus as an Authority for the Text of Thucydides," *CR* 14 [1900] 244-246) has defended the readings of Dionysius
in selected passages. M. Pehle, in a generally overlooked Berlin dissertation
(*Thucydidis exemplar Dionysianum cum nostrorum codicum memoria confertur* [1907]), presents in parallel columns the text of Dionysius and that
of Thucydides. The author groups the texts quoted by Dionysius according
to whether they agree or disagree with the Florence MS. C or the Vatican
MS. B.[4] He concludes (p. 55) that the text used by Dionysius was much
more correct than any of our codices.[5] Pehle also collects (20-24) a group

---

[1] L. Radermacher (*Philol.* 59 [1900] 177-183) has shown that in the *De Dem.*
Dionysius was quoting from an abbreviated text, whereas in the *De Thuc.* his method
of citation of brief passages from Demosthenes is from memory.

[2] A.E. Douglas, *Cicero's Brutus* (Oxford 1966) xxxviii, observes that Dionysius
is exceptional in his use of long quotations. Since orations were accessible in his day,
Cicero in the *Brutus*, for example, does not give a single direct quotation from any
Roman orator.

[3] S.F. Bonner (*Roman Declamation* [Berkeley 1949] 135) has interesting comments on quotations in Roman authors, particularly one attributed to Thucydides by
Livy, Seneca, and Arellius Fuscus which does not appear in our Thucydidean text.
Words attributed to Thucydides by lexicographers, but not found in the received text,
are collected by C. Hude in Appendix 3 of his *editio maior* (Leipzig 1901). As noted
occasionally in the commentary, words found only in Dionysius are not included in
Hude's testimonia.

[4] As to the Thucydidean Vatican manuscript B, which frequently exhibits an
order of words peculiar to it, Roberts (*DHLC* 341) offers the suggestion that the order
is due to a reviser's deliberate effort after greater lucidity. L. Sadée (*Dissertationes
philologicae argentoratenses* 2 [1879] 140) maintains that Dionysius was using a manuscript related closely to an ancestor of BC.

[5] A. Kleinlogel, *Geschichte des Thukydidestextes im Mittelalter* (Berlin 1965)
161, finds that Dionysius' text has an affinity for Λ, the archetype of ABEFM.

of passages where he believes it safe to conclude that the discrepancies in Dionysius' text can be attributed to later scribes. Finally, in a brief but provocative article, J.E. Powell ("The Archetype of Thucydides," *CQ* 32 [1938] 75-79) has concluded that the citations in Dionysius "on the whole agree with the results obtained from a study of the papyri." Moreover, Powell notes that there are twenty-six places where the Oxford apparatus for Thucydides records the agreement of Dionysius either with one of the two families against the other, or with B^2 against the rest, and concludes that in eighteen of these the reading of Dionysius is obviously right, or at least as probable as the other.[1] Not to be overlooked is the fact that there are complete sentences and even paragraphs where very few variants appear. The subject is one deserving of further study.[2]

I have noted in the commentary to each Thucydidean passage quoted by Dionysius any variants from the received texts, together with the preferences of modern editors. It is a rather striking fact that there are few variants which do not find some support from one or more of the able editors Thucydides has had in modern times. Even when Dionysius has not been followed (see on chap. 26.8), I am not at all sure that his readings should be rejected outright.

DIONYSIUS AS A LITERARY HISTORIAN

One of my reasons for undertaking the commentary was to assess the value of Dionysius as a literary historian, and more specifically, his judgment on early prose writers as expressed in his chapter 5 and the conflicting modern evaluations of this chapter, as exemplified in the writings of Felix Jacoby, on the one hand,[3] and Truesdell S. Brown, on the other.

There were classified lists (πίνακες) of authors in the Pergamene Library, as at Alexandria,[4] in which the leading writers of prose, especially the orators, had a prominent place. Dionysius mentions his consultation of such a list in connection with a speech of Dinarchus[5] and also states that

---

[1] The texts of many of the quoted Thucydidean passages are discussed in the appendix to G. Pavano's edition of the *De Thucydide*, but without reference to English scholarship in the field. G. Grossmann (*Politische Schlagwörter aus der Zeit des Peloponnesischen Krieges* [Diss. Basel 1950] 35 n. 23) has a passage defending Dionysius' text of VIII.64.5 against AEFGM.

[2] In presenting interesting emendations to Book VIII, U. von Wilamowitz-Möllendorff (*Hermes* 43 [1908] 613) made the observation that Thucydides suffers from conservative criticism ("Thukydides leidet nun einmal am meisten unter des konservativen Kritik").

[3] Cf. K.J. Dover, "Thucydides" (*G&R Survey* No. 7 [1973]) 9: "Dionysius does not command respect as a historian or as a critic of historiography."

[4] See F. Schmidt, "Die Pinakes des Kallimachos" (*Klassisch-Philog. Studien* 1 [1922. Berlin]), and Regenbogen, *RE* s.v. Pinax (1950) 1424.

[5] *De Din.* 11 (1.317.4).

he found no detailed account of that orator written by Callimachus, the second director of the library at Alexandria.[1] In his list of the genuine speeches of Dinarchus (*De Din.* 10: 1.311.21), after the title *Against Theocrines*, he adds, "Callimachus enters this among the speeches of Demosthenes." As J.E. Sandys remarks,[2] the evidence of the *De Din.* is enough to show that he was "equally prepared to find what he wanted in the lists of the Alexandrian as in those of the Pergamene school."[3] Part of a lost work by Demetrius of Magnesia having the character of literary history was quoted and criticized by Dionysius.[4] In the first chapter of his tenth book, Quintilian suggests a course of reading suitable for the future orator, including Greek and Latin classics arranged under the heads of poetry, drama, history, oratory, and philosophy. He admits that he is giving the criticisms of another. Sandys remarks that "it is practically impossible to dispute Quintilian's indebtedness" to Dionysius.[5]

The depth of his study and wide research may be illustrated in the *Ep. I ad Amm.*, where he sets out to refute the theses that the *Rhetoric* of Aristotle was earlier than the speeches of Demosthenes and that Demosthenes owed his success to the observance of its precepts. Dionysius is betrayed into overstatement, and his order of the *Olynthiacs* is open to grave dispute; but the essay, short as it is, is one of the cornerstones for the study of the chronology of Demosthenes' speeches.[6] Dionysius proves from

---

[1] *De Din.* 1. This tract is an excellent specimen of Dionysius' literary criticism. He begins by saying how little accurate information could be had about the orator, since neither Callimachus nor the Pergamene grammarians knew anything clearly about him. He sketches the orator's life, chiefly from his own words in a speech against Proxenus, then compares the facts he has gleaned with the Histories of Philochorus on the contemporary events. From these materials he determines his approximate age, and thus establishes a canon for rejecting all speeches bearing internal evidence of being composed before the orator was twenty-five or during his exile to Chalcis (307-292 B.C.). The spurious speeches are separated out into those too early for the orator, those composed during his exile, and lastly those too watery or frigid in style. Dionysius, of course, did not have at his disposal the more refined stylometric techniques available to the modern critic.

[2] *History of Classical Scholarship* 1[2] (Cambridge 1906) 158.

[3] In *De Thuc.* 51.410.17, Dionysius refers to γραμματικαὶ ἐξηγήσεις , which Luschnat (*Philol.* 98 [1954] 22-25) has shown were Alexandrian commentaries (ὑπομνήματα) on Thucydides. Indeed, Luschnat has noted (20, n. 1) phrases in Dionysius which he believes derive from the ὑπομνήματα .

[4] *De Din.* 1.

[5] *Op. cit.* 1[2].206.

[6] See, for example, A. Schäfer, *Demosthenes und seine Zeit* 2[2] (Leipzig 1886) 67ff. Dionysius rejected many speeches on the ground of style, and also of historical inaccuracy. He accepted as genuine twenty-two public, and twenty-four private, orations. Schäfer, following investigations similar to those of Dionysius, reduced the number to twenty-nine. Dionysius' judgment on the score of style was doubtless far keener than ours, and it seems to me that when he, who had his attention closely fixed on style, allows a work to pass unchallenged, and even quotes from it, the strongest arguments are required to convince us on the grounds of stylistic defects that it is spurious.

the reference to the Olynthian War in *Rhet.* 3.10.1411a.7 that Aristotle's
work is later than 349 B.C.; his evidence for the dating of the war is drawn
from Philochorus.[1]

W. Jaeger in *Demosthenes* (Berkeley 1938) 115-116 comments:

The rhetor Dionysius of Halicarnassus, to whom we owe this date, gets
much of his chronological material from good sources; these, however, do
not give him the dates of his speeches, but only the time of the events
which he regards as having provoked them. Unfortunately he has gone too
far in linking the speeches with the most definite historical situations. It is
no longer possible to ascertain exactly what prompted each individual
speech; and so Dionysius' efforts to date them, which are the sole basis of
our chronology, often leave us on uncertain ground.

Dionysius realized that a knowledge of dates was necessary to establish the authenticity of speeches and for this reason he published a list of
Athenian fourth-century archons.[2] His list to the number of seventy names
forms the backbone of Athenian chronology and is indispensable to students
of the calendar. Its accuracy, with due allowance for errors of orthography
in transmission, has been sustained time and again.[3] A good example of the
application of the chronological test may be quoted from the *De Din.* 13,
where the conclusion, "Dinarchus was not ten years old at the time" is noteworthy. He quotes several important passages from the historian Philochorus[4]
and was sufficiently familiar with the historical writings of Ephorus and
Theopompus to characterize their style.[5] In *De Din.* 2 (1.299.14), he refers

---

[1] *Ep. I ad Amm.* ch. 9.

[2] *De Din.* 9. M.J. Lossau, "Untersuchungen zur antiken Demosthenesexegese,"
Palingenesia 2 (1964) 68-75, discusses the three criteria used by Dionysius for testing
authenticity under the headings, chronology, style, and technique. See also M. Untersteiner, *AFC* 7.1 (1959) 72-93. Why Lossau follows Jacoby in ascribing Dionysius'
source for the archons to Philochorus is not clear. Archon lists were inscribed on stone
in Athens (Meritt, *Hesperia* 8 [1939]60) and were known at Alexandria (E.G. Turner,
Greek Papyri [Oxford 1968]104). The picture of Alexandrian scholarship set forth by
Turner differs markedly from that to be inferred from the writings of Jacoby.

[3] Dionysius used the *Chronicles* of Eratosthenes, which constituted the first sci-
entific attempt to fix the dates of literary history, and in *AR* 1.74.2, he refers both to
Eratosthenes and to a chronological treatise of his own, now lost, which is cited by
Clement of Alexandria (*Strom.* 1.102) under the title of Χρόνοι.

[4] *Ep. I ad Amm.* 9.

[5] *De Comp.* 22. After the discovery of the Oxyrhynchus historian, W.R. Roberts
(*CR* 22 [1908] 118-122) expounded the view that Theopompus could hardly be the
author of the new historical fragments. The interesting feature of the article, which is
based on Dionysius' treatment of Theopompus, is the proof it affords that Dionysius
was thoroughly familiar with the diverse treatises of the historian. G. Kaibel (*Hermes*
20 [1885] 497-513) has argued that it was the school founded by Isocrates and continued by Ephorus, Theopompus, and others, rather than Plato or Thucydides, which
was the model and ideal of Dionysius in his historical writings. A. von Mess (*RM* 70
[1915] 337-357), in a detailed study of the work of Theopompus, maintains that Dionysius presents a graphic account and a just appreciation of the historian.

to his own efforts to discover the facts in the life of that orator: ἃ οὖν
ἐγὼ αὐτὸς δι᾽ ἐμαυτοῦ κατελαβόμην, ταῦτ᾽ ἐστίν. In *De Isaeo* 1 (1.93.13-
16), he tells that he explored the book of Hermippus, the disciple of Callimachus, on the pupils of Isocrates (Περὶ τῶν Ἰσοκράτους μαθητῶν), but
had discovered only two facts about Isaeus.

Although Prof. K.J. Dover (*Lysias and the Corpus Lysiacum* [Berkeley
1968]) has athetized the entire surviving corpus of Lysias with the exception of the twelfth oration, he has drawn the conclusion (p. 23) that Dionysius was working with a corpus of speeches known to Callimachus of the
Alexandrian school. Dionysius knew that the inclusion of a speech was not
a guarantee of authenticity and that it was up to him to do the job from
the beginning. His determining principle was χάρις, in effect the *Gefühl* of
someone who knew his Greek and his author well.[1] The corpus included
four hundred and twenty-five speeches and Dionysius concluded that no
fewer than two hundred juridical orations were the work of Lysias.

The only surviving hypotheses to Lysias are excerpts from Dionysius.
The part which we have preserved of the speech *Against Diogeiton* (32) is
found in Dionysius who quotes the speech with two other pieces and adds
comments after each rhetorical subdivision. Unfortunately, he does not give
the last part of the proof or the epilogue. In discussing the genuineness of
the *Trapeziticus*, he quotes the opinions of Isokrates' adopted son Aphareus
and of Kephisodorus, "a most devoted listener to Isocrates."[2] Dionysius
quotes an extract from Thrasymachus the Chalcedonian (*De Isaeo* 20) by
which he illustrates the character of his style, of which L. Spengel (*Artium
scriptores* [Stuttgart 1828] 95) says that Dionysius' encomium is justified
by the excellence, though the passage is very corrupt. Dionysius affirms
that Thrasymachus confined himself to technical treatises and the composition of declamations for use in his school. A genuine fragment of a funeral
oration of Gorgias has been preserved by one of the scholiasts on Hermogenes as copied from one of the lost works of Dionysius and is quoted in
H. Diels, *Fragmente der Vorsokratiker* 2⁷ no. 6.

Something of the extent of the accumulated mass of Greek literature
which Dionysius had before him can be gleaned from the following comment of S.F. Bonner (*LTDH* 14-15):

He had the advantage of being able to examine the lists of "canons" of the
Alexandrian or Pergamene scholars who had preceded him. It is noteworthy,
however, that Dionysius did not always accept the opinion of others; for he

---

[1] Dionysius explains his criticism in *De Lys.* 11-12. It was not hiatus, as some
have inferred. This is to confuse Dionysius with G.E. Benseler (*De hiatu in oratoribus
Atticis et historicis libri duo* [Freiberg 1841]). Although Dionysius is regarded as a
pedantic teacher of rhetoric, in the end impressionism wins the day. Lysias, for instance, he tells us, has all the virtues of style, purity of diction, clearness, conciseness,
vividness. The arrangement of his narrative is faultless. But after all his analysis, Dionysius is forced to declare that in a question of genuineness he has to rest his judgment
on an indefinable χάρις, which in the case of Demosthenes becomes a more untrans-
latable αὐτάρκης χάρις.

[2] *De Isoc.* 18.

pays no attention whatever to the canon of the orators, employed by Caec-
ilius as the basis of his work on the orators, but makes his own selection.
The chief authors upon whose work he makes some critical comment are as
follows: Homer, Hesiod, Antimachus, Panyasis, Simonides, Stesichorus,
Sappho, Alcaeus, Pindar, Aeschylus, Sophocles, Euripides, Menander; Hero-
dotus, Thucydides, Philistus, Xenophon, Theopompus; Gorgias, Thrasymachus,
Lysias, Isocrates, Isaeus, Demosthenes, Aeschines, Hyperides, Lycurgus, and
Dinarchus.[1]

Of the minor historians of the third and second centuries B.C., he
mentions Antigonus, Demetrius of Callatis, Duris, Hegesianax, Heracleides,
Hieronymus and Psaon. He cites a large number of fragments of verse, including two in chap. 9, which can only be referred to some lyric poet or to
the lyric portions of some tragic poet.

Dionysius was clearly one of the leading literary historians of his day,
a role, incidentally, which seems to have suited him far better than that of
the general historian. As a Professor of Classics,[2] with a complete mastery
of Greek and a wide acquaintance with the Greek classics, at the same time
enjoying a privileged life with apparent ease of movement and communication,[3] he had available a great amount of classical prose literature now lost.
To attempt to cast Dionysius in the role of one who says that he consulted
works which were actually unavailable to him, or to follow Jacoby in attrib-
uting to him the error of mistaking an historical treatise of the fifth century
for a "pseudepigraphon" of the third,[4] runs counter to what we know of
his authority as a literary historian. Furthermore, in matters of style it
seems perverse to challenge Dionysius' view that Thucydides was idiosyncratic
and obscure, with an economy of expression and variety of form which did
not commend themselves to other prose writers. Dionysius was a man of
remarkable industry, who read extensively in his sources.

DIONYSIUS AS A LITERARY CRITIC IN THE *DE THUCYDIDE*

Modern estimates of Dionysius' place in literary criticism vary.
To start with the adverse opinions, G.L. Hendrickson (*CP* 5 [1910]
372) takes exception to Rhys Roberts' "enthusiastic proclamation of his
critical merits" as follows:

---

[1]Plutarch (*Antony* 58) told the story that Cleopatra was presented with 200,000
volumes from the Pergamene libraries; cf. R. Pfeiffer, *History of Classical Scholarship*
(Oxford 1968) 236.

[2]See G.P. Goold, *TAPA* 92 (1961) 190.

[3]A. Momigliano, *The Development of Greek Biography* (Cambridge, Mass. 1971)
99, comments on the great concern which the Romans had for biography at the time
of Dionysius' arrival in Rome about 30 B.C. In *De Dem.* 53.244.20, Dionysius refers
to biographies of Demosthenes including one written by Demetrius of Phalerum.

[4]*FGH* 330, Text pp. 598-599; Notes pp. 487-490.

Dionysius possessed a receptive mind and a graceful but garrulous pen. He was a perfect product of that new rhetoric to which (like Cicero) he gives the fair name of "political philosophy." He was well read in a large mass of rhetorical and aesthetical criticism and, for his immediate purposes in this work <the *De Comp.*>, had turned over a good deal of more technical matter relating to the aesthetics of sound in music and in verse. He has preserved for us priceless material, and it is not easy to say what is his own and what he has derived from his betters. But side by side with so much that is admirable are to be found such fatuity, such unhistorical scholasticism, such naïveté as must place him in a class far below his nearest contemporaries in the same field of writing, Cicero, Horace, and the writer *On the Sublime*.

A. Parry (*Yale French Studies* 45 [1970] 5) writes as follows:

Dionysus (*sic*) writing from a strict school-rhetorician's point of view, and condemning Thucydides accordingly, is rather like Bentley criticizing Milton from the point of view of a stricter, and tamer, standard of English than Milton's own. And he is valuable as a critic in the same way as Bentley: what he is least capable of understanding is likely to be most characteristically Thucydidean.

B. Jowett (*Thucydides* 1 [Oxford 1881] xviii) says:

The treatise of Dionysius on the style of Thucydides, except in so far as it confirms the text in a multitude of passages, adds nothing to our knowledge of the book; but it throws a striking light on the narrow and feeble intelligence of the Graeco-Roman rhetorician and historian of the first century B.C., and of the world for which he wrote.

G. Saintsbury, *History of Criticism* 1 (2nd ed., New York 1902) 136-137, by contrast, takes an entirely different view of Dionysius:

Yet on the whole, it need not interfere with the emphatic repetition of the opinion, with the expression of which this notice of the Halicarnassian began, that he is a very considerable critic and one to whom justice has not usually, if at all, yet been done. Great as is the place which he gives to oratory, there is no ancient writer (except Longinus) who seems so free from the intention to allow it any really mischievous primacy. If he is, as might be expected from a teacher, sometimes a little meticulous in his philology and lower Rhetoric, yet this very attention to detail saves him from the distinctly unfortunate and rather unphilosophical superciliousness of Aristotle towards style, and from the equally unfortunate divagation, both of that great man and of all his followers, into questions vaguely aesthetic instead of questions definitely literary. The error which, at the new birth of criticism in Europe, was so lucklessly reintroduced and exaggerated by the Italian critics of the sixteenth century—the error of wool-gathering after abstract questions of the nature and justification of poetry, of the *a priori* rules suitable for poetic forms, of Unities, and so forth—meets very little encouragement from Dionysius, and it is perhaps for this very reason that he has been slighted by high-flying aestheticians. Not thus will the wiser mind judge him, but as a critic who saw far, and for the most part truly, into the proper province of literary criticism—that is to say, the reasonable enjoyment of literary work and the reasonable distribution of that work

into good, not so good, and bad. Here, and not in the Laputan *meteroso-
phia* of theories of poetry, is criticism's main work; not that she may not
justly imp her wings for a higher flight now and then, but that she must beware of flapping them in the inane.

B.L. Gildersleeve (*AJP* 31 [1910] 236) reminds us that Dionysius was
the heir of precious traditions, not to be cast aside lightly in favor of an
impressionistic aesthetic:

What if the best of Dionysios goes back to Theophrastos? That only en-
hances his value. For the stylistic study of the orators, Dionysios is simply
indispensable and his criticisms of Thukydides and Plato are interesting
problems of taste. Barring his lack of sympathy, which, to be sure, means
everything, he is nearer right in his judgment of Thukydides than some
modern Thukydidean scholars who have failed to appreciate the conscious-
ness of his art and its subtlety. The architecture of Greek style has not
many Penroses. As a critic of Plato Dionysios' disqualification is largely due
to his lack of a sense of humour. But unfortunately, Plato's humour is
divine and being divine, it hides itself. Who can say that he knows all the
secrets of Plato's tabernacle? True, Wilamowitz calls Dionysios "ein be-
schränkter Rhetor" and I will not undertake to defend the applied rhetoric
of the Ἀρχαιολογία, but the same mordant critic says, *Kultur der Gegen-
wart*, S. 148 "Es ist ein hohes Lob, dass er im Grunde dieselbe stilistische
Überzeugung vertritt wie Cicero, und wir sind ihm für die Erhaltung von
ungemein viel Wichtigem zu Dank verpflichtet; seine Schriften über die
attischen Redner und über die Wortfügung sind auch eine nicht nur belehr-
ende, sondern gefällige Lektüre." The broader sympathies of the author of
the περὶ ὕψους have won for him more admirers than Dionysios can claim
and yet there are stretches in Dionysios that have all the charm of the best
critical appreciation; especially where, not content with minute analysis, he
passes over to what has been happily called "plastic criticism" and now in
metaphor, now in simile, reproduces the feeling of the style he has labori-
ously analyzed. The process is akin to that of the Platonic myth.

No less a student of Greek style than F. Blass, *Die attische Beredsamkeit* 1^2 (Leipzig 1887) 208, writes:

Immerhin müssen seine Ausführungen wenigstens in Bezug auf Form und
Ausdruck die Grundlage auch unsres Urtheils bilden; denn er zeigt auch in
ihnen seine ausgezeichnete Gabe, die Eigenthümlichkeiten einer künstler-
ischen Form herauszufühlen und in beredten Worten darzulegen.

The universality of Dionysius' rhetorical rules can be recognized in the
light of the fact that they are rediscovered by almost every generation. When
Ben Jonson tells us, for example, that "for a man to write well, there are
required three necessaries: to read the best authors, observe the best speakers, and much exercise of his own style. In style to consider what ought to
be written, and after what manner, he must first think and excogitate the
matter <εὕρεσις>, then choose his words and examine the weight of either
<λέξις>. Then take care in placing and ranking <τάξις> both matter and
words, that the composition <σύνθεσις> be comely,"[1] we could be reading

---

[1] *Timber or Discoveries* ed. R.S. Walker (Syracuse 1953) 57.

a τέχνη of rhetoric written by Dionysius. The same judgment could be made about the closing remarks of R.L. Stevenson's "On Style in Literature: Its Technical Elements,"[1] "the work of five days in bed," which appeared in the *Contemporary Review* for April, 1885, 560-561: "We may now briefly enumerate the elements of style. We have, peculiar to the prose writer, the task of keeping his phrases large, rhythmical and pleasing to the ear, without ever allowing them to fall into the strictly metrical <ἁρμονία>;... the task of artfully combining <σύνθεσις> the prime elements of language into phrases that shall be musical in the mouth; the task of weaving their argument into a texture of committed phrases and rounded periods <τάξις>; and, again, the task of choosing apt, explicit, and communicative words <λέξις>."[2] The recent book of A. Scaglione, *The Classical Theory of Composition* (Chapel Hill 1972) is designed to show that "the stylistic criteria of sentence structure as first theorized in antiquity ... <were> regularly transmitted through the centuries down to our own day" (p. 3).

Dionysius was of an age that looked back at the classical Greek achievement. The genuine creative impulse was channeled by the practice of imitation. Dionysius' own discussion of the history of literature up to his time is illuminating (Introduction to his treatise *On Ancient Orators*, translation of J.D. Denniston[3]):

We ought to feel very grateful to the times we live in, my dear Ammaeus, for improvement in many studies, and most particularly for the great advance made in political oratory. In the epoch before ours, the old philosophic type of Rhetoric, subject to monstrous ill-treatment, was being destroyed. From the death of Alexander of Macedon she had gradually withered and declined, till in our own day she was almost gone. A new type of Rhetoric had supplanted her, an ill-bred, pretentious Rhetoric of intolerable effrontery, devoid of philosophy and every form of liberal

---

[1]This article of Stevenson's is highly praised by S.H. Butcher, "Greek Literary Criticism," *Harvard Lectures on Greek Subjects* (London 1904) 242, as a "pretty precise modern parallel to the speculations of Dionysius." Butcher prefixes his remarks with the following comment: "The modern world has grown dull to the cadences of prose. We read of Greek and Roman audiences being painfully affected by inharmonious combinations of sound. There is probably no conceivable dissonance which would cause neuralgia to the unfastidious ears of a British audience. English is itself in truth a most difficult language to render musical."

[2]Cf. B.L. Gildersleeve, *JHUCircular* Vol. 5 No. 50 (1886) 106-107: "Now for the study of literature as an art we have everything to learn from the old critics and what our own Sylvester, our own Lanier have re-discovered as to the science of verse is a chapter from antique rhetoric. Mr. Lowell has recently pointed out the great secret of Gray's abiding popularity. That consummate master did not disdain the close analysis of the sensuous effect of sound, and the melody of Coleridge is due in a measure to a conscious though fitful study in the same line. Of late an author, whose charm of style was first appreciated in this country, has written an essay in which he applies phonetic analysis to the works of our great prose writers, and strikes the dominant chord of what seems unconscious music. The essay might have been written in the beginning of the first century as well as the end of the nineteenth, and have been signed Dionysius of Halicarnassus as well as Robert Louis Stevenson."

[3]*Greek Literary Criticism* (London 1924) 150-151.

education. Undetected by the ignorant and deluded mob, this new Rhetoric not only lived in greater wealth and luxury and magnificence than the other, but had actually attached to herself the posts of honour and political importance which should have belonged to her philosophic sister. She was a thoroughly vulgar and disagreeable person, and finally she made Greece resemble the house of a miserable debauchee. Just as in such a house the free-born, respectable wife sits deprived of all power over her possessions, while a giddy lady of pleasure, who is there to ruin the property, claims to rule the whole establishment, terrorising the other and treating her like dirt: so it happened in every city in Greece, and, to crown all, in the educated ones as much as any. The ancient, indigenous Muse of Athens was reduced to a position of insignificance, expelled from her own possessions, while her rival, a parvenue from some Asiatic jail, some Phrygian or Carian or barbarous creature, claimed to administer Hellenic cities, driving the other out of public life. Thus the ignoramus expelled the philosopher, the mad the sane.

However, it is not only of just men that, as Pindar says: "time is the surest saviour," but of arts and studies and all else that is good. Our own day has proved that. Whether the initiative came from some god, or from nature's cycle bringing round the ancient order again, or from an impulse in mankind urging many people in the same direction: whichever it was, the present age has restored to the ancient, sober Rhetoric her former merited repute, and has compelled the new, silly Rhetoric to cease enjoying the fruits of a distinction to which she has no claim, and living luxuriously on the good things of another.

In judging the *De Thuc.*, Dionysius' general outlook upon his subject must always be kept in mind. The critic's aim in studying Thucydides is, in his own words (25.364.15-16): τὴν ὠφέλειαν αὐτῶν τῶν βουλησομένων μιμεῖσθαι τὸν ἄνδρα. His true distinction as a critic is his purity of taste. Laying aside any temptation to follow later and more pretentious writers, he reverts to the real masterpieces of Greek literature. He is eager to restore the great authors to their rightful supremacy. We know that he made a great effort to distinguish their genuine and their spurious works. Practical in his aims, he desired to determine the highest standard achieved by Attic prose and to mould thereby the writing of his Roman pupils. Much has been written about the fact that Dionysius was a harbinger of a classicism tied to Attic models who were mainly notable for him as masters of style. This has been adequately discussed by others, who have demonstrated that "discussion from the Hellenistic age onward was chiefly determined by the rhetorical criterion of appropriateness."[1] Dionysius, however, romanticized τὸ πρέπον in history as he romanticized τὸ πρέπον in style. His sentimental view of Periclean Athens led him to misread history. His criticisms of the appropriateness of the speech given to Pericles (II.60-64) in chapter 43 have to do with decorum: "I do not know how," "words not fit to be spoken," "they, who have had such a humanizing influence". While taking no exception to Thucydides' accuracy and impartiality, he nonetheless saw signs of a biased temperament (διάθεσις πικρὰ καὶ τῇ πατρίδι τῆς φυγῆς μνησικακοῦσα);

---

[1]The quotation is from C.O. Brink, *Horace on Poetry* (Cambridge 1971) 191. πασῶν ἐν λόγοις ἀρετῶν ἡ κυριωτάτη τὸ πρέπον : *Ep. ad Pomp.* 3.240.10.

for instance, all Athenian reverses are recorded with great minuteness of detail, whereas successes are dismissed with the briefest notice. Dionysius' preoccupation with τὸ πρέπον is the direct result of his rhetorical training and it leads to criticisms which are not convincing, such as his argument in the same chapter that Thucydides should not have represented Pericles as defending his policy by reprimanding the citizens in so outspoken a manner but by soothing the anger of the mob. His problems with τὸ πρέπον then, are twofold, and the two strands of style and history are interwoven.

A study without the historical context that shows the relevance in his own time of the author's speaking as he did is a work only half-understood, and to that extent misunderstood. Three passages selected out of many will illustrate the extent to which the practice of rhetoric was cultivated in the Roman world. Persius, who lived in the time of Nero, intimates (1.85-87) that the cultivation of rhetoric in his days had gone so far that a man could not defend himself from a criminal charge without displaying his mastery over the figures of speech. Caligula had established at Lyons a regular contest in Greek and Latin eloquence, in which the defeated candidates were compelled to compose orations in their praise; while those who did the worst were commanded to obliterate their own writings with a sponge or with their own tongues, unless they preferred to be chastised with rods or ducked in the Rhone (Suetonius, *Caligula* 20; cf. Juvenal 1.44). Juvenal (15.110-112), who wrote at the end of the first century, tells us that chairs of education in oratory were found in every province of the empire and that even the distant Thule was speaking of engaging a rhetorician.

Some of the passages which puzzle us the most in Dionysius can perhaps be better understood if we recognize that rhetorical principles propounded for oratory were carried over into history and that Dionysius' own historical writing followed the rules laid down in the *De Thucydide*. Just as in his great historical work called *Roman Antiquities*, Dionysius, interpreting and modifying the old legendary history, suppressed whatever was unfavorable to his hypothesis that the Romans were, after all, not barbarians, but a pure Greek race, so in his rhetorical treatises the historical standards of his day permitted him to make statements which we today consider entirely erroneous. U. von Wilamowitz-Möllendorff, "Die Thukydideslegende," *Hermes* 12 (1877) 326-367, showed that the most varying traditions were current about Thucydides' exile. Apparently Dionysius selected a version according to which Thucydides had spent the whole of the war in Thrace after his banishment and he duly reported this (41.396.11). The modern scholar, on the other hand, works on the principle that he cannot be sure of anything about Thucydides save what he tells us himself.

Dionysius' attitude about history is on a level with that of Plutarch when the latter took as true the famous story, told by Herodotus, that Solon visited Croesus of Lydia. Plutarch (*Solon* 27) knew that the story conflicted with the accepted chronology of Eratosthenes or Apollodorus or some successor; but he judged that the statements of the chronographers were less reliable than the premise that Solon's known character made the story prob-

able. It was a reasonable position for the period.[1] Dionysius did not put
his rhetoric and his history into separate compartments; he is remarkably
consistent. Dionysius composed his own history, the *Roman Antiquities*,
according to patterns of thinking which were natural to a *rhetor* and *gram-
maticus*. This is not to say that Dionysius would ever have suggested that
the historian would have been justified in sacrificing truth,[2] although the
remark that Thucydides sinned against good taste in making his own coun-
trymen responsible for the war, when he might have found other ἀφορμαί,
comes rather near it. At the beginning of the *AR* (1.1.2) he proclaims that
Truth is to be enshrined, and in the *De Thuc.* (2.326.18) he regards nothing
more precious than Truth (τιμιώτερον τῆς ἀληθείας), which he later names
as the high-priestess of history (8.334.15). But the whole tone of his writings leaves the feeling that considerations of what would be appropriate and
impressive were to his mind the most important. In theory, he classed
εὕρεσις above λέξις (*De Thuc.* 34). His estimate of the importance of the
former is brought out at the beginning of the *De Compositione*: "But the
science which guides us to selection of matter, and to judgment in handling
it, is hampered with difficulties for the young; indeed, for beardless strip-
lings, its difficulties are insurmountable. The perfect grasp of things in all
their bearings belongs rather to a matured understanding, and to an age that
is disciplined by grey hairs,—an age whose powers are developed by pro-
longed investigation of discourse and action, and by many experiences of its
own and much sharing in the fortunes of others" (Roberts' tr.). And the
criterion which he applies to his treatment of subject matter (πραγματικὸς
τόπος, chaps. 5-20) is upon occasion openly acknowledged to be that of the
rhetorical manuals (19.353.13-14).

A training in rhetoric might be expected to produce a rhetorical mind.[3]
The encyclic subjects, or liberal arts, did not include history as one of the
seven disciplines.[4] The reason may have been practical. Every member of the

---

[1] E. Auerbach, *Mimesis* (tr. by W.R. Trask, Princeton 1953) 33-40, has perceptive remarks about the rhetorical nature of Tacitean historiography in relation to the
concept of reality.

[2] Cf. B. Walker, *The Annals of Tacitus* (Manchester 1952) 146: "Literary theory was not to blame if an historian failed in accuracy. When the literary critics pre-
scribed 'oratorical writing', they meant simply that the historian should present not so
many bare and disconnected facts, but an ordered whole, artistically composed in outline and in detail."

[3] J.W. Duff's opening sentence of chap. 2 of his *Literary History of Rome in the
Silver Age*[2] (London 1960) reads, "The main clue to the literary qualities of Silver
Latin is to be found in education, and particularly in rhetorical education."

[4] According to H.I. Marrou (*A History of Education in Antiquity* tr. by G. Lamb
[New York 1956] 167), ἱστορίαι ('stories') "meant anything mentioned by the poet—
persons, places, times and events." Cf. p. 280: "This hallowed word *historiae* must
not be misunderstood; it did not mean 'history' in the restricted modern sense of the
word, but, in a very general way, everything 'that was told' in the passage concerned."
A collection of ancient testimonia which would help to define the role of history in
the instruction in the rhetorical and philosophical schools has never been assembled.

Roman upper class wished his son to be able to speak effectively in public; but not many wished them to be able to write history.[1] A theory of historiography was never fully worked out; historical truth was neglected by the *rhetores* to a degree which modern taste would find intolerable.[2] Tacitus (*Dial.* 29) complains that history was ignored in the schools of rhetoric. His complaint is borne out by the elder Seneca, who apologizes to his sons for an historical digression which he makes toward the end of his *Suasoriae* (6. 16.27). It is needless to point out that the convention was almost universally adopted that speeches need not be accurate but were introduced into history as more or less fictitious elements. Indeed, the composing of speeches for given historical occasions was a regular part of the training; and Theon, perhaps a contemporary of Quintilian, reckoned it under "character-drawing." In his *Progymnasmata* (Spengel, *Rh. gr.* 2.115) he judges success according as a historical character is made to deliver speeches "appropriate to himself and to the underlying situation."[3] So when Dionysius turns to an examination of the Melian Dialogue, he begins by asking whether it was "appropriate to the circumstances and befitting the persons who came together" (41.395.18-19). Similarly, when Dionysius expresses censure (*Ep. ad Pomp.* 3) of Thucydides for not introducing more digressions (ἀναπαύσεις) into his work,[4] he is reflecting a widely recognized rhetorical theory that such digressions were desirable in oratory. Indeed, Cicero regarded history

---

P. Scheller's Leipzig dissertation (*De hellenistica historiae conscribendae arte* 1911) is indispensable for information about theories as to how history should be written; but he does not specifically treat this subject. Similarly, we need more light on the problem of historical composition for recitation and for reading aloud. There are several passages in the *De Thuc.* which suggest a vocal and aural nature of ancient literature. See the commentary on chaps. 15.2, 16.7, 24.16, and 31.9. We know that Asinius Pollio may have recited his history of the Civil Wars (Seneca *Controv.* 4. pt. 2), and that his friend Timagenes read aloud his historical writings (Seneca *De ira* 3.23). Pliny (*Ep.* 7.17.3, 9.27) testifies that historians recited their works. The practice would naturally impress on history a rhetorical character. The narrative of the Parthian wars which Lucian (*How to Write History* 14ff.) heard recited gives us a fair measure of the use of rhetoric in his day. W.W. How and J. Wells (*Commentary on Herodotus* 1 [Oxford 1912] 6-7) would trace this practice back to the time of Herodotus.

[1] For bibliography on the rhetorical view of history, see F.H. Colson, *PCA* 14 (1917) 149-173; J.F. D'Alton, *Roman Literary Theory and Criticism* (London 1931) 491-524; B.L. Ullman, *TAPA* 73 (1942) 25-53; V. Paladini, *Latomus* 6 (1947) 329-344; B. Walker, *The Annals of Tacitus* (Manchester 1952) 144-146; A.D. Leeman, *REL* 33 (1955) 183-208. The force of Colson's article is to warn that the really corrupting influence on history of the pedagogy of rhetoric did not appear until the teachings of the *declamatores*. Seneca's *Controversiae* is a collection of the *declamationes* made by celebrated rhetors.

[2] See A. Gwynn, *Roman Education* (Oxford 1926) 171.

[3] F.W. Walbank, *Speeches in Greek Historians* (Third J.L. Myres Memorial Lecture, Oxford n.d. [1967]) 19.

[4] For digressions in Thucydides, see W. Schmid, *Geschichte der griechischen Litt.* 7.1.5 (Munich 1948) 149 and 193.

as in part a store-house of rhetorical illustrations.[1]

Dionysius' judgments on Thucydides, except for passing comments in the *De Compositione* and *De Demosthene*, extend over three treatises, chapters 3 and 4 of the *Letter to Pompeius*, the *De Thucydide*, and the *Second Letter to Ammaeus*. Herodotus, to paraphrase Dionysius in the *Letter to Pompeius*, has the advantage of Thucydides both in his choice of subject and in his ἀρχή. Thucydides is at fault both in the selection of the misfortunes of Greece as an ἀρχή and in Cynossema as a τέλος. In Herodotus we get relief from time to time, in Thucydides we have only μάχη ἐπὶ μάχῃ, παρα-σκευὴ ἐπὶ παρασκευῇ. In the sequence of the narrative, Thucydides keeps close to the chronological order, Herodotus to the natural grouping of events. Thucydides is the more concise, although both are equally vivid (ἐναργεῖς).[2] Thucydides excels in expressing the emotions, but Herodotus is a better delineator of character. Thucydides is the more impressive, Herodotus the more enjoyable; Herodotus is more natural in diction, Thucydides the more intense: in short, the main distinction is that Herodotus' style is ἱλαρός ("radiant"), Thucydides' φοβερός ("awe-inspiring").

In the *De Thucydide*, Dionysius' preoccupation with rhetorical purposes is responsible for some of the more shortsighted criticisms in the essay. This is particularly true in the first half where he treats of τὸ οἰκονομικόν, the arrangement of the material. Thucydides is constantly interrupting his narrative; for example, the siege of Plataeae breaks off short at II.78 and is not resumed until III.20. His chronological method is peculiar to himself; his descriptions fluctuate between pathos and triviality. He is inconsistent; for example, to the victims of a βραχεῖα ἱππομαχία he devotes a lengthy funeral oration, whereas to the memory of those who fell at Pylos he pays no tribute, although that victory brought Sparta on her knees to Athens. In this section, although there are chapters of sustained analysis, he is writing mainly as a rhetorician whose preconceptions concerning διαίρεσις, τάξις, and ἐξεργασία are the direct result of his training and vocation. It has been piquantly observed that Dionysius cruelly expiated any injustice in his judgments on Thucydides by coming before the world as an historian himself.[3] In this matter he falls short of the ideal sketched by Polybius (1.14.4) before him, and after him by Lucian (*How to Write History* 41).

An anonymous literary critic in a papyrus of the first or second cen-

---

[1]See A. Gwynn (*op. cit.* supra p. xxix n. 2) 105.

[2]The words ἐναργής and ἐνάργεια are not used by Dionysius in the *De Thuc.*, although ἐνάργεια was placed first of the "accessory virtues" in the *Ep. ad Pomp.* 3.239. 15. Plutarch *Mor.* 347a writes about the vividness of Thucydides as follows: "The most effective historian is he who, by a vivid representation of emotions and character, makes his narrative like a painting. Assuredly Thucydides is always striving for this vividness (enargeia) in his writing, since it is his desire to make the reader a spectator, as it were, and to produce vividly in the minds of those who peruse his narrative the emotions of amazement and consternation which were experienced by those who beheld them" (trans. of Babbitt). Plutarch gives several examples.

[3]H. Weil, *Denys d'Halicarnasse* (Paris 1879) 6.

tury of our era replied to the criticisms of Dionysius about διαίρεσις and τάξις. The Grenfell-Hunt translation of this fragmentary papyrus is given in Appendix I. The author justly retorts that there was no reason why Thucydides should have chosen to reckon by archons and that the Herodotean method of narrating events according to localities was inapplicable to a history of the Peloponnesian War, for such a system would in fact disturb the narrative far more than Thucydides' division into the seasons of the year. As to Dionysius' criticisms directed against the τάξις, the author points out that Thucydides was under no obligation to give an elaborate account of events preceding the Peloponnesian War. Here the text breaks off.

When Dionysius in the second half of the essay turns to the λεκτικὸς τόπος, he produces a more thorough investigation of an author's style than in any other extant treatise. He credits Thucydides with the choice of an archaic and figurative style, which he regards as inappropriate to the dignity of history. Most characteristic of him is his condensation, his endeavor to compress into brief compass much thought, with resulting obscurity. He chose a diction which frequently uses words in other than their primary sense and which is full of rare and strange locutions. His four great instruments, or devices (ὄργανα), are summarized as poetical vocabulary, great variety of figures, harsh collocations of sound, and rapidity of expression. Dionysius reaches the general conclusion that the narrative passages are, with few exceptions, altogether admirable and adapted for every kind of service, whereas the speeches are not at all suitable for imitation. Dionysius' criticisms of the speeches in Thucydides are regarded almost exclusively from the point of view of contemporary rhetoric, not at all from the historian's. For this very reason, his comments are inferior to those in his excellent essays on the orators. Speech and narrative are two rigidly separated categories, and it never occurs to Dionysius to examine the narrative surrounding a speech which shocks his notion of τὸ πρέπον to see if it supplies some justification for the speech.

The thoroughness of Dionysius' exposition is illustrated by the fact that some eighteen times in the letters to Tubero and Ammaeus he recasts Thucydides' remarks. Unfortunately, a very long lacuna of nine *folia* occurs in that chapter (25) of our treatise in which Dionysius gives illustrations (apodeixeis) of how periods of Thucydides might be reworked.[1] It is necessary to remember that in the rewritten passages Dionysius is not so much professing to write finer sentences as to clarify his objections by writing in a more normal style. It has often been observed that this method of recasting

---

[1] K.O. Mueller (in the Mueller-Donaldson, *History of the Literature of Ancient Greece* 2 [London 1858] 134 n. 4) notes that in a number of the Thucydidean sentences where the result is placed at the end, the cause or motive being expressed by causal sentences, circumstantial participles, prepositional constructions, or coordinations of the loosest kind, Dionysius "resolves them into more intelligible and pleasing, but less vigorous forms, by taking out of the middle a number of the subordinate clauses and adding them, by way of appendix, at the end." In the opening part of chap. 3 of the *De Comp.*, Dionysius makes it clear that he thinks that sentence movement is more important than the choice of words.

an author's remarks is one which calls for great exertion on the part of the critic.

Dionysius closes his essay by comparing Thucydides and Demosthenes. He finds great similarity in the avoidance by both of a natural manner of expression, but finds a frequent tendency to obscurity in Thucydides as contrasted with the intelligibility of Demosthenes.

At times in the *De Thucydide* he is betrayed to a strange extent into that βραχύτης γνώμης which he taught his pupils to avoid. Thucydides passes no judgment on Demosthenes the general, as Dionysius (8.335.4) contends. At the close of chap. 14, Dionysius blends the accounts of the Spartan embassy sent from Pylos (IV.15-22) and one sent later from Sparta (IV. 41). In chap. 37.388.13ff., Dionysius states that the interlocutors in the Melian Dialogue were an Athenian general and the Melian commissioners; but Thucydides (V.84.3) actually reports that the Athenian generals sent envoys to make proposals to the Melians. In the course of his criticisms of this same dialogue, Dionysius (38.390.11) attributes to "the Athenian" words spoken by the Melians (V.88). In 41.395.11, Dionysius reports that Thucydides, after his banishment from Athens, spent the whole of the rest of the war in Thrace, whereas Thucydides (V.26.5) tells us that he was better able to travel after his exile and became conversant with affairs on both sides.

There are also examples of passages in which Dionysius is thought by commentators to misinterpret the Greek. In 31.377.19-21, he fails to understand the phrase οὐκ ἐχόντων ἄλλοθεν δύναμιν of III.82.7. In 32.378.17-18, the word παρατυχόν of IV.82.7 is wrongly interpreted as meaning παραχρῆμα; and in the following line Dionysius is thought by some to be incorrect in saying that ἄφρακτον is equivalent to ἀφύλακτον.

On the other hand, editors from Krüger to Pavano judged Dionysius (29.375.6-7) wrong in apparently referring the phrase εἰς τὰ ἔργα of Thucydides III.82.4 to δικαίωσις rather than to ἀξίωσις; but Gomme (*HCT* 2. 374) believes that the phrase goes with ἀντήλλαξαν and that Dionysius construed it correctly. G.E.M. de Ste. Croix (*The Origins of the Peloponnesian War* [London 1972] 54) maintains that "what Thucydides is saying in I 23.6, although misunderstood to a greater or less degree by nearly everyone in modern times, was thoroughly grasped by Dionysius of Halicarnassus two thousand years ago." In any case, the misinterpretations with which Dionysius is charged derive from III.81-82, probably the most difficult passage in the *History* and one which still affords puzzlement to modern scholars. Steup has reminded us that the modern scholar comes to the text of Thucydides equipped with decades of critical exegesis. After citing a page (*Einleitung*[7] lxxxiii) of ancient testimonia about the obscurities of Thucydidean speeches, he refers to the following extract from K.O. Müller (in the Müller-Donaldson, *History of the Literature of Ancient Greece* 2 [London 1858] 136:

Even at that time these speeches must have produced much the same effect upon the Attic taste as that which Cicero, at a later period, endeavored to convey to the Romans, by comparing the style of Thucydides with old, sour, and heavy Falernian. Thucydides was scarcely easier to the later Greeks and Romans than he is to the Greek scholars of the present time; nay, when Cicero declares that he finds the speeches in his history almost unintelligible, modern philologists may well congratulate themselves that they have surmounted all these difficulties, and left scarcely anything in them unexplained or misunderstood.

In chapter 24 of the *De Thucydide*, Dionysius gives a long list of criticisms of diction but without illustrations. At the request of Ammaeus, Dionysius then composed the so-called *Second Letter to Ammaeus*, in which he took up the various points with specific examples for each.[1] The *Second Letter*, then, is in effect an appendix to the *De Thucydide* and linguistically of considerable interest. I have incorporated into the commentary on chapter 24 many of the illustrations which Dionysius uses.

Dionysius did not understand how history should be written, at least by modern standards; but he did most thoroughly understand the qualities of the austere style, and he appreciated the best qualities of Thucydides on the artistic side—his power in narrative, his dignity and unsurpassed pathos.

The most detailed critique of those chapters of the *De Thuc.* and of the *Ep. II ad Amm.* having to do with diction is the work of E.F. Poppo, director of a gymnasium at Frankfurt and a scholar who wrote on Thucydides from 1815 to 1856. The bulk of his studies is published in an eleven-volume edition (Leipzig 1821-40) of the History, containing prolegomena, text, scholia and annotations of immoderate prolixity. The first volume of the prolegomena (Leipzig 1821) is a defence of Thucydides against accusations of Dionysius, who, Poppo (p. 248) says, was devoid of sense (*cuius menti tanta caligo offusa erat*). Poppo maintains that the supposed irregularities of Thucydides are not real confusions but are attributable to an unfixed state of grammar, or obey the sequence of thought rather than the rules of grammar, or are due to some attraction of sound or sense. Poppo concludes that Thucydides' diction blended the language of poetry and prose at a time when the two were not distinguished, that what Dionysius regarded as solecisms were at variance, not so much with the language of Thucydides' time, but with the practice of later Greek, and that Thucydides allowed himself few liberties not to be found in other writers of his period. These conclusions he bases upon a large number of examples and of references to works (by author only) of the eighteenth century, not available to me.[2] Poppo's prolegomena is not reproduced in the emended edition of

---

[1] Unfortunately, there seem to be some lacunae in the manuscripts.

[2] Poppo's conclusions are criticized by E.A. Junghahn, *NJPhP* 119 (1879) 353-402, and J. Ehlert, *De verborum copia Thucydidea quaestiones selectae* (Diss. Berlin 1910) 4-5. They are supported by E. Zarncke, *Die Entstehung der griechischen Litteratursprachen* (Leipzig 1890), who gives a large bibliography in his end-notes, but does not refer to Poppo. In a subsequent article, "Zur griechischen Kunstprosa" (*Griechische Studien Hermann Lipsius* [Leipzig 1894] 120-126), Zarncke stressed the evidence of Strabo 1.2.6. Although I question that we have anything like a sufficient

J.M. Stahl.

In the light of Dionysius' critique, it seems curious to us that one of the ablest editors of Thucydides, J. Classen, could characterize the style of Thucydides as one of simplicity and naturalness (*Einleitung*[3] lxxviii), "Daher ist grösste Einfachheit und Natürlichkeit der Grundcharakter der Sprache des Thukydides." Partly to contradict this judgment of Classen's,[1] F. Blass wrote his chapter (*Attische Beredsamkeit*[2] 1 [Leipzig 1887] 203-244; see p. 212) on the style of Thucydides. Other studies of Thucydidean style include E. Norden, *Antike Kunstprosa*[5] 1 (Stuttgart 1958 [reprint edition]) 96-101; R.C. Jebb in E. Abbott's *Hellenica* (London 1880) 306-310; A. Croiset, *Thucydide* (Paris 1886) 102ff. and *Histoire de la littérature grecque* 4 (Paris 1899) 155-170; G. Wille, "Zu Stil und Methode des Thukydides" (*Synusia*, Festschrift W. Schadewaldt [Pfullingen 1965]) 53-77; and O. Luschnat, *RE* s.v. Thukydides, Suppl. vol. 12 (1970), 1258-1266. The best study of the subject which exists today is that of W. Schmid in the Schmid-Stählin, *Geschichte der griechischen Literatur* 7.1.5 (Munich 1948) 181-204, an essay which surveys in the most illuminating fashion the investigations of scores of the best students of the Greek language, particularly those living in Germany in the nineteenth century. Yet there is hardly a page in the later part of Schmid's essay which does not refer to Dionysius, and he frequently vindicates the judgments of the Greek rhetorician as against the modern scholar. Of words in the English language, the introductions to Book I by C.D. Morris (Boston 1887, based on Classen) and E.C. Marchant (London 1905) are distinguished by sobriety of judgment. Finally, K.J. Dover has a chapter on Style in his monograph, "Thucydides" (*Greece and Rome,* Survey No. 7 [1973]), which will be informative for any student of Thucydides. In my commentary, I have collected material relating to individual aspects of Thucydides' style as they are mentioned by Dionysius.

---

number of documents, especially of early Attic inscriptions, ever to disprove the judgments of Dionysius (see, in particular, G.U. Yule, *The Statistical Study of Literary Vocabulary* [Cambridge 1944, reprinted 1968]; cf. D. Young, *G&R* 6 [1959] 96-108), who had far more material than we have, the consensus of scholarly opinion now leans in the direction of regarding Thucydides' diction as representing that of the old Attic speech of the educated class. We find no bold compounds or poetical experimentation. Thucydides was a creator of words, especially abstract and verbal compounds, but the formations were in a manner normal for writers of the fifth century. Forms common to both the Attic and Ionic of the time occur frequently; but this does not mean that he was Ionicizing. Although we have had many studies of this difficult subject, it is apparent that more research is required. See the commentary on chap. 24.7.

[1] Cf. also A. Croiset, *Thucydide* (Paris 1886) 124.

OUTLINE OF *DE THUCYDIDE*[1]

---

[1]Cf. G.M.A. Grube, *Phoenix* 4 (1950) 95-100.

RHETORICAL SYSTEM OF DIONYSIUS

According to E. Kremer, *Über das rhetorische System des Dionys von Halikarnass* (Diss. Strassburg 1907), the rhetorical system of Dionysius was organized as follows:

I. πραγματικὸς τόπος
  a) στοιχεῖα
    1. α) εὕρεσις
      β) κρίσις
    2. οἰκονομία
      α) τάξις
      β) ἐξεργασία
  b) γένη
  c) ἰδέαι
    1. προοίμιον
    2. πρόθεσις
    3. διήγησις
    4. πίστεις
    5. ἐπίλογος

II. λεκτικὸς τόπος
  a) ἐκλογή
    1. κυρία φράσις
    2. τροπικὴ φράσις
  b) σύνθεσις
    1. κόμμα
    2. κῶλον
    3. περίοδος
  c) σχήματα
  d) ἀρεταί

The χαρακτῆρες were organized as follows:

1. λέξεως
  a) ὑψηλός
  b) μέσος
  c) ἰσχνός

2. ἁρμονίας
  a) αὐστηρά
  b) μέση
  c) γλαφυρά

Kremer's analysis is substantially the same as that of G. Ammon, *De Dionysii Halicarnassensis librorum rhetoricum fontibus* (Munich 1889).

TRANSLATION

DIONYSIUS OF HALICARNASSUS

ON THUCYDIDES

325 **Chapter 1.** In my treatise *On Imitation*,[1] already published,[2] O Quintus Aelius Tubero,[3] I have reviewed those whom I thought to be the most important writers of poetry and prose.[4] I have given a brief sketch of the points of excellence in the realm of subject matter and in the realm of style which each of them shows. And I have given the points of inferiority where each falls short of his capacity either because the chosen topic is not always illuminated[5] by the most exact reasoning or because the effect has not been successful throughout the entire work. My purpose[6] was to give good and tested rules for those who propose to be successful writers or orators according to which they could compose their exercises, not by trying to imitate all the characteristics in those writers, but by trying to adopt their virtues and avoid their defects. Touching on historians, I made clear what I thought of Thucydides, giving a brief

326 and summary treatment not because of carelessness or negligence, nor for lack of arguments which would confirm my propositions, but having as my goal that what I wrote should be appropriate to the circumstance, as I have done with the other writers.[7] It was not possible for me to give an accurate and detailed treatment for each of these writers once I had chosen to reduce my work to the shortest size possible. Since you wished me to compose a separate work on Thucydides encompassing all that merits to be said, I have postponed the treatise on Demosthenes, which I have already commenced, and agreed to do as you wish.[8] Now that I have finished, here is my promise executed.

Chapter 2. Now that I am about to take up the detailed consideration of Thucydides, I desire first to say a few words about myself and the nature of my treatise, not for your benefit—good heavens!— nor for those, like you, who judge facts with perfect rectitude and consider nothing to be more precious than truth,[1] but for those others who share a mania for criticism on account of the excessive admiration which they have for the ancients or of disdain for contemporaries or of a combination of these two sentiments which are common in human nature. In fact I sus-

327 pect that there will be some who will read this work and find fault with me for venturing to show that Thucydides, the very best of all historians,[2] at times fails in the purpose of his work and shows a falling off in power. For this reason there has come upon me the conviction[3] that I shall seem to be the first and only one to say new and unexpected things[4] if I begin to quibble about some of the things which Thucydides wrote, thus not only running counter to general opinion which everyone has accepted for a long time and maintains firmly, but also denying credence to the testimony of the most distinguished philosophers and rhetoricians who accept him

as the norm for historic method and the standard for skill in forensic oratory. Nor are the assumptions of these philosophers solid ... [lacuna in text].
In order to free myself from these accusations, which have something of
the theatrical[5] in them and are capable of moving the masses, it will be sufficient to say of myself only this, that I have all my life up to the present
moment shown no signs of a contentious, quarrelsome and carping spirit
against people generally at random.[6] I have never published any writing in
which I denounce anyone, except for a single treatise which I composed on
political philosophy[7] against those who unjustly attacked it.[8] I certainly
would not start now for the first time to manifest against the foremost of
historians a malice which is not suitable to the character of a free man and
which is counter to my disposition. Concerning the nature of this writing
328 I might have many things to say, but a few will suffice. If my arguments
are truthful and worthy of me, you and men of letters generally will be the
judges.[9]

Chapter 3.   The object of the present treatise is not to make an onslaught[1]
on the plan and ability of Thucydides, nor to make an enumeration of his
faults, nor to disparage his merits, nor to engage in any other undertaking
of the sort, in which I would pay no attention to the author's felicities and
merits and would dwell only on his less happy utterances. The present
work is an evaluation of the style (charakter)[2] of his discourse; it embraces
all the qualities that he possesses either in common with others or distinct
from them. Hence, it was inevitable for me to mention also faults that
were found side by side with the virtues. Human nature is never so well endowed as to be unerring in either word or action,[3] and that nature is best
which meets with the greatest success and the least failure. Let everyone
therefore examine from this point of view what I am about to say, and let
him not question the purpose of this work instead of examining the peculiar
products of the genius (charakter) of the man. But I am not the first to
attempt such a thing as this. There have been many men both ancients and
contemporaries, who have chosen to write treatises inspired not by malice
but by a desire to know the truth; and I could furnish tens of thousands of
examples, but I shall be content to cite two of them, Aristotle and Plato.
Aristotle is persuaded that not everything that his teacher Plato has said is
329 of the highest excellence; so, for example, what he has to say about ideas,
and the good, and the state. Then, too, Plato himself desires to show that
Parmenides and Protagoras and Zeno, and not a few of the other natural
scientists,[4] have been guilty of mistakes. Yet no one censures him for this
in view of the fact that the aim of natural science is the knowledge of the
truth, and it is this too that reveals the true end of life. So when no one
finds fault with the honest intentions (proairesis)[5] of those men who differ
in matters of dogma, if they do not speak well of all the views of their
elders, surely no one will censure those who have chosen to reveal the peculiarities of genius, if they do not testify to the possession of all virtues by
their predecessors, even those they do not possess.

Chapter 4.   There is still another point that seems to require explanation.

The charge is an odious one and one that gives much pleasure to the rabble, and yet it will be easy to show that it is not sound. It does not follow that if we are inferior in ability to Thucydides and other men, we therefore forfeit the right to form an estimate of them. For men who do not possess the same skill as Apelles, Zeuxis, Protogenes, and other famous artists, are not thereby prevented from judging the art of these men, nor are men of inferior skill debarred from judging the works of Phidias, Polyclitus and

330   Myron.[1] I forbear to state that the layman is often a better judge of many works than the artist himself,—I mean all such works as appeal to irrational impression (alogos aisthesis)[2] and emotion... [lacuna]; and these are the criteria that every form of art has in view, and upon them it is based. But enough of this lest my whole treatise seem to be nothing more than an introduction.

Chapter 5.[1] Before beginning to write about Thucydides, I would like to say a few words about the other historians, both the more ancient ones and those who flourished in his period. These few words will illuminate his choice of subject (proairesis), in which he went beyond his predecessors, and his ability to deal with it (dynamis).[2] Now, the ancient historians flourished in great numbers and in various places before the Peloponnesian war; including Euagon[3] of Samos, Deïochus <of Cyzicus, Bion> of Proconnesus,[4] Eudemus of Paros,[5] Democles of Phygela,[6] Hecataeus of Miletus,[7] Acusilaus of Argos,[8] Charon of Lampsacus,[9] and Amelesagoras[10] of Chalcedon.[11] Those who were a little before the Peloponnesian war and extended down to the time[12] of Thucydides are Hellanicus of Lesbos,[13] Damastes of Sigeum,[14] Xenomedes of Ceos,[15] Xanthus of Lydia,[16] and many others. All of these showed a like bent in the choice of their subjects and there was little difference in their ability. Some wrote treatises dealing with Greek history, the others dealt with non-Greek history. And they did not blend

331   together these histories <into one work>, but subdivided them by nations and cities and gave a separate account of each,[17] keeping in view one single and unvarying object, that of bringing to the common knowledge of all whatever records or traditions[18] were to be found among the natives of the individual nationalities or states, whether recorded in places sacred or profane,[19] and to deliver these just as they received them without adding thereto or subtracting therefrom,[20] rejecting not even the legends which had been believed for many generations nor dramatic tales[21] which seem to men of the present time to have a large measure of silliness.[22] For the most part they used the same style[23]—as many of them as adopted the same type of dialect[24]—which was characterized by perspicuity (saphes),[25] the use of current words (koine), purity (kathara),[26] conciseness (syntomos),[27] adaptation (prosphyes) to subject matter,[28] and the absence of any display of technical[29] elaboration (skeuoria).[30] And withal their works are invested[31] with a certain charm[32] and grace, greater with some than with others, but possessed by all, and it is for this reason that their writings are even now extant.

In contrast with these men, Herodotus of Halicarnassus, being a little

before the Persian Wars[33] and extending down to the Peloponnesian war,
expanded and rendered more splendid[34] the scope of his subject-matter.
Not deigning to write the history of a single city or a single nation,[35] but
forming the design of comprising within a single treatise many varying deeds
of people of Europe and Asia, he started with the Lydian empire and
332   brought his history down to the Persian Wars and narrated in a single work
the history of the intervening period of two hundred and twenty years,[36]
and he invested his style with qualities that his predecessors had failed to
acquire.

Chapter 6.   Then came Thucydides who was unwilling either to confine[1]
his history to a single region as did Hellanicus, or to elaborate into a single
work the achievements of Greeks and barbarians in every land, as did Herodotus; but scorning the former as trifling[2] and petty and of little value to
the readers, and rejecting the latter as too comprehensive to fall within the
purview of the human mind, if one would be very exact, he selected a single
war, the war that was waged between the Athenians and Peloponnesians,
and gave his attention to writing about this. Since he was physically robust
and sound of mind, living through the duration of the war, he put together
his narrative not from chance rumors but on the basis of personal experience, in cases where he was present himself, and on information from the
most knowledgeable people, where he was in the dark as a result of his
exile. In this way, then, he differed from the historians before him, and I
333   say this since he chose a subject which neither consists entirely of one member (monokolon)[3] nor is divided into many irreconcilable parts. Moreover,
he did not insert anything of the mythical into his history, and he refused
to divert his history to practice deception and magic upon the masses, as all
the historians before him had done, telling of Lamias issuing from the earth
in woods and glens, and of amphibious nymphs arising from Tartarus and
swimming through the seas, partly shaped like beasts, and having intercourse
with human beings; telling also about demi-gods, the offspring of mortals
and gods, and many other stories that seem incredible and very foolish to
our times.

Chapter 7.   I have not been led to say these things by the desire to censure
those writers, since, on the contrary, I have much indulgence towards them
for mentioning the fictions of myths when writing national and local history.
For among all men alike there are preserved some records of both national
and local traditions of the kind that I have mentioned, which children have
received from their parents and have taken care to hand down to their children in turn and they have insisted that those who wished to publish them
should record them as they have received them from their elders.[1] These
historians, then, were compelled to embellish their local histories by such
334   mythical digressions. On the other hand, it was not suitable for Thucydides,
who chose just one subject in which he participated, to mix theatrical en-
ticements with the narrative, or to practice the deceit against readers which
those compilations customarily exhibited, but to be useful, as he himself
explained in the introduction to his history,[2] writing thus (I.22.4): "The

absence of the story-telling element from my history makes it seem less attractive to the ear,[3] but for all who wish to investigate the clear truth of past events and of those likely at some future time[4] (in accordance with the course of human nature) to recur in such or similar fashion—for such persons to judge that my history is useful will be enough <for me>. And so it has been composed rather as a treasure for all time[5] than as a prize composition to please the ear for the moment."

Chapter 8.   Philosophers and rhetoricians, if not all of them, yet most of them, bear witness to Thucydides that he has been most careful of the truth, the high-priestess of which we desire history to be.[1] He adds nothing to the facts that should not be added, and takes nothing therefrom, nor does he take advantage of his position as a writer,[2] but he adheres to his purpose without wavering, leaving no room for criticism, and abstaining from envy and flattery of every kind, particularly in his appreciation of men of merit. For in the first book, when he makes mention of Themistocles,[3] he unstintingly mentions all of his good qualities, and in the second book in the discussion of the statesmanship of Pericles,[4] he pronounces a eulogy such as was worthy of a man whose reputation has penetrated everywhere. Likewise, when he was compelled to speak about Demosthenes the general,[5] Nicias the son of Niceratus,[6] Alcibiades the son of Clinias,[7] and other generals and speakers, he has spoken so as to give each man his due. To cite examples is unnecessary to readers of his history. This then is what may be said about the historian's success in connection with the treatment of his subject-matter—points that are good and worthy of imitation.

Chapter 9.   The defects of Thucydidean workmanship and the features that are criticized by some persons relate to the more technical side of his subject matter, what is called the economy[1] of the discourse, something that is desirable in all kinds of writing, whether one chooses philosophical or oratorical subjects.[2] The matter in question has to do with the division (diairesis),[3] order (taxis)[4] and development (exergasia).[5] I shall begin with division and state by way of introduction that whilst the writers that preceded Thucydides adopted either topographical or chronological subdivisions that were easily followed,[6] Thucydides did not see fit to adopt either of these divisions.[7] In the division of his work he was guided neither by the places in which the events narrated took place, as were Herodotus and Hellanicus and some others of his predecessors,[8] nor by the times after the manner chosen by those who published local histories, who determined their subdivisions by kingly or priestly successions, or by Olympiads, or by the appointees to annual offices. But Thucydides chose to follow a new path and one that had not been trodden by others, and divided his work by the events of summers and winters. The effect of this was different from what he had expected. The chronological division has not become clearer, but it is more difficult to follow.[9] What is a source of astonishment, is the fact that he failed to observe that 'far-shining light' and 'pure'[10] would not light up his narrative if divided, like so much small change,[11] into small sections, <but there would be a state of confusion> resulting from the fact

335

336

that many events were occurring in many different places at the same time.
This is clear from the events themselves. In the third book (for I shall limit
myself to this, needing no other) the author starts to write about the Myti-
337   lenaeans,[12] but before completing the narrative passes on to Lacedaemonian
affairs.[13] Yet, without bringing these to a head, he mentions the siege of
Plataeae.[14] Leaving this also unfinished, he speaks of the Mytilenaean war.[15]
Thereupon he transfers his narrative to Corcyra, stating that the Corcyraeans
split into two factions, the one faction inviting the aid of the Lacedaemonians, the other that of the Athenians.[16] This too he leaves half-finished, and
gives a little information about the first Athenian expedition to Sicily.[17]
Thereupon, after starting to tell of an expedition of the Athenians to the
Peloponnese and the campaign of the Lacedaemonians in Doris,[18] he runs
through the exploits of Demosthenes the general around Leucas and the war
against the Aetolians.[19] Thence he moves to Naupactus.[20] Leaving the wars
on the continent unfinished also, he touches on Sicily a second time,[21] then
purifies Delos[22] and ... [lacuna] Amphilochian Argos attacked by the Am-
praciots.[23] But what need is there of saying more? The whole book has
thus been chopped up into small bits and has lost the continuity of the narrative. We lose our way, as is natural, and it is hard for us to follow the
narrative, our mind being confused by the tearing asunder of the events,[24]
and being unable easily and exactly to remember the half-finished reports it
has heard.[25]   The events narrated in an historical treatise must follow without interruption,[26] especially when the events are many in number and hard
to follow. It is plain, then, that the Thucydidean canon is not suited to
history.[27]   For none of the later writers divided his history by summers
338   and winters,[28] but all of them followed the beaten paths that lead to clearness (sapheneia).[29]

Chapter 10.   Some critics also find fault with his order (taxis), claiming
that he has neither made a proper beginning nor brought it to a suitable
close. These people say that the most important feature of a good arrangement of material (oikonomia) is to adopt as a starting-point something that
is not preceded by anything else, and to bring the treatise to such a close
that it will seem to be really complete and lack nothing, but Thucydides
has not properly attended to either of these two matters. The writer himself furnished the basis of such an accusation. Having first stated that the
Peloponnesian surpassed all previous wars in length and in the occurrence
of many disasters, he desires at the close of his proem first to state the
causes (aitiai) that led to the beginning (arche) of the war.[1] These he claims
to be two in number—first the true cause, which was not however stated to
everybody, to wit, the growth of the Athenian state; the second cause,
which was not the real one but was invented by the Lacedaemonians, was
the dispatch by the Athenians of an auxiliary force to help the Corcyraeans
against the Corinthians. He does not, however, start his narrative with the
true cause of the war, what he himself believed to be the cause, but he begins with the other, writing as follows verbatim: (Thuc. I.23.4-24.1) "The
war was started by the Athenians and Peloponnesians by the breaking of the

thirty years' truce, agreed upon by them after the capture of Euboea. As
339 for the reason why they broke it, I have first written the grounds of complaint (aitiai) and the differences <between the two> that nobody[2] might
ever seek the cause that gave rise to so great a war among the Greeks. The
truest explanation (prophasis), but the one least mentioned, I believe to be
that the increase of Athenian power frightened the Lacedaemonians and
forced them into the war. The grounds of complaint that were openly
stated were the following.[3]   There is a city by the name of Epidamnus,
which lies to the right[4] as one enters the Ionian Gulf. Its neighbors are the
Taulantians, who are barbarians, an Illyrian tribe." Hereupon he tells the
story of Epidamnus and Corcyra, the events centering about Potidaea, and
the meeting of the Peloponnesians at Sparta and the speeches there pronounced against the city of the Athenians. Drawing out this narrative to
two thousand lines,[5] he then delivers his statement about the other cause
(aitia), which was the real cause and the one he thought to be such, starting
with these words: (Thuc. I.88) "The Lacedaemonians passed a resolution
that the truce had been broken and that they would go to war with the
Athenians[6] not so much because they had been convinced by the arguments
of their allies, as because they feared that the Athenians might become still
more powerful, now that the larger part of Greece was already subject to
them. Now it was in the following manner that the Athenians were involved
340 in the affairs that brought about their aggrandizement." This is followed by
the things achieved by the city after the Persian war up until the Peloponnesian war, stated in a summary and cursory[7] fashion in less than five hundred lines. Having mentioned that these events preceded the Corcyraean
affairs and that the war originated in them and not in the Corcyraean
trouble, he again writes word for word as follows: (Thuc. I.118) "Now it is
after these events, not many years later, that there occurred the events already mentioned, the Corcyraean trouble, the troubles in regard to Potidaea,
and all those things that furnished an explanation of the war. The whole
period, embracing all the conflicts of the Greeks with one another and with
the barbarian, was approximately a period of fifty years that intervened
between the withdrawal of Xerxes and the beginning of this war.[8]   In these
years the Athenians established their empire more firmly and the city itself
rose to great power. The Lacedaemonians on the other hand, fully aware
of this, made but feeble attempts to prevent it, and remained inactive during
the greater part of this time. Indeed, even before this, they were not very
quick <to go> to war, except under compulsion, but then they were somewhat prevented by wars of their own.[9]   All the same[10] the power of the
Athenians was clearly rising and was breaking in on the <Lacedaemonian>
341 confederacy.[11]   Then, however, they <the Lacedaemonians> thought matters
were no longer endurable, and that they must bend every effort and put
down this power, if they could, by embarking on the present war."

Chapter 11.   He ought instead, when he began his search for the causes
(aitiai) of the war, first to give an account of the real cause and the one he
believed to be so. For the very nature of things (physis) would require the

earlier to take precedence over the later and truth over falsehood, and the introduction (eisbole)[1] of his narrative would have been far more effective, if such had been the method of arrangement (oikonomia). For none of those who would like to defend him could offer as an excuse that the events were small and insignificant, or a matter of common treatment and worn out by his predecessors, so that it was better for him not to start with them. For the historian himself considers this point as worthy of mention on the ground that it had been omitted by the older authors, writing in these very words: (Thuc. I.97.2) "I have recorded these events and made this digression because[2] this particular topic is wanting in the works of all my predecessors. They either composed the Greek history of the period preceding the Medic wars or the history of these very wars. But Hellanicus, who in his Attic history actually did touch upon the matter in question, treated of it lightly and was careless about his chronology. Moreover, <the insertion of this material> gives an account of the way in which the Athenian empire was established."

Chapter 12.   This one point, then, the unnatural beginning of the history, 342   would of itself be a sufficient proof that the history had not been shaped by him in the most advantageous manner. There is added to this the fact that the history does not conclude with the proper chapters (kephalaia). For though the war lasted twenty-seven years and though the author lived till the conclusion, he brought his history down only to the twenty-second year, extending his eighth book only to the naval battle at Cynossema, and that too after having stated in advance in the proem that he would embrace <in his narrative> all the events of the war, and in the fifth book he again reckons up the time from the beginning to the point it reached when it was terminated, writing verbatim as follows: (Thuc. V.26.3) "And for those who made any assertion on the basis of oracles, this was the only matter that really came to pass. For I remember that at all times at the beginning of the war and up to the time it came to a close the statement was made by many people that the war was destined to last thrice nine years. I lived through it all, being of an age that would enable me to understand it, and directing my mind to the accurate[1] ascertainment of facts. I also had the experience of being an exile from my native city for twenty years after my command at Amphipolis,[2] and being present on both sides of the conflict,– 343   and quite as long a time with the Peloponnesians <as with the Athenians>,– <I had the advantage> because of my exile of seeing some of the events a little more at ease.[3] So I shall narrate the differences that arose after the ten years and the breach of the truce and the subsequent events of the war."

Chapter 13.   To show that in the elaboration (exergasia) of his chapters he is rather careless, either giving more space to matters that demand less or else indolently treating in a cursory manner matters that require more detailed treatment,[1] I might offer many proofs but shall use only a few. After starting at the close of the second book to describe the first two naval battles that were fought by the Athenians and the Peloponnesians (Thuc. II.83-84, 85-92), in which the Athenians by themselves fought with twenty ships

against the forty-seven of the Peloponnesians ... [long lacuna] in a naval
battle against many times their number of barbarians they destroyed some
of the boats, and captured others, men and all, to a number not less than
those they had originally dispatched to the scene of the war. I shall also
give his very words: (Thuc. I.100.1) "Thereupon at the river Eurymedon
in Pamphylia both a land-battle and a naval battle were fought by the
Athenians and their allies against the Medes, and the Athenians under the
command of Cimon, son of Miltiades, were victorious in both engagements
344   on the same day and they either captured or destroyed in all two hundred
ships of the Phoenicians."[2]   Similar to this are anomalous extensions or
contractions of the descriptions of land-battles. So having started to tell in
the fourth book of the achievements of the Athenians at Pylos and at the
island called Sphacteria on which they shut up the Lacedaemonians and after a siege forced them to capitulate, and after incidentally adding a few
other events belonging to this war and again returning to tell the sequel, he
has given a detailed and effective description of all the battles that were
fought by the contending parties, devoting more than three hundred lines
to the battles, and this in spite of the fact that the number of those who
perished or surrendered their arms was small. At any rate he himself thus
sums up the battle writing as follows word for word: (Thuc. IV.38.5) "The
number of those that were killed in the island or captured alive was as follows: four hundred and twenty hoplites in all had gone across. Of these two
hundred and ninety-two were recovered alive, the rest of them died. And of
the number of those who remained alive one hundred and twenty were
Spartans, but only a few Athenians perished."[3]

345   **Chapter 14.**   Speaking of the campaign of Nicias, when he sailed to the
Peloponnesus with sixty ships and two thousand[1] Athenian hoplites, and,
after shutting up the Lacedaemonians in their forts, he took by storm the
Aeginetans who dwelt in Cythera and in Thyrea, and pillaged a large portion of the rest of the Peloponnesus, whence he sailed home to Athens with
a multitude of prisoners, the author has spoken thus cursorily regarding the
events at Cythera: (IV.54.2) "A battle ensued and the people of Cythera
held their ground for some little time; then they took flight and sought
refuge in the upper city and later agreed with Nicias and his fellow-com-
manders to submit the decision of their fate to the Athenian people, death
excepted." And in regard to the capture of the Aeginetans in Thyrea <he
writes> as follows: (IV.57.3) "Landing in the meantime and straightway
marching with all their forces, the Athenians captured Thyrea, burning the
city and sacking everything that was in it, and taking to Athens all of the
Aeginetans who had not perished in the hand-to-hand encounter." Although
right at the beginning of the war great disasters befell the cities, which
caused both of them to desire peace, and the Athenians, seeing their country
346   laid waste and their city depopulated by the plague,[2] despaired of other help
and sent ambassadors to Sparta to sue for peace, the author has reported
neither the men who were sent nor the speeches there spoken by them, nor
the opposing speeches by which the Lacedaemonians were persuaded to

reject the truce, but in a sorry and careless fashion, as though he were talking about small and insignificant events, he has used the following language:
(II.59.1) "After the second invasion of the Peloponnesians, the Athenians
underwent a change of feeling, when their land had been ravaged a second
time and the war and the plague together were afflicting them. They blamed
Pericles for having persuaded them to go to war and held him responsible
for the misfortunes which had befallen them; and they were anxious to come
to terms with the Lacedaemonians. They sent envoys to them, but they met
with no success."[3] But when the Lacedaemonians, proposing to recover the
three hundred prisoners who were taken at Pylos, sent an embassy to Athens,
he has recorded the speeches delivered by the Lacedaemonians on that occasion and has given the reason which prevented the consummation of the
treaty. (Cf. IV.15-22.)[4]

Chapter 15. Now, if, in the case of the Athenian embassy, a statement
comprising merely a summary of the events was sufficient, and there was no
need of the speeches and pleas made by the ambassadors, though the Lacedaemonians were not prevailed upon and did not accept the proposals for a
truce, why, pray, did he not follow the same plan also in the case of the
envoys who came from Sparta to Athens? For they too went away without
securing peace. If the details of the latter events had to be stated, why was
the author so careless as to omit the former? Surely it was not feebleness
of ability that prevented him from finding and stating the possible arguments
in both cases. But if he had some special purpose in view in working out
the details of one of the embassies, I cannot conjecture why he should have
preferred the Lacedaemonian to the Athenian, the later in time to the earlier,[1] the foreign one to the one sent out by his own city, and the one that
resulted from the lesser evils to the one that resulted from the greater.

Having often been compelled to write of the capture, overthrow, and
enslavement of cities, and other similar disasters, he sometimes makes the
sufferings appear so cruel, so terrible, so piteous, as to leave no room for
historians or poets to surpass him.[2] And then again he represents them as
so insignificant and so slight, that the reader receives not an inkling of the
terrors.[3] When he says what he has said about the city of the Plataeans
(III.52-68) and that of the Mytilenaeans (III.27ff., 35-50) and that of the
Melians (V.84-116), I need not cite those words in which he has made use
of all his powers to elaborate their misfortunes.[4] But the language in which
he cursorily treats of their (? = text)[5] sufferings and minimizes them,...
[lacuna] in many passages of his history, of these I shall make mention.[6]
So for example (V.32.1): "About this same time, the Athenians captured
the city of Scione by storm, slew all the male inhabitants who had reached
the age of manhood, enslaved the women and children, and gave the land
to the Plataeans to occupy."[7] (I.114.3): "The Athenians under the command of Pericles crossing to Euboea a second time subdued the whole of it.
The rest of the island they received in submission by surrender, but the
Hestiaeans they drove out of their homes and took possession of their territory themselves."[8] (II.27.1): "At this same time the Athenians expelled

347

348

the Aeginetans from Aegina, themselves, their wives and their children, charging them with being chiefly responsible for the war in which they were involved and feeling that it was safer for them to send colonists of their own to have possession of Aegina, lying as it did off the coast of the Peloponnesus."[9]

Chapter 16. There are many other portions throughout the whole history that one may find either to have been worked out with the most consummate elaboration and that admit of neither addition nor subtraction, or else to have been carelessly skimmed over and to present not the slightest suggestion[1] of that former skill, and this is especially true of his harangues and dialogues and other pieces of oratory.[2] In his anxiety for these,[3] he seems to have left his history incomplete.[4] Such, too, is the view of Cratippus, who flourished at the same time as he,[5] and who collected the matter passed over by him,[6] for he says that not only have the speeches been an impediment to the narrative, but they are also annoying to the hearers. At any rate he maintains that Thucydides noticed this and so put no speech in the closing portions of his history,[7] though there were many events in Ionia and many events at Athens that called for the use of dialogues and harangues. Certainly, if one compares the first and eighth books with each other,[8] they would not seem to form part of the same plan nor to be the work of the same genius. The one book comprising a few, small events is full of oratory, whereas the other embracing many great events shows a scarcity of public speeches.

Chapter 17. I have even thought that in his very speeches the man has given evidence of the same failing, so much so that in dealing with the same subject and on the same occasion[1] he writes some things that he ought not to have said, and omits others that he ought to have said, as, for example, he has done in regard to the city of the Mytilenaeans in the third book. After the capture of the city and the arrival of the captives, whom the general Paches had dispatched to Athens, though two meetings of the ecclesia were held at Athens (Thuc. III.36), our author has omitted as unnecessary the speeches that were made by the leaders of the people at the first of these meetings,[2] in which the demos voted to kill the prisoners and the rest of the Mytilenaeans who had reached manhood, and to enslave the women and children; but the speeches (III.36-49) that dealt with the same subject and that were delivered by the same persons at the later meeting at which the majority experienced a sort of repentance, the historian has admitted as necessary.

Chapter 18. And as for the much talked-of funeral speech (II.35-46),[1] which Thucydides recounted in the second book, for what reason, pray, is it placed in this book rather than in another?[2] For whether on the occasion of great disasters that had befallen the city when many brave Athenians had perished in battle it was befitting for the customary lamentations to be made over them, or, by reason of the great services which brought conspicuous renown to the city or added to its power, it was meet for the dead to be honored with the praises of funeral speeches, any book that one might

choose would be a more suitable place for the funeral oration than this
book. For, in this book, the Athenians who fell during this first invasion of
the Peloponnesians were very few in number, and not even these performed
any illustrious deeds, as Thucydides himself writes (II.22): After first saying
351   of Pericles that "he watched the city and kept it as quiet as possible, but he
continually sent out small numbers of horsemen[3] to keep patrols of the
<hostile> army from sallying forth into the farms near the city and doing
damage," he says that a brief cavalry conflict took place "at Phrygia between
a single squad of Athenian cavalry accompanied by Thessalians and the
Boetian horsemen. In this engagement the Thessalians and Athenians were
not worsted until the hoplites came to the assistance of the Boeotians and so
they were put to flight and a few of the Thessalians and Athenians were
killed. But the dead were recovered on the same day without a truce. And
the Peloponnesians erected a trophy on the following day."[4] But in the
fourth book (cf. Thuc. IV.9-23, 26-40) the men who fought with Demosthenes at Pylos against a force of the Lacedaemonians, attacking them by
land and from the sea and conquering them in both the battles, and who
thereby filled the city with boasting, were far superior in numbers and worth
to the above-mentioned soldiers. Why then, pray, in the case of the few
horsemen who brought neither reputation nor additional power to the city,
does the historian open the public graves[5] and introduce the most distinguished leader of the people, Pericles, in the act of reciting that lofty[6] tragic
352   composition; whereas, in honor of the larger number and more valiant who
caused the people who declared war against the Athenians to surrender to
them, and who were more worthy of obtaining such an honor, he did not
compose a funeral oration? To dismiss all the other battles on land and on
sea, in which many perished who much more deserved to be honored with
the funeral eulogy than those frontier guardsmen of Attica, amounting to
about ten or fifteen horsemen, how much more worthy of the funeral lamentations and eulogies were those of the Athenians and allies who met their
death in Sicily along with Nicias and Demosthenes in the naval engagements
and in the land battles and lastly in that wretched flight, who numbered no
less than forty thousand and who were not even able to obtain the customary mode of burial?[7] But the historian was so neglectful of these men that
he has even omitted to state that the city went into public mourning and
duly made the customary offerings to the shades of those who had died in
foreign lands, and appointed as the orator of the occasion the man who was
the most competent speaker of the orators of that time.[8] For it was not
likely that the Athenians would go into public mourning for the fifteen
horsemen, but would not deem worthy of any honor the men that fell in
Sicily, among whom ... [lacuna] and of the muster-roll of citizens[9] those
that perished were more in number than five thousand. But it seems that
the historian (for I shall say what I think), desiring to use the personality
353   of Pericles and to put in his mouth the funeral eulogy that he had composed,
since the man died in the second year of the war and did not live at the
time of any of the disasters that subsequently befell the city, bestowed upon
that small and insignificant deed a praise that went far beyond the real worth

of the matter.

Chapter 19. One may see still better the fluctuations of the writer in his method of elaboration (exergasia) when one reflects that though he has omitted many important events he stretches out the proem of his history to a length of five hundred lines, simply because he wants to show that the acts that were done by the Greeks before this war were slight and not worthy of comparison with this war.[1] For neither was this the truth, as it is possible to show by many examples, nor do technical considerations suggest such a manner of amplification (auxesis)[2] (for it does not follow that if a thing is larger than small things, it is therefore actually large, but this is only so if it exceeds large things); and, furthermore, his proem after receiving so much elaboration by way of demonstrating the proposition, has become a history all by itself. But the composers of rhetorical treatises lay down the rule that one ought to make the proem an exposition of the speech,[3] stating in advance a summary of what is to be set forth. And this is exactly what the author has done in less than fifty lines at the close of his proem, when he is about to start his narrative (Thuc. I.23). So that those endless petty details that are calculated to diminish the greatness of Greece, did not have to be dragged in by him, such a statement as that (I.3) at the time of the Trojan war Greece was not yet collectively called by a single name, and that (I.5) those who were in need of sustenance started to cross the sea in ships to visit one another, and falling upon cities that were without walls and distributed in villages, they plundered them and gained the greater part of their living in this way. What necessity was there of speaking about the luxurious mode of life in which the Athenians of olden times indulged (I.6), stating that they plaited their hair into "buns" on the nape of the neck[4] (krobulos) and wore golden cicadas on their heads and that (I.6.5) the Lacedaemonians "were the first to strip themselves and openly removing their clothes anointed themselves with oil as they exercised"? What suitable occasion (kairos)[5] was there for telling (I.13) in advance of the narrative (diegesis)[6] about the Corinthian shipbuilder Aminocles, who was the first man to build triremes for the Samians,—he built four of them,—and of Polycrates (I.13), tyrant of Samos, who captured Rheneia and dedicated it to the Delian Apollo, and of the Phocaeans who founded Marseilles that they had won the victory over the Carthaginians in a naval battle (I.13), and all the other statements like these?

Chapter 20. If it is right and lawful for me to speak what I think,[1] I should say that the proem[2] would have been best if he had attached the close of it to the statement of his subject (prothesis)[3] omitting all of the intervening portion and fashioning it as follows:[4] (I.1.1) "Thucydides, an Athenian, wrote the history of the war waged by the Peloponnesians and the Athenians against one another, beginning to write as soon as it was under way in the expectation that it would be great and the most notable of all wars; inferring this both from the fact that they were at the acme of their strength on both sides in all manner of preparation for war, and also because he saw the rest of Greece siding with one or the other state, some at once, the rest at least

intending so to do. For this was the greatest disturbance that had ever
arisen among the Greeks,[5] extending also to a considerable portion of the
barbarians, and, one might say, to most of mankind. As to the events that
preceded this and those again that are still older, it was impossible to get
clear information on account of the lapse of time, yet from necessary
inferences,[6] which, upon inquiring to the utmost point, I find that I can
trust, I think that they (= events) have not been on a large scale either as
regards wars or other affairs. (I.21.1) Instead of believing what the poets
have sung, adorning and amplifying events, or what prose-writers have composed with a view to what was more attractive to the ear rather than to
truth, stories which cannot be proved or disproved, most of which having
from the lapse of time won their way into myth destitute of all credibility,
but thinking them here searched out on the basis of the clearest signs and
sufficiently, considering their antiquity, <one, I say, shall not err.>[7]   (2)
And though men always judge the present war when they are engaged in it
to be the greatest, but when it is over admire more events which were earlier, yet this war will show to persons who form their opinions on the basis
of facts that it proved to be really greater than those that went before.
(22.1) What particular persons have said in speeches when they were about
356   to go to war or when they were already in it, it was hard to recall the exact
words that were spoken, both for myself with regard to what I heard in
person and for those who reported to me from various other sources. I
have given the speeches as I thought the several speakers would have spoken
what was necessary on the various occasions, adhering as closely as possible
to the overall purport[8] of what was actually said. (2) As to the deeds which
were done in the war I thought it my duty to set them forth, not <as ascer-
tained> from the first chance-comer, nor as I think probable, but only after
examining as accurately as possible each event both where I was present myself and <when I rely on reports> from others. (3) It was with labor that
the facts were ascertained, because those who were present at the various
events did not give the same account about the same things, but as one was
inclined to either party or as he remembered. (4) And the absence of the
story-telling element from my history will perhaps make it seem less attractive to the ear, but for all who wish to investigate the clear truth of past
events and of those likely at some future time (in accordance with the
course of human nature) to recur in such or similar fashion—for such persons
to judge that my history is useful will be enough <for me>.[9] And so it has
been composed rather as a treasure for all time than as a prize composition
to please the ear for the moment. (23) Of deeds of former times the greatest
was the Persian War, and yet this was decided in two sea-fights and two land-
battles. But this war <=Peloponnesian War> was protracted to a great
length and in the course of it disasters befell Greece such as had never oc-
357   curred in any equal space of time. For never had so many cities been taken
and made desolate, some by the barbarians and others by the Greeks themselves warring on one another, while some cities after they were captured
changed their inhabitants. Nor <had there been> so many banishments of
men or such slaughter, whether in the course of the war itself or as a result

of civil strife. And so stories of former times reported on hearsay, but too scantily confirmed by fact, ceased to be incredible, for instance, about earthquakes which prevailed over the greatest part of the earth and were most violent at the same time, and eclipses of the sun which took place more frequently as compared with those remembered from former times, and great droughts in some places with resultant famines, and what wrought most harm and to a considerable degree destroyed them—the plague. All these <evils> fell upon them simultaneously with the war. And the war was started by the Athenians and Peloponnesians by the breaking of the thirty years' truce, agreed upon by them after the capture of Euboea. As for the reason why they broke it, I have first written the grounds of complaint and the differences <between the two> that nobody might ever seek the cause that gave rise to so great a war among the Greeks."

Chapter 21. These then are the faults and the merits of the author in so far as the arrangement of the material (to pragmatikon meros) is concerned.[1] I am now going to speak about his style (to lektikon)[2] in which the individuality of the author is most clearly seen. Perhaps it may be necessary in connection with this topic (idea)[3] also, to state in advance into how many parts diction (lexis)[4] is divided and what are the qualities it embraces; then to show without concealing anything what was the state of literary expression when Thucydides received it from his predecessors,[5] and what parts of it were due to his innovations, whether for better or for worse.

Chapter 22. That all diction (lexis)[1] is divided into two primary divisions, (1), the choice of the words by which things are designated, and, (2), the composition[2] <of these> into larger and smaller groups (lit. parts), and that each of these is subdivided into still other divisions, the choice of the elementary parts of speech (nominal, verbal, and conjunctive, I mean) into literal (kyria)[3] and figurative (tropike) expression,[4] and composition into phrases (kommata),[5] clauses (kola),[6] and periods (periodoi);[7] and that both of these classes (I mean simple and uncompounded words and the combination of these) happen to be capable of assuming certain figures (schemata); and that of the so-called virtues (aretai) some are essential[8] and must be found in every kind of discourse, whilst others are accessory (epithetoi)[9] and receive their peculiar force only when the former are present as a foundation,—<all those matters> have been stated by many before.[10] Hence I need not now speak about them, nor state the considerations and rules which are many in number, upon which each of these qualities is based. For these matters also have been most carefully worked out.

Chapter 23. Which of these features all of Thucydides' predecessors used and which of them they used but slightly, taking up from the beginning as I promised,[1] I shall summarize. For thus one will more accurately recognize the individual style (charakter) of our author. Now I have no means of conjecturing what was the language used by the very ancient writers who are known only by their names, whether they used a style that was plain (lite),[2] unadorned (akosmetos),[3] and had nothing superfluous (perittos),[4] but only what was useful and indispensable, or whether they employed a style that

was stately (pompike),[5] dignified (axiomatike)[6] and elaborate (egkataskeu-
os)[7] and provided with accessory embellishments (kosmoi).[8] For neither
have the writings of the majority of them been preserved up to our times,
nor are those that have been preserved believed by everybody to belong to
those men, among others the works of Cadmus of Miletus[9] and Aristaeus of
Proconnesus,[10] and the like.[11] But the authors who lived before the Peloponnesian war and survived up to the time of Thucydides, all of them as a
rule followed the same plan, both those who chose the Ionic dialect which
flourished more than the others at those times, and those writers who chose
the old Attic dialect which showed only a few slight differences from the
Ionic. For all these writers, as I stated, were more concerned about the
literal meaning of the words than about their figurative use,[12] and they admitted the latter only to impart flavor (hedysma),[13] as it were, to their
style; and as to their composition all of them used the same kind, the plain
and unstudied,[14] and in the framing[15] of their words and their thoughts
they did not deviate to any considerable extent from the everyday (tetrim-
360   mene),[16] current (koine) and familiar manner of diction (dialektos).[17] Now
the diction (lexis)[18] of all of these writers possesses the necessary virtues—
it is pure (kathara), clear (saphes), and fairly concise (syntomos), each preserving the peculiar idiom (charakter) of the language;[19] but the accessory
virtues, which to the largest extent reveal the power of the orator,[20] are not
found in their entirety nor in their highest state of development, but only
in small numbers and in a slightly developed stage,—I refer to such qualities
as sublimity (hypsos),[21] elegance (kalliremosyne),[22] solemnity (semnologia,)[23]
and splendor (megaloprepeia).[24] Nor does their diction reveal intensity
(tonos),[25] nor gravity (baros)[26] nor sentiment (pathos)[27] that arouses the
mind,[28] nor a vigorous (erromenon) and combative (enagonion)[29] spirit,
which are productive of so-called eloquence (deinotes).[30] <This is true of
all> with the single exception of Herodotus. This author in the choice of
words, in his composition, and in the variety (poikilia) of his figures far
surpassed all the others,[31] and made his prose utterance resemble the best
kind of poetry, by reason of his persuasiveness (peitho),[32] graces of style
(charites),[33] and great charm (hedone).[34] In the greatest and most conspicuous qualities <he was second to none.> ... [Text defective] ... Only
the qualities of a forensic nature seem to be lacking, whether he was not
naturally gifted with these, or, whether in pursuance of a certain design he
voluntarily rejected them as unsuited to history.[35] For the author has not
made use of many deliberative or forensic speeches,[36] nor does his strength
(alke)[37] consist in imparting the elements of passion (pathainein) and forcefulness (deinopoiein) to his narrative.[38]

Chapter 24.[1] Following this author and the others whom I previously men-
361   tioned, and recognizing the qualities that each of these authors possessed,
Thucydides was the first man to endeavor to introduce into historical composition a certain peculiar style (charakter)[2] and one that had been disre-
garded by all others. In the choice of his words he preferred a diction that
was figurative (tropike),[3] obscure (glottematike),[4] archaic (aperchaiomene),[5]

and foreign (xene)[6] in the place of that which was in common use and familiar to the men of his time;[7] in the composition of the smaller and larger
divisions <of the sentence> he used the dignified (axiomatike),[8] austere
(austera),[9] sturdy (stibara),[10] and stable (bebekuia),[11] and one that by the
harsh sound of the letters[12] grates roughly on the ears instead of the clear
(liguros),[13] soft (malaka),[14] and polished (synexesmene)[15] kind, and one
in which there is no clashing of sounds.[16] On the use of figures, in which
he desired to differ as far as possible from his predecessors, he bestowed the
greatest effort. At any rate, during the twenty-seven years' period of the
war, from its beginning to its end, he continued to work at the eight books,
which were all that he left, turning them up and down[17] and filing and
planing them,[18] handling each individual part of speech. Sometimes he
made a phrase (logos)[19] of a word (onoma),[20] and sometimes he would
contract a phrase into a word;[21] and at times he expressed the verb (rhema-
tikon) in the form of a noun (onomatikos)[22] and then, again, he made a
verb of the noun;[23] and even of these he would pervert the <normal> use,
in order that a substantive (onomatikon) might become an appellative (pros-
egorikon),[24] or an appellative be used as a substantive.[25] He made actives
(drasteria)[26] of passives (pathetika),[27] and passives of actives,[28] and changed
the nature of singular and plural,[29] substituting the one for the other in the
predicate. He attributed feminine genders to masculines and masculines to
feminines and to some of these even neuter genders,[30] a procedure which
violates the natural sequence (akolouthia).[31] The inflections of substantives
(onomatikoi) and participles (metochikoi),[32] he sometimes diverts from the
form (semainon) to the meaning (semainomenon),[33] sometimes from the
meaning to the form. In the conjunctions (syndetikoi)[34] and the prepositions
(prothetikoi),[35] and still more so in the parts of speech[36] that complete the
meanings (dynameis) of words (onomata),[37] he takes liberties after the
fashion of a poet.[38] Then, too, one may find an abundance of figures which,
in consequence of apostrophe of person,[39] interchange of tense, and variation
of tropical signification[40] differ from the familiar ones and have taken on the
appearance of solecisms: ever so many cases in which things (pragmata) are
used for persons (somata) or persons for things;[41] or enthymemes[42] and conceptions (noemata)[43] in the case of which the introduction of a large number of parentheses causes too great an interval before the conclusion is
reached.[44] Also things that are tortuous (skolia), tangled (polyploka), hard
to unravel (dysexelikta), and the like.[45] One may also find not a few of
the showy (theatrika) figures in this author,[46]—I refer to balance of phrases
(parisoseis),[47] assonance (paromoioseis),[48] play on words (paronomasiai),[49]
and antithesis (antitheseis),[50] which were used to excess by Gorgias of
Leontini,[51] by the school of Polus and Licymnius,[52] and by many others
who flourished in his time.[53] The most conspicuous and characteristic
features of the author are his efforts to express the largest number of things
in the smallest number of words, and to compress a number of thoughts into one, and his tendency to leave his hearer still expecting to hear something
more, all of which things produce a brevity that lacks clearness. To sum it
up, there are four instruments, as it were, of Thucydidean diction (lexis):

362

363

poetical vocabulary (to poietikon ton onomaton),[54] great variety of figures
(to polyeides ton schematon), harshness of sound combination (to trachy
tes harmonias),[55] and swiftness in saying what he has to say (to tachos ton
semasion).[56] Its qualities (chromata)[57] are solidity (striphnon)[58] and
compactness (pyknon),[59] pungency (pikron)[60] and harshness (austeron),[61]
gravity (embrithes),[62] tendency to inspire awe and fear (deinon kai phobe-
ron),[63] and above all these the power of stirring the emotions (pathetikon).[64]
That is about the kind of author Thucydides is as regards the characteristics
of his diction (lexis), in which he differed from all the other authors. Now
when the author's powers keep pace with his purpose, the success is perfect
and marvelous; but when the ability lags behind and the tension (tonos)[65]
is not maintained throughout, the rapidity of the narrative makes the diction
obscure,[66] and introduces other ugly blemishes. For the author does not
throughout his history observe the proper use of foreign[67] and coined[68]
364   words nor the limit to which he may go before he stops, though there are
principles regulating their use that are good and binding in every kind of
writing.[69]

Chapter 25.   After the summary account that has just been given of these
features, it is now time to proceed to the illustrations (apodeixeis).[1] But I
am not going to give a separate account of each individual point, arranging
the Thucydidean diction under the respective heads, but taking his works by
chapters and paragraphs,[2] and selecting portions of his narrative and of his
speeches, and placing by the side of his successes or failures in the handling
of his subject-matter or in the use of his diction the reasons that make them
such.[3] And I will once more ask you and other men of letters who will
read this treatise to bear in mind the object of my undertaking, that it is a
description of a peculiar style, which embraces all the characteristic qualities
of the writer that require discussion, its object being to aid those very men
who desire to imitate our writer.[4]

     At the beginning of the proem having made the statement that the
Peloponnesian war was greater than any that preceded it, he writes word for
word as follows: (I.1.2) "As to the events that preceded this and those
again that are still older, it was impossible to get clear information on account
of the lapse of time, yet from necessary inferences, which, upon inquiring to
the utmost point, I find that I can trust, I think that they <=events> have
not been on a large scale either as regards wars or other affairs.[5] (I.2.1)
For it is plain that the country now called Hellas had in ancient times no
settled population; on the contrary, migrations were frequent in former times,
365   the several tribes readily leaving their own land when forced to do so by any
who from time to time were more numerous. (2) For there was no com-
merce and people did not have dealings with one another without fear either
on land or on sea, each cultivating his own land so far as to get a livelihood
from it, having no accumulation of capital and not planting trees[6]... [Lacuna.
MS. M left nine empty folia. After the gap, the text continues with an incomplete citation from Thuc. IV.34.1] "...cowed in their spirits at the
thought of marching against the Lacedaemonians. So they had learnt to

despise them and with a yell they proceeded in a body to attack them."[7] This section ought not to have been worked out in this fashion, but in a manner that is more commonly used and that is more useful. I mean that the last part should have been appended to the first and the portion that intervenes should have followed after the two. But framed as the narrative has been, it has become terser (agkylotera)[8] and more forceful (deinotera), but it would have been clearer and more agreeable (hedion) if it had been done the other way, viz.: "When the Lacedaemonians were no longer able to sally forth at the point where the attack was made, the light-armed soldiers seeing that they were by this time slackening <in their defence> formed a compact body and starting to yell hurled themselves in one solid mass upon the Lacedaemonians (lit. them); for they had taken courage from seeing that they (the Athenians) were many times the number <of the enemy>, and they had conceived contempt for the Lacedaemonians because they no longer appeared so terrible to them, since they had not forthwith met with the punishment they had expected when first they disembarked for the attack, cowed in their spirits at the thought of marching against Lacedaemonians."[9]

Chapter 26. Excepting the circumlocution, all the rest has been expressed in the most appropriate words and has received the most suitable form, and does not, so to speak, show a lack of any of the virtues of style and subject-matter, which virtues there is no need of my enumerating once more.

In the seventh book when he relates the last naval encounter between the Athenians and Syracusans, he has expressed and shaped what took place as follows: (VII.69.4) "Demosthenes, Menander and Euthydemus (for these had embarked on the Athenian ships as generals) weighing anchor left their naval base and proceeded at once towards the barricade of the harbor and the exit that had been left,[1] desiring to force their way out. (70) But the Syracusans and their allies, weighing anchor in advance[2] and starting out with about the same number of ships as before, kept guard with a portion of them at the mouth of the harbor and <posted themselves> in a circle in the rest of the harbor in order that they might make a simultaneous attack on the Athenians from all sides. Besides the infantry came to their assistance[3] and met the ships wherever they tried to land (Dionys. = where the ships were present in force).[4] The fleet of the Syracusans was commanded by Sicanus and Agatharchus, each of them having charge of one wing of the whole force, whilst Pythen and the Corinthians formed the center. But when the other[5] Athenians also advanced to the barrier, bearing down on them with their first charge, they had the better of the ships that were stationed near the barrier and they tried to burst it. But afterwards when the Syracusans and their allies bore down on them from all directions the fight was not limited to the neighborhood of the barrier but spread over the whole harbor, and the battle was fiercely contested, and wholly unlike any of the previous engagements. Great zeal was manifested on both sides on the part of the sailors to proceed to the attack at the word of command, and the pilots displayed great rivalry in the employment of their skill, and the marines

366

367

saw to it when[6] ship met ship that the skill of those upon the decks did not fall short of that of the others, and, in fact, every one was eager to appear to be the first to whatever post he had been assigned. Inasmuch as there was a clash of a large number of ships in a little space (for the number of the boats that fought in the small space[7] was very large; for the combined number fell little short of being two hundred), there was but little maneuvering (lit. = departures from the line)[8] because there was no backing and no chance of rowing between ships. But collisions, as vessel happened to strike vessel either when trying to escape or in attacking another ship, were more frequent. As long as a ship was bearing down, the men on the decks made use of a profusion[9] of javelins and arrows and stones against it. But after they had clashed, the marines engaged in hand to hand encounters and tried to board one another's ships. And in many places it came to pass on account of the narrow space that on one quarter they had rammed an enemy ship, while on another quarter they had themselves been rammed, and that two ships were forcibly bound together with one or at times even more ships. And the pilots had to ward off attack and provide for attack not one by one, but they were confronted on all sides at once, and the noise resulting from the collision of a large number of boats was so great as to cause dismay and make it impossible to hear the orders of the boatswains.[10] For the boatswains on both sides indulged in a great deal of ordering and shouting, some of it of a technical nature, some by way of stirring up nautical[11] rivalry, the Athenians shouting to their men to force the outlet, and now, if ever,[12] with a will to essay the task of making their way in safety to their native cities,[13] the Syracusans and their allies exclaiming that now was a fine time to keep them from escaping, and by winning the victory each one to magnify his own native country. And besides, the generals on each side, when perchance they saw any one backing water without compulsion, would call out the trierarch by name and ask him, the Athenians whether they were withdrawing[14] because they deemed a land that is most hostile to be now more their own than the sea which had been acquired by not a little labor,[15] the Syracusans whether they were now themselves going to run away from the Athenians[16] who were already on the run and who they knew full well were trying in every possible way to effect their escape. (71) The land troops also on both sides while the outcome of the naval battle was hanging in the balance were subjected to a great mental struggle and conflict,[17] the natives being ambitious for even greater glory, whilst the invaders feared that they might fare even worse than they had. For the Athenians their fate depended on their ships, and their fear for the future was like unto none they had ever felt before; and because of the inequality <of the places they occupied> their view of the battle from the land must needs also be unequal.[18] Their sight being at short range and not all looking at the same point at the same time, when some would see their men at some point getting the upper hand, they would gain fresh courage and would begin to call upon the gods not to deprive them of their salvation. Others having cast their eyes upon a spot where their men were losing would vary their shouting with lamentation and by the sight of what was going on were more cowed in spirit than the men

368

369

who were actually fighting. Still others, looking at a point where there
was an even fight, because of the continued indecisiveness of the battle
were in a state of the greatest distress, their very bodies swerving, in the ex-
tremity of their fear, in sympathy with their thought. For all the time they
were almost on the point of escaping or of perishing. Within the army[19] of
the Athenians, while the contest was evenly waged, all sorts of sounds might
be heard at the same time, wailing and shouting, winners and losers, and all
the other various sounds that were inevitable in the case of a large army in-
370 volved in great danger. The men on the ships had the same experience, until
the Syracusans and their allies, after the fight had remained undecided for a
long time, finally routed the Athenians and making a brilliant charge with
shouts and cheers started to pursue them to the land. Then the ships making
land, in various directions, as many as were not caught out in the open,
cast themselves ashore at their encampment. Then the land forces without
a varying note as by one impulse gave vent to groans and lamentations,
grieved at the sight of what was going on, and some of them ran to give
assistance to the ships, others to what remained of their wall to guard it,
and still others—and these constituted the largest number,—thought it was
time to look out for themselves and see how they might be saved. There
was for the time being consternation such as has never been exceeded. The
Athenians themselves had had the same experiences and had accorded the
same treatment at Pylos. For after the Lacedaemonians had lost their ships,
the men who had been transferred to the island were also destined to be
lost, and on this occasion the Athenians had no hope of saving themselves
by land, unless something contrary to calculation[20] should happen. (72)
The engagement having been a fierce one and both sides having lost many
ships and men,[21] the Syracusans and their allies, who had been victorious,
after recovering their wrecks and their dead, sailed off to their city and
erected a trophy."

371 **Chapter 27.** Now to me these and similar passages appeared worthy of
emulation and imitation,[1] and I am persuaded that the elevation (megalegoria),[2]
elegance (kallilogia),[3] forcefulness (deinotes),[4] and other qualities are <ex-
hibited> in these works in their highest perfection. My judgment is based
upon the fact that every type of mind is affected by this kind of discourse,
and neither the irrational critical element of the mind, which enables us to
comprehend what is pleasing (hedy) and what is disagreeable (aniaron), feels
a stranger to it, nor the reasoning element which is the touchstone by which
beauty (kalon) in the various arts is discerned.[5] Neither could those who
are not experts in parliamentary discourse mention a word or figure that
excites their displeasure, nor could the most fastidious, who look with scorn
upon the ignorance of the multitude, find fault with the ornamentation
(kataskeue)[6] of this style, but the many as well as the few will form the
same opinion. Neither will your layman, who exists in such large numbers,
have occasion to be displeased with the vulgarity (phortikon),[7] tortuosity
(skolion),[8] and obscurities (dysparakoloutheton)[9] of the style, nor will the
rarer trained stylist, who has enjoyed an unusual education,[10] find fault with

it as common (agennes),[11] vulgar (chamaitypes),[12] and inartistic (akata-skeuon).[13] But there will be perfect agreement between the rational and the irrational criterion[14] by both of which according to our opinion all works of art must be judged.[15] [lacuna] ...he has worked out the one, he does not keep up the beauty and the perfection in the execution of the other.

Chapter 28. I at any rate am not able to commend all those passages, which, though seeming grand and admirable to some, do not even possess the cardinal and most common virtues, but by reason of over-elaboration (periergon) and excess (peritton)[1] have lost their charm and their usefulness. I shall present a few specimens of such passages and will at once place by the side of them the reasons that have caused them to lapse into faults that are the very opposite of the desirable virtues. So in the third book when he narrates the cruel and impious acts perpetrated in the course of the civil war by the common people of Corcyra against the men of influence,[2] so long as he narrates the events in the common and familiar style of discourse, he says (lit. has said) everything clearly, concisely, and effectively. But when he begins to adopt a tragic style[3] in the narration of the common disasters of the Greeks and to depart from the common meaning of the words,[4] he falls far below his normal level. The first part of this narrative, which nobody could censure as being faulty,[5] is as follows: (Thuc. III.81.2) "When the Corcyraeans saw the Attic ships sailing up and those of the enemy gone, they took the Messenians,[6] who before had been outside, and brought them into the city. Then they gave orders for the ships that they had fitted out to sail around to the Hylaic harbor and while these were being taken around, they proceeded to slaughter whatever enemies they found, and disembarking all those whom they had persuaded to embark, they made away with them.[7] They also went to the Heraeum, and, after persuading about fifty of the suppliants to submit to trial, they condemned every one of them to death. The majority of the suppliants, who had not been persuaded, on seeing what was happening, killed one another in the sanctuary,[8] and some hanged themselves on the trees, and still others killed themselves the best way they could. For seven days, during which Eurymedon who had arrived remained with the sixty ships, the Corcyraeans butchered those among themselves who seemed to be enemies, stating the charge in the case of those who had been trying to undermine the demos. But there were some who were killed on account of private hatred, whilst others were put out of the way because money was owed to them by those who captured them. Thus every manner of death was resorted to, and as is wont to happen under such circumstances, there was nothing that did not happen, and even worse. For father slew son, and men were dragged away from sanctuaries, and were slain close to them, and a few were even walled up in the sanctuary of Dionysus and thus met death. (III.82) To such cruel lengths did party strife go. And it seemed all the more cruel, because it was among the first that took place.[9] For later all of Greece, one may say, was in a state of convulsion, there being quarrels everywhere, on the part of the

democratic leaders to bring in the Athenians, and on the part of the olig-
archs the Lacedaemonians."[10]

Chapter 29.[1] The passages that follow these[2] are contorted, hard to follow,
and contain figures so curiously constituted as to look like solecisms,[3] and
<devices> that were not used by writers of that time nor by those of later
374   times when the cultivation of prose style was at its zenith.[4] I shall now
quote the passage: (Thuc. III.82.3) "So the <affairs> in the cities[5] were
rent by civil dissensions, and those that for some reason or other were a
little late <in starting dissensions>, through hearing of what had been done
before far outstripped the others in the invention of plans both in the matter of the extreme ingenuity of their enterprises and by the strangeness of
their reprisals."[6] In this passage the first of the clauses has been periphras-
tically expressed without there being any need: "So the <affairs> in the
cities were rent by civil dissensions." It would have been better to say, "the
cities were rent by civil dissensions." The expression that follows this, "and
those that for some reason or other were a little late" is hard to interpret.[7]
It would have been clearer if it had been expressed thus: "and the cities
were late." This is followed by "through hearing of what had been done
before far outstripped the others in the invention of plans." <This too is
obscure> for he wishes to say, "The tardy on hearing what had happened
in other states took occasion to go to excess in the matter of devising new
schemes." Aside from the involved manner of speaking (ploke), not even
the framing of the words is pleasant to the ear. This passage he follows up
by another conclusion (kephalaion) that belongs more to the elaborate workmanship[8] of poetic, or rather dithyrambic,[9] art: "Both in the matter of the
extreme ingenuity of their enterprises as well as by the strangeness of their
reprisals, and for the ordinary value of words as applied to acts they changed
<the accepted signification of words> with a view to their actions as they
thought fit."[10] For what he wishes to indicate in this intricate mass of
words is about as follows: "They made great progress in innovations con-
375   nected with the technical contrivances of their undertakings and with the
monstrous punishments they inflicted, and changing the names as ordinarily
applied to acts, they claimed the right to call them by other names." The
expressions "extreme ingenuity" and "strangeness of their reprisals" and
"ordinary value of words" and "the justification for changing with a view to
their actions"[11] belong rather to poetical circumlocution. He next adds the
following showy figures: "reckless daring came to be regarded as bravery in
the interests of the party, and cautious delay as specious cowardice." Both
of these examples show assonance (paromoiosis)[12] and balance of clauses
(parisoseis)[13] and the epithets are used purely for purposes of ornament
(kallopismos).[14] For the structure of the sentence, if free from desire for
theatrical effect[15] ... [lacuna] and containing only what is essential, would
be about as follows: "daring was called bravery, and delay cowardice."
Similar to this is also what follows in the context, "wise restraint was called
the coward's mask, and prudence in everything <was construed as> an in-
disposition to do anything." It would have been more properly expressed

thus: "men of self-restraint were cowards, and those who were prudent in
all things were <regarded as> lazy in everything."[16]

Chapter 30. If after going thus far he had stopped embellishing his discourse in some places and toughening it up[1] in others, he would have been
less annoying (ochleros). But, as it is, he adds: "Intrigue was regarded as
safety and was a specious pretext for desertion <of one's party>.[2] The
violent man was always trusted, he that opposed him became an object of
suspicion." For in this passage again it is not clear to whom he refers by
376   "the violent man" nor in regard to what this violence is manifested, nor on
the other hand whom he means by his opponent and on what his opposition
is based. He continues: "One who plotted and was successful[3] was looked
upon as a shrewd fellow, and if he foresaw another's plot was even cleverer.
But if he exercised forethought and provided against future need[4] it was
said that he was a subverter of his party and smitten with fear of his enemies."[5] For neither does the expression "successful" help to clear up what
he wishes to say, nor can the same person be considered at one and the
same time as "successful" and "having foreseen," if the expression "successful" is used of the man who is successful and attains the object of his hope,
whereas the term "having foreseen" is used of the man who has foreseen
harm that has not yet been done but is still impending. The sense would be
clear[6] and luminous <if the section had been written> thus: "Those that
plotted against others were <considered> clever, if successful; those that
suspected hostile designs in advance and kept on their guard, were <thought
to be> still cleverer; but he who had taken measures in advance to need
neither intrigue nor protection <against intrigue> was thought to be bent
on breaking up the clubs and to be afraid of his enemies."

Chapter 31. After adding to this a single period which has been expressed
in a manner which in addition to clearness possesses also the quality of
terseness (angulos)[1] and effectiveness: "In plain words he that anticipated
the person who was about to do some harm was praised and no less the man
who had urged on <to intrigue> a man who had no idea of doing any such
thing," he is bound to indulge in poetical substitution (metalepsis),[2] thus:
377   (Thuc. III.82.6) "Moreover the <tie> of blood became weaker than that of
party because <those with the latter were[3]> more ready without an excuse
to engage in deeds of daring." For the expressions "the <tie> of blood"
and "the <tie> of party," used instead of "kinship" and "party,"[4] are substitutions, and it is not clear whether the expression "without an excuse to
engage in deeds of daring" is used of the friends or of the relatives. For,
assigning[5] the reason why they judged relatives greater strangers than friends,
he added "because they displayed a daring <that required> no excuse <to
act>."[6] The speech would have been clear if, framing it according to his
own meaning, he had expressed it after this fashion: "Moreover, even one's
associates were considered closer to oneself than one's relatives because they
were more ready to engage in deeds of daring without having any excuse for
so doing." Circumlocution also characterizes the passage that follows, and
it has been neither forcibly nor clearly expressed: "Such associations were

not <formed> in accordance with the established laws for the <public> good, but contrary to established laws for private gain."[7]   The sense is about as follows: "The associations were formed not for purposes of lawful mutual assistance but for gain by illegal means."   "And as for oaths," says the author (III.82.7),'if ever they *were* given[8] to make a reconciliation binding, being offered to meet a difficulty by one side or the other, they held good only for the time being while the parties had no resource from

378   any other quarter."   In this passage there is hyperbaton and circumlocution. The expression "oaths of reconciliation" has some such meaning as this: "If oaths ever were taken to bind a friendship."   The word "held good" being used in hyperbaton[9] belongs to "for the time being" for he means to say "they were in force for the time being."   The portion which reads "being offered to meet a difficulty by one side or the other while they had no resource from any other quarter," might have been expressed more clearly thus: "<oaths> being offered by each in his difficulty because each had no other power."   The proper sequence of thought would have been something like this: "If ever oaths were taken in matters of friendship, being offered by each for lack of any other pledge, they were in force only for the time being."[10]

Chapter 32.   More tortuous[1] than this is the passage that follows: "In any event that might chance the man who was the first to pluck up courage[2] if he saw <his enemy> off his guard was more delighted in revenging himself because of the other's faith <in the oath> than <when he attacked him> as an open enemy, and he took into consideration not only the safety of his course but also the fact that by having gotten the better of the fellow by deceit he was looked upon as the winner in a contest of shrewdness."   The term "that might chance" is used instead of "at the moment;"[3] "off his guard" instead of "unguarded,"[4] and the phrase "more delighted in revenging himself because of the other's faith than <when he attacked him> as an open enemy" is an obscure periphrasis and there is missing an element to complete the sense.   One may conjecture that this is what he wanted to say: "If by some means the opportunity presented itself to some one and he learned that his enemy was unguarded, he took greater pleasure in his revenge for attacking him when trusting <in himself> than when on his guard. For he also won a reputation for shrewdness because he took into consideration the safety of his course and the fact that he had worsted his enemy by

379   deceit."   He continues, "The majority are more readily called clever if they are rascals or ignorant if they are honorable, and they are ashamed of the latter but are exultant over the former."[5]   The statement is catchy and concise, but the meaning lies hidden in obscurity.   It is hard to find out whom he means by the ignorant and the honorable.   For if he contrasts them with the rascals, it would not follow that the people that are not bad are ignorant; but if he applies the term "ignorant" to fools and dullards on what basis does he call them honorable?   And of whom does he say "they are ashamed"?   It is not clear whether it is both groups or the ignorant.   In the case of "they are exultant" it is also uncertain who are meant.   For if he is speaking of both, it makes no sense; for neither do the honorable take

delight in the rascals nor are the rascals ashamed of the ignorant.

Chapter 33.   This obscure and involved way of talking in which the charm
of utterance (thelxis)[1] is far exceeded by the author's annoying habit
(ochlesis) of obscuring (skotizousa) the sense, is kept up for a hundred lines.
I shall quote also the sequel without adding a word of my own: (Thuc. III.
82.8) "The cause of this whole state of affairs was <the desire of> government for selfish gain and self-aggrandizement, and from these sprang eager-
ness <to quarrel> as men settled down into factional strife.[2]   The leaders of
both parties in the cities made a fine show of names, the ones by champion-
ing 'political equality (isonomia) of the masses,' the others a 'moderate
aristocracy,' and while saying that they were promoting the interests of the
state, they treated these as prizes in a contest.   Striving in every way to get
380   the better of one another they did not balk at the most terrible acts, and
the punishment they meted out was still more terrible, not confining themselves within the limits of justice and to what was of advantage to the state,[3]
but determining it by what at any time might give pleasure to the members
of the respective parties.   And in the attempt to gain the ascendency by an
unjust vote of condemnation or by open violence, they were ready to satisfy
the grudge of the moment.   Neither of the two factions placed any value on
piety, but those who happened to have accomplished some purpose in an
odious way under cover of some fine phrase were spoken of more highly.
Those of the citizens that were affiliated with neither party fell victims to
both factions, either because they refused to enter the fray or from envy
that they might survive.   (83) Thus factional life in Greece caused the prevalence of every kind of wickedness, and simplicity of which nobility of mind
is so large a part[4] became an object of derision and vanished.   <Instead> an
attitude of mutual distrust prevailed over a wide area.   There was no language
powerful enough and no oath terrible enough to reconcile them.   All men
when stronger <than their enemies>, by consideration of the hopelessness of
security <in word or deed>, took precautions not to suffer and were incap-
able of trusting anyone.   The men of inferior mental calibre as a rule got the
upper hand <of their adversaries>.   For fearing that as a result of their own
deficiency and the shrewdness of their adversaries they might be worsted in
arguments or might be anticipated in some plot by reason of their opponents'
intellectual versatility,[5] they boldly proceeded to act.   The other party, con-
temptuously assuming that they would foresee <an attack> and that there
was no need of getting by force what they could gain by cunning, were off
381   their guard and so perished in greater numbers."   Though I might adduce
many other examples to make it clear that Thucydides is better in his narratives (diegemata)[6] when he does not depart from the customary and familiar style of speech, and worse, when, instead of the ordinary method of
talking, he resorts to strange words and forced figures, some of which even
present the appearance of solecisms, I shall content myself with the above
specimens in order that my treatise may not be drawn out beyong the proper length.[7]

Chapter 34.   Since I have promised to state my opinion of his speeches

(demegoriai)[1] in which some people think he displayed the height of his genius,[2] I shall divide this treatment also into two sections, one on subject-matter (pragmatikon) and the other on style (lektikon), and speak about each separately, starting with the subject-matter. In the handling of the subject-matter the first place belongs to the invention (heuresis)[3] of enthymemes (enthymemata)[4] and conceptions (noemata),[5] the second place being held by the use of the prepared material. The first derives its force mainly from nature, the second from technique. Of the two the one that has a larger measure of natural endowment (to physikon) than of technical skill and that stands in need of a smaller amount of instruction (didache) is marvelously developed in our writer. For, as though from a rich source (lit. spring),[6] he draws forth an inexhaustible supply of conceptions (noemata) and enthymemes that are unusual (perittos), strange (xenos) and paradoxical (paradoxos).[7] But the part that involves a higher degree of technical skill and imparts additional luster to the other is less than it ought to be in many cases.[8] Now all those who admire the author excessively, so that <in their eyes> he does not differ from divinely inspired men, seem to feel this way on account of the great number of enthymemes. And if any one
382 attempts to instruct them in each matter, presenting the reason why it was not appropriate for this <statement> to be spoken on such and such an occasion and by such persons and that <another statement> should not have been used about such and such matters nor to such an extent, they are annoyed, experiencing the same feeling as those who are overpowered by so strong a love of some vision (opsis) as to border upon madness. For just as persons of this description imagine that the visions which have enchanted them possess all the qualities that belong to beautiful forms <in general> and accuse as slanderers and sycophants those who attempt to censure any defect that may adhere to them, so the former <the admirers of Thucydides>, having been stupified by this one quality, testify to the presence of all the other qualities, even such as are not present. For the characteristics that one desires to see (lit. to be) in connection with the object of one's affections and admiration, these one also believes to exist. All those who preserve an unprejudiced mind and base the criticism (exetasis) of writing upon correct principles, whether endowed with a natural gift for criticism or by reinforcing their critical faculties through the medium of instruction, neither praise all things alike nor take offence at everything, but they offer proper testimony to successful features, and withhold praise from any portion of the writing that may be a failure.[9]

Chapter 35. At any rate I, who base all my speculations upon fixed principles <of criticism>,[1] have not heretofore been reluctant to publish my
383 views, nor shall I now desist. Now granting as I do the first point, as I said in the beginning,[2] namely that Thucydides is successful in hitting the mark in the matter of invention (heuresis),—even if another critic, whether from a spirit of contentiousness or a lack of critical discernment (anaisthesia), has formed an opinion adverse to this, believing Thucydides to be at fault,—I no longer grant the other point, namely the possession of technical skill (tech-

nikon) in the arrangement of material (oikonomiai), except in the case of a
very few of the speeches (demegoriai).³ I note that the faults of diction
(lexis), about which I have already spoken,⁴ are most numerous and grave
in these forms of discourse. For as a matter of fact, obscure (glottematikai),
foreign (xenai) and coined (pepoiemenai) words are most in evidence in
these compositions, and the involved (polyploka), intricate (agkyla) and
strained (bebiasmena) figures are most numerous in them. Whether my judgment be right, you and every one else⁵ will judge as you are drawn to the
scrutiny (exetasis) of his works. The citation (lit. juxtaposition) of these
passages will be made after the same fashion, for over against the passages
that seem to me to be best, I shall marshall up for comparison the passages
that are neither a success in the matter of arrangement (oikonomia) nor un-
impeachable (anegkleton) in the matter of expression (phrasis).⁶

Chapter 36.¹ Now in the second book having set out to write of the march
of the Lacedaemonians and their allies against Plataeae he assumes that,
when Archidamus, the king of the Lacedaemonians, is on the point of rav-
aging the land,² envoys from the Plataeans have come into his presence and
he reports such speeches as were likely to have been given by each side,
speeches (logoi) that were suited to the speakers and appropriate to the subject,³ that neither fell short of nor went beyond the proper measure; and
he embodied them in language (lexis) that is pure (kathara), clear (saphes)
and concise (syntomos),⁴ and that does not lack the other qualities. And
the harmony (harmonia)⁵ of it is so inspired⁶ that … [lacuna] <it may> be
compared with the most enjoyable <compositions>: (Thuc. II.71) "The
following summer the Peloponnesians and their allies did not invade Attica,
but marched against Plataeae. The command was exercised by Archidamus,
son of Zeuxidamus, a king of the Lacedaemonians. After encamping his
army, he was about to lay waste the land. But the Plataeans at once dispatched envoys to him⁷ who spoke about as follows: 'Archidamus and men
of Lacedaemon, in making this expedition into the land of the Plataeans
you are committing a wrong and acting in a manner not worthy of you nor
of your ancestors. For <you will remember that> Pausanias, the son of
Cleombrotus, a native of Lacedaemon, after liberating Greece from the Medes
with the help of the Greeks who were willing to share the danger⁸ and <par-
ticipate in> the battle that was fought in our land, offered sacrifice to Zeus
Savior⁹ in the market-place of the Plataeans and after convoking an assembly
of all the allies gave back to the Plataeans their land and their city to keep
and to dwell therein in freedom. And no one was ever to make an expedition against them without a just cause or for their enslavement; and if anyone did, then all the allies who were present <at the meeting> were to assist the Plataeans as they were able. This is the gift that your ancestors
bestowed upon us as a reward for the bravery and the zeal that we displayed
in those times of danger. But you are doing just the reverse of what they
did.¹⁰ For, in company with the Thebans, who are our worst enemies, you
are come to enslave us. But summoning as witnesses the gods that then
served to bind the oaths, and your ancestral gods and the gods of our land,

we call on you not to harm the Plataean land[11] and not to transgress your oaths, but to permit us to dwell in freedom, exactly as[12] Pausanias deemed right.' (II.72) That being about what the Plataeans said, Archidamus makes reply about as follows:[13] 'Your words are just, men of Plataeae, if your acts are like your words. As Pausanias has given you the privilege, live in freedom yourselves and help free the others, as many as shared the dangers of those times and joined you in the oaths but are now under Athenian domination. All this military preparation has been made and this great war has been started to free them and the others. Therein you should take part if possible and yourselves abide by your oaths. Or else, do as we even before[14] called upon you to do, keep peace and dwell in your lands. Take sides with neither, receive both as friends but neither for warlike purposes.

386   With this we shall be satisfied.' Thus much did Archidamus say. Upon hearing this the Plataean envoys entered the city. Having communicated the speech to the populace, they made answer to him that it was impossible for them to comply with his request without <consulting> the Athenians; that children and women of theirs were at Athens. They also feared for their whole[15] city lest, after the Lacedaemonians had departed, the Athenians would come and not permit them to comply, or else that the Thebans, taking advantage of the fact that they were parties to sworn compacts that both sides were to be received, might again make an attempt[16] to seize their city. (II.72.3) Wishing to encourage them, Archidamus said in reply to this: 'Do you hand over for safe-keeping to us, the Lacedaemonians, your city and houses, and designate the boundaries of your land, and <specify> your trees[17] and whatever else is subject to enumeration. But do you yourselves go whither you desire, as long as the war lasts. When it is over, we will return to you what we receive. Up to this time we will hold <these lands> in trust, keep <them> in cultivation, and make returns[18] to you such as will suffice for your wants.' (73) After hearing this they again returned to the city and when they had deliberated with the people they said that they wished first to communicate his proposals to the Athenians, and if they persuaded them they would be willing to do as he asked. They urged him to

387   grant them a truce till that time and to refrain from laying waste their land. Archidamus agreed to a truce for the number of days in which they were likely to complete their journey and refrained from laying waste their land. So the Plataean envoys went to the Athenians and after sharing in their deliberations they returned with some such message[19] as the following to the people in the city. 'The Athenians say that never before since we entered into alliance with them have they allowed you to be wronged in any matter, nor will they permit it now, but will help you to the best of their ability, and they adjure you by the oaths which your fathers swore, not to make any change in the matter of the alliance.' (II.74) When the envoys brought back such a report, the Plataeans[20] resolved not to desert the Athenians but to put up,[21] if need should be,[22] with the sight of their country being laid waste, and with any other suffering that might befall them. <They decreed> that no one should leave the town any more, but that they should give the reply from the city walls to the effect that it was impossible

for them to comply with the proposal of the Lacedaemonians. When they had made the reply, then first of all Archidamus the[23] King addressed himself to the task of calling to witness the gods and heroes of the country with these words: 'Ye gods as many of you as dwell in the land of Plataeae, and ye heroes, be ye[24] my witnesses that neither at the outset <was it due to> any lawlessness <of our own>, but only when these people first[25] departed from the sworn agreement, did we invade this land in which our fathers, after prayers to you, overcame the Medes and thanks to you found it a favorable field for the Greeks to fight in, nor shall we now, if we take any measure, commit any wrong. For having made an appeal to them to do a number of things that are reasonable, we meet with no success. Do ye therefore permit those who were the aggressors to be punished on account of their wrong-doing, and those obtain their revenge who are seeking to exact it lawfully.' (II.75) After this brief adjuration of the gods he got his army to open hostilities."

388

Chapter 37. Let us examine by the side of this dialogue[1] which is so fine and so extraordinary another dialogue of his, which is highly lauded by the admirers of Thucydides' style.[2] After the Athenians had dispatched an army against the Melians, the colonists of the Lacedaemonians, and before they started hostilities, he represents the Athenian general and the Melian delegates (probouloi)[3] as holding a conference about the settlement of the war.[4] In the beginning he in his own person states what was spoken by each side, but preserving this narrative form[5] in one reply only, he introduces persons in the remainder of the dialogue and uses a dramatic form.[6] The Athenian begins with the following statement: (Thuc. V.85) " 'Inasmuch as our remarks are not directed to the assembly, evidently in order that the people[7] may not be deceived by hearing from us once for all in uninterrupted discourse statements which are seductive and untested—we know that this is the meaning of our[8] being taken before the few—do you, the presiding body,[9] act in a still safer way. You also[10] must not make up your mind in a brief space of time,[11] but you must instantly challenge every statement of ours that seems to be amiss. And first state whether our proposal suits you.' (V.86) The Melian commissioners replied: 'The fairness[12] of the proposal to engage in quiet interchange is not questioned <by us>. But your <acts> of war, which are already at hand and not a thing of the future, are plainly at variance with it.' " As to this last statement if any one would see fit to reckon it as an example of a figure of speech,[13] he must forthwith call figures of speech all the solecisms that constitute violations of number and case. After leading off with the statement, "The fairness of the proposal to engage in quiet interchange is not questioned," he attaches to that which is singular and expressed in the nominative case (i.e. epieikeia), the words "the <acts> of war which are already at hand and not a thing of the future" and adds to these a singular in the genitive case, namely the word αὐτοῦ, whether one chooses to call this a demonstrative article (dektikon arthron)[14] or a pronoun (antonomasia). Now by refusing to make this word conform to either the feminine singular nominative

389

<ἐπιείκεια and hence αὐτῆς> or the plural neuter accusative <τὰ τοῦ πολέ-
μου and hence αὐτά> he has destroyed the concord.[15] The sentence would
390 have had been rightly construed[16] if framed in this wise: "The fairness of
the proposal to engage in quiet interchange is not questioned: but the <acts>
of war, which are already at hand and not a thing of the future, are plainly
at variance with it (feminine = "fairness")." After these words, he puts an
enthymeme which is indeed conceived in a normal way, but is not expressed
in a manner that can be easily followed: (Thuc. V.87) "Now then, if you
have met to consider conjectures about the future or for some other purpose
than to plan[17] for the safety of your city in the light of present conditions
and what you see, we <shall> stop.[18] But if this is your purpose, we will
continue the discussion."

Chapter 38. Hereupon turning the dialogue from the narrative form to the
dramatic, he makes the Athenian (*sic*)[1] reply as follows: (V.88) "It is natural and pardonable for men in such a plight as ours to turn[2] their words
and thoughts upon divers things." Then after setting up a very fine statement of the case (prothesis), to wit: "This meeting, however, has met to
consider the question of our safety and, if you so desire, let the discussion
proceed in the way that you propose," he first makes use of <the following>
enthymeme which is neither worthy of the Athenian state nor fitting to be
used of such events: (V.89) "Neither are we ourselves going to make use of
a lot of fine words and inflict on you a long speech without being believed,[3]
claiming that because we defeated the Medes we are justly continuing in the
exercise of our rule or that we have been wronged and are now coming to
exact vengeance." These are the words of a man who admits that the expedition is directed against people who have done no wrong, since he is unwilling to speak on either point.[4] He then adds, "Nor do we expect you to
391 think to prevail by saying either that you are colonists from Lacedaemon
and did not join us (or her[5]) in the war, or that you have done us no wrong,
but <we expect both> to negotiate <the best> possible terms on the basis
of the real state of mind of both of us." This amounts to saying: "Do you,
though correctly believing that you are being wronged, plead necessity and
yield. We, on the other hand, being well aware that we are wronging you,
shall overcome you in your weakness by force. These are the possibilities
on either side." Then wishing to state the grounds for such a decision he
adds: "Because justice as human beings see things is determined by equal
compulsion <on both sides>, but superiors exact what they can and the weak
submit."

Chapter 39. Words like these were appropriate to oriental monarchs addressing Greeks, but unfit to be spoken by Athenians to the Greeks whom
they liberated from the Medes, to wit, that justice is the normal conduct
of equals to one another, but violence is <the law> of the strong against
the weak.[1] After a brief reply on the part of the Melians to the effect that
it would be well for the Athenians to be considerate of justice, lest they
too might some day meet with misfortune and come under the authority of
others and be subjected to the same treatment by those stronger <than

themselves>, he represents the Athenian as replying: (V.91) "As for us, we
are not gloomy about the termination of our empire, even though it be dis-
solved," giving as the reason of this <optimism> that even if the Lacedaemonians put an end to the <Athenian> empire, they will pardon the Athenians because they themselves were guilty of much similar conduct. I shall
392   also put down his words: (V.91) "It is not those who like the Lacedaemonians exercise dominion over others who are to be feared by the vanquished."
This is like saying that tyrants are not hated among tyrants. He then adds:
"And as regards this matter just leave it to us to run the risk," words such
as a pirate or robber would hardly utter, saying "I don't care about the
vengeance to follow if only I gratify my present desires." Then after a brief
dialogue when the Melians were ready to agree to a fair compromise: (V.94)
"So <you mean to say>[2] that you would not accept a proposition for us to
be neutral and be your friends instead of enemies, but the allies of neither
side?", he makes the Athenian reply: (V.95) "No, your enmity is not half
so mischievous to us as your friendship; for the one is in the eyes of our
subjects an argument of our power, the other of our weakness."[3] This is a
bad enthymeme and tortuously expressed.[4] If one wishes to have a clear
view of his thought, it is something like this: "If you love us, you will make
us appear weak before the eyes of others, but if you hate us, <you will
make us appear> strong. For we do not seek to rule our subjects by good-
will but by fear."

Chapter 40. Adding to this some more elaborate and stinging repartee, he
represents the Melians as saying that the fortunes of war[1] favor neither side
and: (V.102) "To yield cuts off all hope forthwith, but action holds out
the hope that we may yet stand upright." In answer to this, he makes the
Athenian reply <in a statement that is> more tortuous than a labyrinth as
393   to the hope that men entertain in misfortune, writing word for word as follows: (Thuc. V.103) "Hope, which is a solace in danger,[2] though it may
injure, yet does not utterly destroy those who have recourse to her if they
have a superabundance <of other support>, but when men stake all they
have <upon hope> (hope is a spendthrift by nature), her true nature is only
recognized when disaster has come upon them, and at the same time she
leaves no further opportunity for men to guard against her, when once she
is known. Of such an experience as this, do you who are weak and who
have but a single place of vantage[3] beware, and do not liken yourselves to
the many, who though still capable of being humanly saved, when hard
pressed and bereft of visible hopes[4] seek refuge in hopes that are invisible,
in divination, oracles, and all the other things which as the attendants of
hope bring ruin." I do not know how one could commend words like these
as fit to be spoken by Athenian generals, namely, that hope proceeding
from the gods brings ruin upon men, and that there is no use of either
oracles or divination to those who have chosen a life of piety and righteous-
ness. Even though there be other reasons, it is one of the chief glories of
the city of the Athenians to follow the gods in every matter and on every
occasion and to execute nothing without divination and oracles. And when

the Melians said that in addition to help from the gods they put their faith also in the Lacedaemonians, who, if for no other reason, would at least from a sense of shame come to their rescue and would not permit them,

394 related by blood as they were, to be destroyed, he introduces the Athenian making a still bolder reply: (V.105) "As for the favor of the gods, we too do not expect to be left behind. For we make no claims and commit no act that runs counter to recognized human views in matters relating to the gods, or that is not comprised within the ordinary wishes that men entertain for themselves.[5] For of the gods we believe and of men we know clearly that throughout the ages they rule whomever they rule by the iron hand of necessity as a result of the very nature of their being."[6] The meaning of these words is hard to guess even for those who seem to be very well versed in the author, but the statement winds up with some such conclusion as this, that everybody's knowledge of the gods is a matter of opinion, but justice between man and man is determined by the common law of nature; <the mandate of> which is that one should rule over whomever one can hold in subjection. These words are in a line with the first[7] and are not fit to be spoken by either Athenians or <any other> Greeks.

Chapter 41. Though I might cite many other sentiments which reveal a depraved shrewdness, yet to keep my essay from extending beyond the proper limits I shall adduce no more than the final conclusion which the Athenian spoke as he was about to leave the meeting: (V.111.2) "But your strength,[1] resting <merely> upon hope, is subject to delay, and your present[2] <means of resistance> are too slight to prevail[3] against forces that

395 are already drawn up against you. You[4] show a great lack of brains if, after letting us withdraw,[5] you do not determine upon some other more sensible course than this." To this he adds: (V.111.3) "For surely you will not seek refuge in that sense of shame which often brings men to ruin when they are confronted by dangers involving disgrace and clearly foreseen. For many men, while yet foreseeing <the destruction> for which they are heading, are lured on by the powers[6] of a seductive word, so-called shame, and so, victims of a word, they have plunged in fact with eyes wide open[7] into irreparable disaster."

That the historian was not present on that occasion at the meeting, and that he did not hear these speeches from the Athenians or the Melians who recited them, may readily be seen from what the author writes about himself in the preceding book,[8] that after serving as a general at Amphipolis he was banished from his native city and spent the entire remaining period of the war in Thrace.[9] So it remains to be examined whether he has made the dialogue appropriate to the circumstances and befitting the persons who came together at the conference, "adhering as closely as possible[10] to the overall purport of what was actually said," as he himself has stated (I.22.1)

396 in the proem of his history. Is it true, then, that as the speeches about freedom which called upon the Athenians not to enslave a Greek city that was doing no wrong against them were appropriate and suitable to the Melians, so also propriety characterized <the speeches of> the Athenian

generals who permitted no examination of or reference to the justice of the
case, but who introduced the law of violence and greed and declared that
the pleasure of the stronger constituted the justice of the weak? I for my
part do not believe that such words were appropriate for commanders who
were sent from a city that enjoyed the very best of laws to foreign cities,
and I should say that it ill befitted Athenians, who preferred to leave their
country and city at the time of the Persian War in order that they might
not have to submit to any disgraceful command, to accuse those who chose
the same course of being fools, whereas the Melians, who were citizens of a
small state and who had performed no signal act, took greater thought of
honor than of safety and were ready to endure all possible suffering in order that they might not be compelled to do any unseemly thing. I believe
that even if any other people attempted to say such things in the presence
of the Athenians, they who have exercised such a humanizing influence on
everyday life would have grown indignant. So for these reasons I do not
approve this dialogue when I compare it with the other one. For in that
other Archidamus the Lacedaemonian makes a just request of the Plataeans
and makes use of language (lexis) that is pure (katharos) and clear (saphes)
and containing no figure that has been twisted on the rack[11] and no anaco-
397   luthon. In the present dialogue, however, the wisest of the Greeks advance
the most disgraceful arguments (enthymemata) and clothe them in most un-
pleasing language. Unless it be that the historian is harboring a grudge
against the city on account of his condemnation and is showering upon it
these reproaches which were bound to cause it to be hated by all men.[12]
For the views and statements which the leaders of the cities and the men
entrusted with such great power <seem>[13] to hold and to express before
<other> cities on behalf of their own city,—these <views and statements>
all men look upon as shared by the city which dispatches them. Thus much
then for the dialogues.

Chapter 42.[1] Of the harangues, I greatly admire the one in the first book
that was spoken at Athens by Pericles (I.140-144) on the question of not
yielding to the Lacedaemonians, which has this beginning,[2] "My opinion,
men of Athens,[3] is ever the same. We ought not to yield to the Peloponnesians." The arguments (enthymemata) are marvelously expressed and the
hearer is not annoyed by the way in which the parts are put together nor
by an unusual use of figures that are strained and are characterized by anacoluthon;[4] but this speech embraces all the fine qualities that harangues
may have. <I also admire> the speeches of Nicias, the general, which were
spoken at Athens in reference to the Sicilian expedition (VI.9-14, 20-23),
and the letter sent by him to the Athenians (VII.11-15) in which he asks
398   for auxiliary forces and a successor <to himself>, his body being weakened
by disease; also his hortatory address to his soldiers, which he made before
the last naval battle (VII.61-64); also the consolatory address delivered when
he was on the eve of leading off his army by land after the loss of all his
ships (VII.77); and whatever other similar addresses there may be that are
characterized by purity[5] and perspicuity[6] and are suitable for actual plead-

ings.[7]   But more than all the speeches presented in the seven books I admire the defence of the Plataeans (III.53-59), and that for nothing so much
as for the absence of distortion[8] and excessive elaboration[9] and the use of
true and natural embellishments.[10]   The arguments (enthymemata) are presented with a great deal of feeling, and the language is not repulsive to the
ear.   For the composition is euphonious[11] and the figures are appropriate to
the matter.[12]   These are the works of Thucydides that are worthy of emulation, and I advise historians to draw their material for imitation from
these.[13]

Chapter 43.   The defence of Pericles (II.60-64) in the second book which
he made on behalf of himself when the Athenians were exasperated because
he persuaded them to undertake the war, I do not approve in its entirety.
Neither do I commend the speeches on the city of the Mytilenaeans which
Cleon (III.37-40) and Diodotus (III.42-48) made and which are recorded in
the third book; nor the speech of Hermocrates of Syracuse (VI.76-80) to
the people of Camarina; nor the speech in reply by Euphemus (VI.82-87),
399   the ambassador of the Athenians; and others like these.   For there is no need
to enumerate all those that are written in the same style of language (dialektos).   That no one may think that I am making statements which are not
susceptible of proof (though I might furnish an abundance of proofs) yet in
order that my discourse may not become too long I will content myself
with two speeches, the defence of Pericles and the invective of Hermocrates
against the Athenian state addressed to the people of Camarina.

Chapter 44.   Pericles speaks as follows: (Thuc. II.60) "This outburst of
your anger against me is just what I expected, for I see the reasons, and I
have called this assembly for the express purpose of calling to your attention
and remonstrating with you if in any respect you are wrong either in being
angry with me or in giving way to your misfortunes."   Such language as this
was suitable for Thucydides writing about the man in the form of a narrative,[1] but it was not appropriate for Pericles who was defending himself
against an angry crowd[2] especially so at the beginning of his defence before
he had tempered the anger of men, who were naturally out of sorts because
of their misfortunes, with arguments of another nature.   For the best of
their land had been laid waste by the Lacedaemonians, a great multitude
had died during the prevalence of the plague, and the war, which they had
undertaken at his advice, had provoked these troubles.   Besides, the form
of censure was entirely inappropriate[3] to the thought where there was need
400   of conciliation.[4]   For orators ought not to stir up but to calm the anger of
the masses.   The words discussed are followed by a sentiment that is true
enough and well expressed but inapplicable to the occasion: (II.60.2) "For
I am of the opinion that a city which is flourishing as a whole is of greater
benefit to the individuals than one that is prosperous as regards its individual
citizens but is collectively going to ruin.   For the man who is prospering in
his own private affairs none the less perishes in the general ruin of his native
city, but if he is suffering from misfortune in a city enjoying general prosperity his final salvation is far more likely."   As a matter of fact if some of

the citizens had suffered losses individually, whilst the state as a whole had been prosperous, the language would have been appropriate; but, inasmuch as all were plunged into the very depths of misfortune, it cannot be said to be appropriate. Neither was there any ground for optimism as to the future in the thought that terrible sufferings would turn out to be an advantage to the city. For to a human being the future is dark, and the vicissitudes of fortune change one's views of the future in the light of the present.

Chapter 45. These words are followed by a still more commonplace thought[1] and one that is not at all appropriate for the occasion: (II.60.5) "But I, the person against whom you are directing your anger, am a man of such ability that I believe myself inferior to no one in recognizing the needs of a situation and expounding these needs,[2] and I am a patriot and superior to bribes." It would be an astonishing thing, if Pericles, the greatest of the orators of his time, had not known what any man of even moderate sense knew, that everywhere men who unsparingly praise their own merits appear to annoy their hearers, and especially so in speeches before courts and the public assemblies, in which the danger is not one of honors but of punishment. For in such cases they are not only an annoyance to others, but the cause of misfortune to themselves, provoking as they do the envy of the multitude. When one has the same men as judges and plaintiffs, one needs countless tears and appeals to pity to secure the very first thing of all, namely, the good will of the audience. But the popular leader (Pericles) is not content with the statements already made. He works it up anew in the following manner and repeats in different words what he has already stated: (Thuc. II.60.6) "For he who has seen the needs, but has not clearly stated them, is no better off than if he had had no conception of them, and he who possesses both qualities, but is hostile to his country, cannot speak with the same degree of ease as a loyal citizen; but even supposing that he possessed patriotism, but was subject to bribes,[3] he would sell everything for this single consideration." I do not know who would assert that the propriety of such utterances on the part of Pericles, addressing Athenians who were in a state of irritation, was equal to their truth. Indeed the invention (heuresis) of the very best arguments and thoughts is not in itself an object worthy of serious effort, if they are not appropriate to the events, the speakers, the occasions, and everything else <connected with them>. But <the fact is> as I said at the outset, the historian, giving expression to his own views about the merits of Pericles, seems to have spoken these words contrary to the proprieties of the occasion (topos).[4] The writer ought himself to have expressed whatever views he desired about the statesman, but ought to have put in his mouth, when he was in danger, words that were humble and calculated to conciliate the anger <of his audience>. Such a course would have been befitting a writer who was desirous of giving a picture of the truth.

Chapter 46. Annoying, too, are these puerile[1] embellishments[2] of speech and intricately constructed arguments: (II.62.3) "to go and meet the enemy and drive them off[3] not only with spirit (phronema) but with the spirit of contempt (kataphronema). For even a coward may be filled with spirit as the result of ignorance when good luck attends it,[4] but the spirit of contempt is found only in one whose judgment makes him confident that he is superior to his opponents, as is the case with us. And courage based upon an equal <share of> fortune[5] is rendered more secure by intelligence which springs from a superior feeling.[6] And it[7] trusts less in hope, whose strength lies in perplexity, than in judgment based upon facts, which gives a surer insight into the future."[8] The <paranomasia of> "spirit" (phronema)[9] is rather frigid and more in keeping with the style of Gorgias, and the interpretation of the terms partakes of sophistry[10] and is devoid of good taste.[11] And the courage which "based upon an equal <share of> fortune is rendered more stable by the intelligence which springs from a superior feeling" is stated in terms that are more obscure than the dark sayings of Heraclitus,[12] and the "strength of hope in perplexity" and a "surer insight of judgment based upon facts" are poetical periphrases. What the writer means to say is that one must trust a judgment derived from existing circumstances more than hopes whose strength lies in the future.

403   **Chapter 47.**[1] I have even observed that while attempting to allay the anger that had taken possession of them because of the disasters from which they were suffering, the majority of which had befallen them contrary to calculation and expectation,[2] and calling upon them to bear their misfortunes in a noble manner[3] and not to mar the distinction of the city,[4] but putting away their private sorrow to apply themselves to the safety of the commonwealth,[5] and thereupon having related that in view of the firmly established possession of their naval empire they will not be put down by either the King, or the Lacedaemonians, or any other nation on earth (cf. II.62.2)[6] (the proof of which was not a present one but belonged to the future, nor one that was founded on foresight but upon hopes), then forgetting all this he asks them not to trust in hope whose strength lies in perplexity.[7] These statements are contrary to each other if indeed pain produced a sensation that was already present, whereas the manifestation of help was yet absent (cf. II.61.2).[8]

　　　But to the same degree as I find fault with the preceding from the point of view of the subject-matter and the style, so I admire the following for its accurate thought, elegant[9] expression and agreeable composition: (II.61.1) "for those who are otherwise prosperous and have the choice <between peace and war>, it would be sheer folly to go to war, but if it were necessary either to yield at once and submit to one's neighbors or else to incur danger and survive, one who shuns danger is more to be blamed than one who stands to face it. And I am ever the same <in opinion> and

404   do not change my mind, but it is you who change, since as luck has it you followed my advice when still unscathed, but repent now that you are suffering." This passage too <is admirable>: (II.61.3) "For the spirit is cowed by the sudden and unexpected[10] and by what happens most contrary to calculation. ... [lacuna][11] (4) nevertheless as you are citizens of a great state and have been brought up amid customs corresponding to her greatness, you

ought to be willing to endure affliction[12] and not lose your distinction; for
men think it equally right to blame the man who falls short through cowardice of the reputation he already enjoys[13] and to hate the man who
through over-boldness tries to reach out for that which is not deserved."
Likewise the following words which arouse in the hearts of the Athenians
their ancestral pride: (II.63.1) "And furthermore it is reasonable for you to
try to maintain the honorable position of your city that has been won by
your leadership, in which you above all others[14] take pride, and not to shrink
from hardships unless you also stop coveting those honors. And you must
not imagine that the contest involves but a single issue, the substitution of
servitude for freedom, but it is a question also of the loss of empire and
danger from the enmities you incurred in the exercise of the empire. And
from this <empire> it is impossible for you to withdraw, even if anyone,
prompted by his present alarm and an indolent spirit, wishes to play the role
of honest man. For by this time the empire you hold is a tyranny, which it
seems wrong to have assumed, but it is hazardous to abandon."[15] And <I
admire> all those passages which like these exhibit variations from the normal use of words and figures which are moderate and not too elaborate or
hard to follow.[16]

405   **Chapter 48.** Of the speech of Hermocrates I am able to praise the following
successful efforts[1] of the writer: (VI.77.1) "But we have not come now to
point out in the presence of those who already know how many injustices
the city of the Athenians has committed, although she is open to accusation,
but <we are here> rather to remonstrate with ourselves for having before
our eyes examples of how Greeks over there (= of the Aegean)[2] were reduced
to slavery from failing to help one another and <seeing> the same deceptive
tricks now being practiced upon ourselves—resettlements of Leontine relatives
and succourings of Egestaean allies—we are not willing to unite and to show
them with more spirit that this is not a case here[3] of Ionians or of Helles-
pontians and islanders, who are forever changing masters, be it a Mede or
some other <tyrant>, and continuing in a state of servitude, but Dorians,
free men who have come from a free country, the Peloponnesus, and have
settled in Sicily. Or do we mean to wait[4] until we are taken one at a time,
city by city, knowing that this is the only way we can be conquered?" For
this passage which is expressed in clear and pure language has the added
qualities of rapidity (tachos),[5] beauty (kallos),[6] tension (tonos),[7] grandeur
(megaloprepes)[8] and forcefulness (deinotes),[9] and is full of oratorical passion. And one might use this language[10] at the bar, at public meetings, and
in conversation with friends. And here is another fine passage: (VI.78.2)
"And if there is any one who is filled with envy of us or even fears us (for
406   greater <powers> incur both these sentiments), and for this reason wishes
the Syracusans to suffer harm in order that we may be humbled in our pride,
and yet out of consideration for his own safety wishes her to be saved, he is
cherishing a wish that does not lie within human power. For the same man
cannot at one and the same time be the steward of his wishes and of fortune."
And so the passage at the close of the speech: (VI.80.3) "We beseech you,

then, and asseverate,[11] should we fail to persuade you, that the plot against us is being hatched by Ionians, our perpetual enemies, but we are being betrayed by you, Dorians by Dorians. (4) And if the Athenians subdue us, they will prevail by your decisions, but will be honored in their own name, and they will receive as the prize of their victory none other than the one that made the victory possible." These and similar passages I deem beautiful and worthy of emulation. But I do not see how I could praise passages like the following: (VI.76.2) "For now <they have come>[12] to Sicily on a pretext that you have heard, but with an intention that we all suspect. And it seems to me they do not so much want to settle the Leontinians in the land as to drive us out of it."[14] The paronomasia is frigid,[14] and adds no real feeling but gives a studied appearance. The same is true of the following involved and many-twisted figures:[15] (VI.76.4) "Resistance to the Mede was not offered by these[16] for the freedom of the Greeks, nor by the Greeks for their own freedom, but by the ones <the Athenians> for the enslavement

407   of the others to themselves instead of to him <the Mede>, and by the others <the Greeks> for the sake of getting a new master who was not more empty-minded, but more evil-minded."[17] And the same judgment must be rendered about the violence[18] of the transfer from the plural to the singular and from discourse about persons to the person of the speaker:[19] (VI.78.1) "And if it actually occurs to someone that not he, but the Syracusan, is the enemy of the Athenian and thinks it a hard thing to fight for *my* country let him consider that he is fighting[20] not so much for my country as <that he is fighting> to an equal degree for his own country while fighting in mine, and all the more safely because if I have not previously been destroyed, he will fight with me as an ally and not alone. And let him consider that the Athenian <does not want> to punish the hostility of the Syracusan ..."[21] For this language is puerile and over-wrought and not so clear as a so-called enigma. And this is true of the following passages in addition to those above: (VI. 78.3) "And if he were to be mistaken in his judgment, when bewailing his own misfortunes he might perhaps some day conceive the desire again to envy *my* good fortune.[22] But <that would be> impossible for <one> who had abandoned <me> and had been unwilling to assume the same dangers <as I do>, in a matter of deeds not words." And to these words he adds a concluding remark (epiphonema)[23] which one would not expect of a boy. "For nominally he would be preserving our power, but actually he would be promoting his own[24] safety."

408   **Chapter 49.** There are other passages also in this speech which deserve censure, but I need not say any more about them. For I think that even by these I have made my proposition sufficiently clear that that kind of Thucydidean language is best which only moderately deviates from the customary mode of speech and which preserves the first and necessary[1] virtues; but inferior is the kind which makes frequent deviation from words and figures generally used and resorts to such as are foreign (xena), forced (bebiasmena) and show a lack of proper sequence (anakoloutheta),[2] which prevents any of the other virtues from producing their peculiar effect. For such a style

of language (phrasis) is useful neither in public meetings in which citizens
(lit. the cities) meet to deliberate about peace, war, the introduction of laws,
the regulation of the form of government, and the other large affairs of
state, nor in courts, where speeches dealing with death, exile, loss of civil
rights, imprisonment, and the carrying off of money are addressed to those
who have received the authority in such matters (... [lacuna] for they of-
fend the rank and file of the citizens who are not used to hear such language),
nor in private conversations, in which we talk with citizens, friends, or relatives about everyday affairs, narrating some of our own experiences, or consulting them about some of the necessities of life, or admonishing, or making
requests, or rejoicing with them in their blessings, or grieving with them in
409   their misfortunes. I omit to say that even the mothers and the fathers of
persons speaking in this way would be disgusted <with such language> and
would not put up with it but would ask for interpreters as though they were
listening to a foreign tongue.[3]   This is what my conviction is in regard to
the writer, and I have stated it in all candor to the best of my ability.

Chapter 50.   It is necessary also to examine briefly the statements made in
his defence by some, in order that I may not seem to have omitted anything.
It will, of course, be admitted by all those who are of unimpaired mind and
in possession of their natural senses that such a style is not suitable for political debates[1] nor for private conversations, but some professors of repute[2]
venture to state that whilst this style is not suited to those who have fitted
themselves for addressing large crowds nor for court speakers, but that for
those who publish historical treatises, which demand grandeur,[3] solemnity,[4]
and impressiveness (kataplexis)[5] it is desirable above all to cultivate this
mode of expression (phrasis) which is obscure, archaic, figurative and which
deviates from usual figures in the direction of the strange (xenon) and elaborate (peritton).[6]   For the claim is that writings like these are not composed
for the people of the market-place nor for shopmen and artisans, nor for
others who have not shared in a liberal education, but for men who after
passing through the cycle of general studies[7] have advanced to rhetoric and
philosophy, to whom none of these things will appear strange.[8]   Some have
410   even made the attempt to say that the historian wrote his work not with a
view to the people of later times, but to men of his own times, who had a
manner of speaking (dialektos)...[9] [lacuna] this style of language is useful
neither for deliberative nor for forensic speeches in which the members of
the assembly and those of the jury are different from those that Thucydides
assumed.[10]

Chapter 51.   To those who think that only the well-educated are qualified
to read and understand the language (dialektos) of Thucydides, I have this
to say, that, by limiting the work to a very few men exactly as in cities of
an oligarchic or tyrannical form of government, they remove from the general life of mankind[1] that feature of the work <which comprises> its indis-
pensability and its universal utility (for nothing could be more indispensable
and of more varied use). For easily counted are the few who are capable of
understanding the whole of Thucydides, and not even these can understand

some <of the passages> without recourse to a grammatical commentary.[2]
To those who would refer the Thucydidean language to archaic life, claiming
that such language was in common use among the people of those days, a
brief and clear reply suffices. At the period of the Peloponnesian war there
were many orators and philosophers at Athens, and yet none of them has
made use of such language, neither Andocides, Antiphon and Lysias and
their schools, nor the Socratic schools of Critias, Antisthenes, and Xenophon.[3]
411   Of all these men, Thucydides plainly was the first to practice this style of
expression (hermeneia)[4] in order to differ from the other writers.[5]   Now
when he uses it sparingly[6] and with moderation, he is marvelous and not to
be compared with any other writer.   But when he uses it lavishly and without taste,[7] distinguishing neither fitness nor measure,[8] he is blameworthy.
As for myself, I should not want an historical treatise to be jejune (auchme-
ra),[9] unadorned, and commonplace, but to have also a touch of the poetic.[10]
Nor <should I be satisfied with> a style that is altogether poetical, but one
that deviates but slightly from the language in common use.   Excess of even
the most pleasant things is annoying (aniaros), and moderation (symmetria)[11]
is everywhere useful.

Chapter 52.[1]   I have yet to say something about the orators and writers
who have imitated Thucydides. This matter must needs be discussed, like
others, to complete my treatment, but it causes me[2] some hesitation and
much anxiety lest to those who are in the habit of speaking ill (sykophant-
ein)[3] of everything, I afford an occasion for slander that is altogether at
variance with the fair-mindedness which I have displayed in my speech and
my conduct.[4]   To men of this kind I likely shall seem <lacuna: to be doing>
a piece of spitework and malice, if I adduce[5] the writers who have not suc-
cessfully imitated Thucydides and cite the writings on which they most
prided themselves and which were the source of great wealth to them and
412   which caused them to be deemed worthy of brilliant renown.[6]   That no such
suspicion be stirred up against me, I shall forbear censuring some of them
and making mention of their faults, but I shall add a few brief remarks about
those who succeeded in their imitation <of Thucydides>, winding up my
treatise at this point.[7]   Of the older writers, as far as I know, no one imitated Thucydides in those matters in which he seems most to differ from
other writers,[8] to wit, in the use (1) of obscure, archaic, poetical and strange
diction[9] and (2) of ideas which are illogically arranged,[10] involved, and ab-
ruptly[11] admitting of many meanings with long-delayed apodoses, in addition,
(3) of clumsy constructions (schematismoi)[12] which deviate from natural
concord and do not have a place even in any form of poetry—<all of> which
result in that obscurity (asapheia) which spoils all the fine passages and
casts a cloud <even> upon the merits of his work.[13]

Chapter 53.[1]   Demosthenes, alone among orators, imitated Thucydides in
many points,[2] as he imitated other writers who were thought to have
achieved greatness and brilliance in their speeches. He added to his own
political speeches merits received from Thucydides which were possessed by
neither Antiphon, nor Lysias, nor Isocrates, the foremost orators of that

time. The qualities I refer to are swiftness, concentration,[3] intensity,[4] pungency,[5] firmness[6] and vehemence[7] that rouses emotion. But he omitted
413 the far-fetched part of Thucydides' diction,[8] unusual and poetic words as
unsuited to real speeches. Nor did he show any fondness for figures of
speech that deviated from the natural sequence nor for solecisms, but he
confined himself to language in common use and embellished his diction
with varieties of style[9] and diversity,[10] and by expressing absolutely no idea[11]
without the use of a figure.[12] Involved sentences such as say a great deal in
a few words and in which the conclusion is delayed for a long time[13] and
the arguments expressed are full of surprises, he esteemed and used in his
harangues and judicial speeches, more freely in public than in private suits.

Chapter 54. I shall adduce a few examples from his many speeches of both
types,[1] and these will be sufficient for those who have read him. There is a
harangue of his which has for its subject the war against the King. In this
he calls on the Athenians not to enter into it <the war> too readily, claiming that neither were their own military resources a match for the King's
nor would the troops of their allies faithfully and loyally brave the dangers.
But he calls upon them to let the Greeks see that, after making suitable
preparations of their own, they will risk the danger of fighting for the liberty
of the whole of Greece if any one attacks them. And before making suitable
preparations, he would not have them dispatch ambassadors to the Greeks to
summon them to war, claiming that they would address unwilling ears.
Adopting this line of thought, he has built it up and framed it after this
414 fashion: (Dem. XIV.13) "Later on if you go to work and do what we now
purpose,[2] no Greek of the whole Greek world is so conceited as not to
come and entreat you when he sees that you have a thousand cavalry, as
many hoplites as one could wish, and three hundred ships, feeling that with
such support his safety is assured. Inviting them now means that you are
the suppliants, and, if unsuccessful, you fail, whereas to wait and at the
same time to complete your preparations, <means that> you save them at
their request and are assured that they will all join you." This passage is remote
from[3] the language of everyday life and from that with which the majority
of people are familiar, and it is beyond <the understanding of> the layman,
yet it has not been made obscure, but is clear and needs no explanation.
And when he starts to speak in regard to military preparation, he continues
with these words: (14-15) "The first and most important point in military
preparation, men of Athens, is for each one to have the determination to do
without compulsion and zealously whatever may be necessary. For you see,
men of Athens, that nothing ever slipped away from you whenever you have
collectively desired to accomplish some project and thereafter each one has
415 realized that the execution devolved upon himself individually, and, on the
other hand, that you never were successful in anything whenever you had
conceived the project but thereupon looked to one another <to carry it out>,
each expecting to do nothing while his neighbor did all that was required."[4]
Here, too, to be sure, the thought is highly involved, and language has been
used in which the ordinary mode of expression is exchanged for one that is

unusual, but the excellence (peritton)[5] of the language is preserved by its lucidity. In the greatest of his harangues against Philip he has right at the outset constructed his prooemium thus: (IX.1) "Although many speeches, men of Athens, are made at almost every meeting of the public assembly about the wrongs which Philip has been committing against you and the others ever since the conclusion of the peace;[6] and though all, I am sure, would be inclined to say, even though they do not act accordingly, that we must try by word and deed to stop him from his wantonness and bring him to account, yet I see that all our interests have been so betrayed and sacrificed that I am afraid that <what I am about to say> is true though it had better be unsaid.[7] If all the speakers desired to propose, and all of you had wanted to vote, measures that would be calculated to put our affairs into the worst possible shape, they could not possibly, in my opinion, be put into worse shape than they are to-day." Similar to this passage is also the following: (IX.13)[8] "Do you imagine then that if, in the case of men who could have done him no harm, but might perhaps have guarded themselves against suffering any, he preferred to deceive them rather than to resort to compulsion after due warning, in your case he will give a formal declaration of war, especially so long as you allow yourselves to be duped?" In the most powerful of his court speeches, the oration *On the Crown*, he makes mention of the cleverness with which Philip out-generaled the cities and has expressed his thoughts as follows: (XVIII.231)[9] "And I need not add that it has been the ill fortune of others to experience the brutality which may be seen in circumstances where Philip has once become the master of a city, whereas you fortunately have reaped the fruits of the kindness which he feigned when he was trying to acquire the dominion of the remaining cities." Also the passage in which he declares that those who were betraying their governments to Philip were responsible for all the ills that had befallen the Greeks,—he writes word for word as follows: (XVIII.294) "But in the name of Heracles and all the <other> gods, if we should be obliged to conduct an honest investigation and, discarding lying and malicious slander,[10] to state who really were the men upon whom all might fairly and justly saddle the blame for what has happened, you would find that they are men in the several cities who resemble Aeschines, and do not resemble me. For, when the power of Philip was feeble and very slight, and in spite of our predictions, exhortations, and admonitions as to the best course to pursue, these fellows for private gain betrayed the interests of the state, deceiving and corrupting the citizen bodies of the various states until finally they had reduced them to slavery."

Chapter 55. Though I might take the speeches of Demosthenes, both deliberative and forensic, and adduce from them innumerable examples of passages that have been modeled after that style of Thucydides which, though deviating from the ordinary manner of speaking, keeps within the bounds of language that is familiar and used by all, yet, to keep my discourse from becoming longer than it ought, I shall content myself with the examples I have given as being adequate to confirm my thesis, and I do not hesitate to

advise those that practice oratory, that is to say those who still preserve
their judgments unwarped, to use Demosthenes as a counsellor, who we are
persuaded is the best of all the orators who have ever been born, and to
imitate such composition in which the brevity, the forcefulness (deinotes),[1]
the strength (ischus),[2] the vigor (tonos), the elevation (megaloprepeia), and
related qualities are plainly seen by all men. But periods that are enigmatic,
obscure and in need of learned commentary, and that show distortion and
solecism in the use of figures, I advise them not to admire nor to imitate.

418   To sum up then, it is unreasonable to say that both kinds are equally deserving of emulation, the parts of his writings that are not clearly expressed by
the historian and those that along with the other virtues have the added
quality of clearness.[3] One must admit that the more perfect portions are
superior to the less perfect ones, and the passages that are characterized by
lucidity are superior to those that are obscure. Why then do some of us
praise the entire style of Thucydides and insist on saying that to the people
of his own time what Thucydides wrote was familiar and intelligible but
that the author took no account of us who were to follow after, whilst
others banish from courts and public meetings all the language (lexis) of
Thucydides as useless, instead of admitting that with but few exceptions the
narrative portion is admirable and adapted to every purpose, whereas the
speeches are not in their entirety suitable for imitation, but only those parts
which are easily understood by all but whose composition does not lie within the range of everybody?

       I might have written you more pleasant things about Thucydides, my
dearest Quintus Aelius Tubero, but nothing that would be more true.

— THE END —

COMMENTARY

COMMENTARY

Commentary on Chapter 1

[1]The essay on imitation is known to us from an epitome of the second book, together with an excerpt in *Epistula ad Pompeium* chap. 3. This essay, the earliest of Dionysius' writings, was a practical handbook for use in the schools. Literary virtues were set forth and the styles of historians were tested for each virtue. Thucydides, for example, was found superior to Herodotus in συντομία, "conciseness," and ἰσχὺς καὶ τόνος, "vigor and tension."

[2]Dionysius composes his critical writings in the form of letters, addressed to one or another of his literary friends, patrons, or pupils. Tubero was the cognomen of a great patrician branch of the Aelii. Quintus Aelius Tubero is clearly a Roman and is probably the famous jurist, historian, and father of two consuls. It would appear that Tubero had tried to introduce Thucydidean overtones into his own history: see G.W. Bowersock, *Augustus and the Greek World* (Oxford 1965) 129-130.

[3]H. Kallenberg (*RM* 62 [1907] 28-31) devotes a section of an article on hiatus in Dionysius to show that Dionysius was very fond of the interjection ὦ, but that he regularly omits it before a proper name beginning with a vowel, in order to avoid the hiatus. In familiar language, the vocative rarely appears without the interjection.

[4]Dionysius never wearies of telling his readers that this matter or the other has been, or will be, treated in a separate work. The word συγγραφεύς, here used for a prose-writer, sometimes means "historian" in Dionysius: see Roberts, *DHTLL* 205. For συγγραφεύς, cf. Plato *Phaedr.* 235c.

[5]Usener's emendation, θηρώσης for ὀρώσης, is rejected by Roberts, *CR* 14 (1900) 454.

[6]In translating, I have broken up the long sentence which occupies most of the chapter. Actually, the ἵνα clause is to be joined with δεδηλωκώς.

[7] Cf. *De Comp.* 22.98.19: "The right thing, no doubt, is after all to take a middle course, neither to exceed all measure, nor yet to fall short of carrying conviction" (Roberts tr.).

[8]Dionysius composed several works on Demosthenes. S.F. Bonner (*LTDH* 35) states that the reference here can hardly be to the *De Demosthene*, since this was one of a series of essays on the orators and therefore only part of a σύνταξις, not a πραγματεία, as the text here has it. Bonner concludes that the reference is to a treatise on the genuine and spurious speeches of Demosthenes. In his definition of syntaxis, Bonner states that he is following H. Rabe, *RM* 48 (1893) 149, who maintained that Dionysius always used this word in the sense of a work composed of parts. R.H. Tukey (*CP* 4 [1909] 402 n. 1) has shown, however, that Dionysius sometimes uses it to refer to a single essay. The word is found in a second-century commentary

on Thucydides (*Oxy. Pap.* 853) and refers to the present treatise of Dionysius, which was clearly a separate work. In the *De Dem.* (201.22; 252.16-
19), Dionysius promised to take up the subject of Demosthenes again. A
treatise περὶ τῆς πραγματικῆς Δημοσθένους δεινότητος (*De Dem.* 252.16)
has not been preserved, if indeed it was ever completed.

Commentary on Chapter 2

[1] For τιμιώτερον, cf. *Ep. ad Pomp.* 1.222.10 (ἧς οὐδὲν χρῆμα τιμιώτερον), a poetic reminiscense of Soph. *Ant.* 702: οὐκ ἔστιν οὐδὲν κτῆμα
τιμιώτερον.

[2] Dionysius here uses the word ἱστοριογράφος for "historian," a more
specific expression than συγγραφεύς. Dionysius does not use λογογράφος.
For the confusion of terms, see Jacoby, *Mnemosyne*, Series 3, 13 (1947) 26
n. 24. Kurt von Fritz (*Die griechische Geschichtsschreibung* 1 [Berlin 1967]
Text 79) cautions about the use of the word logographer in modern scholarship.

[3] Instead of Unger's text καὶ <διὰ> τοῦθ᾽ οὗτος, Henri Weil (*REG* 12
[1899] 319) would retain the reading of the MSS., construing as follows:
καὶ (ἐπιτιμήσοντας ἡμῖν ὅτι) οὐδ᾽ οὗτος ἡμᾶς ὁ λογισμὸς εἰσῆλθεν ("and
finding fault with me because the realization did not come to me that...").
For another emendation, see H. Richards, *CR* 19 (1905) 254.

[4] Dionysius uses the word καινοτομεῖν, "to break new ground," a min-
ing term for the opening of a new vein.

[5] The word θεατρικός, rare in the rhetorical literature in general, is a
favorite word with Dionysius (see *De Thuc.* 5.331.10, 7.334.2, 29.375.12;
De Comp. 22.100.14, 108.5; *De Dem.* 5.137.6, 18.166.27, 36.209.7, etc.)
and is usually employed in the sense of ostentatious or appealing to the un-
learned multitude.

[6] Throughout his writings, Dionysius took the position that criticism
must be outspoken but not censorious. See Roberts, *DHTLL* 48.

[7] "This πολιτικὴ φιλοσοφία can hardly be anything except rhetoric regarded from the Isocratean standpoint as a preparation for life. ... One of
the wrongs done by the usurping rhetoric was that it deprived the 'philosophic rhetoric' of the leadership in the state which was its lawful possession": H.M. Hubbell, *The Influence of Isocrates on Cicero, Dionysius and
Aristides* (Yale diss. 1913) 44-45. Hubbell finds that the thought expressed
here closely parallels that of Cicero, affirming (p. 42) that "Cicero and Dionysius belong together as the representatives of Atticism in the broad sense
of the word." In Quintilian, too, there is an unusual tone of bitterness in
his reference to philosophers, whom he describes not only as remote from
practical affairs but as arrogant, vicious and hypocritical: 1.pr.15, 5.9.39,
11.1.33, 35, 12.2.6-9. He has a scornful reference (12.3.12) to pupils who,
finding the rhetorical course too difficult, grew beards, underwent a brief

course in the philosophical schools and then assumed an air of superiority which was merely a cloak for private vice. See M.L. Clarke, *Rhetoric at Rome* (London 1966) 113.

[8] H. Usener (*Praef.* to the Teubner edition p. xxxiii), L. Radermacher (*RE* s.v. Dionysius [1905] 962), and Roberts (*DHLC* 250) believe that this polemical treatise, which has not survived, attacked Philodemus and his Epicurean sect. The conclusion rests on two points. Diogenes Laertius (10.4) numbers Dionysius among the enemies of Epicurus. Secondly, the Epicurean School was notorious for its lack of interest in political life, whereas Dionysius taught that rhetoric was subordinate to citizenship. See, in particular, the passage in which he adopts the view of Isocrates: *De Isoc.* 4 (= 1.60-61). For several other lost works of Dionysius, see Roberts, *DHTLL* 7.

[9] For the circle of educated Greeks and Romans who interchanged opinions on literary subjects, see W. Rhys Roberts, "The Literary Circle of Dionysius of Halicarnassus," *CR* 14 (1900) 439-442; and G.P. Goold, "A Greek Professional Circle at Rome," *TAPA* 92 (1961) 168-192.

Commentary on Chapter 3

[1] καταδρομή: "vehement attack." Cf. our own use of "rundown." The word is also used in *De Comp.* 25.131.14.

[2] The word χαρακτήρ (lit. a mark engraved or impressed, the impress or stamp on coins, seals, etc.) was often used to designate the great types or styles of prose composition and appears in the title of the present work in codex P. "The χαρακτῆρες, at any rate in later Hellenistic and Roman theory, are seldom just a matter of diction, or indeed of diction *plus σύνθεσις plus* figures. They are best described as tones or qualities of writing, involving the choice not only of words but of subject": D.A. Russell, *G&R* 14 (1967) 138, who also gives a bibliography on the three "styles" in the rhetorical literature. But G.M.A. Grube (*GCDS* 24-25) points out that the word is often very general in meaning. Cicero (*Orat.* 11) gives the Latin equivalent as *forma*. Conveying the meaning of "characteristic stamp," the word in Dionysius is used for "style" in general, or for one's "peculiarities, genius," etc.

[3] The same idea is found at the opening of the *Ep. ad Pomp.*, where it is clear that Pompeius has complained that Dionysius had taken exception to errors which should be graciously conceded to men of genius. Cf. Horace *AP* 347.

[4] The word φυσιολόγοι is variously translated, "physicists, men of science, pre-Socratics," etc. "φυσιολογίαι are scientific excursuses of any kind": Russell, *'Longinus' on the Sublime* (Oxford 1964) 112.

[5] The word προαίρεσις (lit. "choosing before") has a wide range of meanings. The Loeb edition of Aristotle's *Rhetoric* (pp. 15, 106) translates

"moral purpose." S.F. Bonner (*LTDH* 12) renders "point of view" for *De Isoc.* 4.61.9, Roberts (*DS* 299) "purpose." The example in *De Dem.* 2.130. 16 is translated by D.A. Russell (*ALC* 307) as "persuasion." Elsewhere, "choice of subject, method, plan" seems to be more appropriate. D.W. Lucas in his commentary on Aristotle's *Poetics* (50b 8) writes of Aristotle's use of the word: "A προαίρεσις is a considered decision made by a person of mature judgment after due deliberation." W.H. Fyfe in his Loeb edition of the *Poetics* says that proairesis corresponds "to our use of the term 'Will,' the deliberate adoption of any course of conduct or line of action." H.-M. Hagen (*Ethopoiia* [Diss. Erlangen 1966] 33-35) and W.M.A. Grimaldi ("Studies in the Philosophy of Aristotle's Rhetoric," *Hermes Einzelschriften* 25 [1972] 26) also analyze the nature of the word in Aristotle.

Commentary on Chapter 4

[1]A large number of passages in which comparisons are made to painting and sculpture by Dionysius and Cicero are collected in a separate appendix by J. Brzoska, *De canone decem oratorum atticorum quaestiones* (Diss. Breslau 1883) 81-101.

[2]For the meaning of αἴσθησις in the critical vocabulary of Dionysius, see J.F. Lockwood, *CQ* 31 (1937) 193. The aesthetic criterion is irrational, but plays a necessary part in all artistic judgments. Αἴσθησις is distinguished from logos in *De Lys.* 11.19.1, where it is said that the grace of Lysias, like all other forms of perfect proportion αἰσθήσει ... καταλαμβάνεται καὶ οὐ λόγῳ. ὥσθ' ὅπερ οἱ μουσικοὶ παραγγέλλουσι ποιεῖν ... The Latin equivalent of alogos aisthesis is *tacitus sensus* (Cicero *De Orat.* 3.50.195), which H. Rackham (Loeb) translates as "subconscious instinct." Cf. below on chap. 27.15.

Commentary on Chapter 5

[1]This chapter is quoted in part and translated into English by J.K. (initials only), *Museum Criticum* 1 (1814) 80; Gomme, *JHS* 33 (1913) 225; L. Pearson, *Early Ionian Historians* (Oxford 1939) 3-4; and T.S. Brown, *AHR* 59 (1954) 834.

[2]The δυνάμεις are listed in *Rhet. ad Her.* 3.6.10 as those physical attributes which are bestowed upon the body by nature: agility, strength, beauty, health, and their contraries. The noun is rendered by J.L. Ackrill (*Aristotle's Categories* [Oxford 1963]) as "capability" in chapter 13 of Aristotle's *De interpretatione* and as "capacity" in *Categories* 8.

[3]Adopting the alteration of Jacoby (*FGH* no. 535) for the spelling Εὐγέων of MSS. and Usener-Radermacher. A long inscription of the mid-third century B.C. (H. von Gärtringen, *Inschriften von Priene* [Berlin 1906] 37), now in the British Museum, records the arbitration of the problem of certain lands on the continent by a Rhodian commission. The question at

issue was the ownership of Karion and its neighborhood, the Samians asserting that the occupation by Priene was a modern encroachment. The Samians cited from historians, including Euagon, that Karion and Dryussa were allotted to Samos; but the arbitrators affirmed that the historical testimony was in favor of Priene.

[4] Adopting the supplement of Jacoby (*FGH* no. 332 T 2): Δηίοχος <ὁ Κυζικηνὸς καὶ Βίων> ὁ Προκοννήσιος. Elsewhere Jacoby (*FGH* 330 Notes p. 488) comments about the supposed errors in this list, "it is of little importance for how many of them Dionysius himself is to blame and for how many his copyists." On the other hand, T.S. Brown (*AHR* 59 [1954] 835-838) has vigorously defended Dionysius against Jacoby's criticisms, maintaining that Dionysius was familiar with the works of the early historians on his list. Difficulties in the transmission of lists of names is well exemplified by frg. 2 of Pherecydes of Athens as recently republished by G. Huxley (*GRBS* 14 [1973] 137-138), where Philaios appears in the codices as Philaias, Epilykos as Epidykos, Oulios as Olios, Polykles as Lykes, Autophon as Tophon, etc.

[5] Jacoby (*FGH* 597 Notes p. 246) questions the name and ethnic, "weil Dionys' text sehr schlecht überliefert ist." K. von Fritz (*DGG* 1, Anmerkungen 56) has reviewed the evidence and defends Dionysius' text: "dann mindestens ebenso plausibel ist wie die Identifikation des letzeren mit dem Naxier."

[6] Jacoby (*FGH* no. 1 T 17a) states that his treatment of Democles is reserved for the unpublished part VI ("Unbestimmbare Autoren") of the *FGH*. Strabo (14.1.20) gives the ethnic as Pygela. There seems no doubt but that the place was in the paralia of Ephesus. Our chief information about Democles comes from Strabo (1.3.17). who tells us that he recorded great earthquakes in the Troad.

[7] Jacoby (*FGH* 1 p. 318) indicates that Hecataeus is placed out of order in the list. Jacoby's added statement that Dionysius never got his hands on the works of Hecataeus is contradicted by Dionysius' own words in this chapter: see T.S. Brown (*op. cit.* 835).

[8] The works and date of Acusilaus have been studied by K. von Fritz, *DGG* 1, Text 81-83; Anmerkungen 57-58. Since the thirty-one fragments published in C. Müller (*FGH* 1.100-103) contain hardly any professed quotations of his actual words, the discovery of an Oxyrhynchus papyrus (no. 1611) giving a long extract (lines 58-83) of this early writer on mythology, who was older than Herodotus, affords an opportunity to study the style of one of the earliest prose writers. This has been done by J.T. Kakridis (*CR* 61 [1947] 77-80), from whom I quote: "The narrative is clear, simple, and unadorned. The sentences are nearly all co-ordinate, connected mostly by the conjunction καί, twice by δέ, and once by ἔπειτα. Anyone reading this text, written 2,400 years ago, immediately notes its affinity to modern popular tales, not only in regard to its content, but also in regard to the form of the narrative." The story is free from any mythological symbolism

and shows the influence of Hesiod. The style of the earliest Greek prose writers is the subject of a monograph by S. Lilja, *Suomen Tiedeseura, Commentationes humanarum litterarum* 41, no. 3 (1968).

[9]The analysis of the date and fragments of Charon by K. von Fritz (*DGG* 1, Text 519-522, with notes and bibliography) supersedes earlier studies.

[10]Instead of ὁ Χαλκηδόνιος ᾿Αμελησαγόρας (Us.-R: Με) Jacoby proposes to read ὁ Χαλκηδόνιος <*nomen* καὶ ὁ ᾿Αθηναῖος> ᾿Αμελησαγόρας. W. Schmid (*Gresch. d. griech. Lit.* 7.1.1 707) favors Dudith's emendation of Μελησαγόρας. Jacoby, who writes in denigrating terms of chap. 5 of the *De Thuc.*, believes that Dionysius' "Amelesagoras" is to be identified with Amelesagoras of Eleusis, reported to have written an *Atthis* sometime after 300 B.C. He regards "Amelesagoras" as a "pseudepigraphon," saying that the name is "unheard of for a human being" (*Atthis* 85), although, as he acknowledges (*FGH* 3B Text p. 600), no ancient suggests any suspicion as to the authenticity of the book or its author. He seems to believe that Dionysius mistook the work of a third-century Atthidographer for an early logographer. The man invented a name for himself and the title for his book, and is presumed to have written in archaic language which deceived Dionysius. Jacoby (*FGH* 330, Text p. 599) derives the name "from the river in the underworld ᾿Αμέλης, which Plato *Rep.* X 621A seems to have invented." Jacoby's onomastic theories are at fault. Hansen-Dornseiff (*Rückläufer Wörterbuch der griechischen Eigennamen* [Berlin 1957] 140) list more than one hundred compounds in *-αγόρας*. Similar formations in F. Bechtel, *Die historischen Personennamen des Griechischen* (Halle 1917) 15-19, include Κουφ-αγόρης, Σφοδρ-αγόρης, Φειδ-αγόρας, etc. Amelides is common enough to be found today in the Athens telephone directory. Moreover, fifth-century Greek names are notoriously unpredictable, and any new list of any size usually contains previously unattested ones. Of the four items of testimonia in Jacoby, two (Maxim. Tyr. *Dissert.* 38.3 [ed. Hobein 439] and Antigon. *Hist. mir.* 12) refer to a third-century historian Melesagoras of Athens; two (Dionysius and Clem. Al. *Strom.* 6.26.8) to a fifth-century historian, Amelesagoras (of Chalcedon = Dionysius). The evidence of Clement, who knew far more Greek literature than we have, indicates that Amelesagoras was earlier than Gorgias. He mentions Hellanicus as one of the writers who stole from Amelesagoras. The scholiast on Euripides *Alc.* 1 says that according to Amelesagoras Zeus destroyed Asclepius because he had raised Glaucus from the dead. In the *Bibliotheca* of Apollodorus (3.10.3) we find the same account given on the authority of a writer of the name of Μνησαγόρας. Jacoby's *Index auctorum* to the *FGH* exhibits numerous homonyms of historians from different places, sometimes as many as six or seven. Indeed, a fruitful source of perplexity is found in the existence of so many writers of the same name. To bring some light into existing chaos, one Demetrius Magnes, a contemporary of Cicero, wrote a book entitled Περὶ τῶν συνωνύμων ποιητῶν τε καὶ συγγραφέων, which was quoted by Plutarch, Athenaeus, Diogenes Laertius, and Dionysius. The existence of many of these homo-

nyms rests (for us) on one or two items of testimonia. Whether the correct form of one or both of our names was Melesagoras or Amelesagoras is a moot point. Parenthetically, according to the notes of Savile made in 1581 the form in the 'opuscula' was Amelesagoras: A.B. Poynton, *Journal of Philology* 28 (1901) 181. T.S. Brown (*AHR* 59 [1954] 836) argues that the textual difficulties do not justify us in impeaching Dionysius, an expert in forgeries, about a logographer with those work he claims that he was familiar. *Pace* Jacoby, Dionysius' discussion of the early historians is still valuable. The effort of Dionysius to gain knowledge of the life and writings of an author is well illustrated at the beginning of his tract *De Dinarcho*, where he says how little accurate information could be had about this orator, although he had searched through the writings of Callimachus and the Pergamene grammarians. Presumably, Dionysius refers to the famous Πίνακες of Callimachus, the first scientific literary history, which was in one hundred and twenty volumes. He quotes Demetrius Magnus in illustration of inaccuracy. Dionysius read eighty-seven orations, sixty of which he judged to be authentic. He sketched the orator's life, chiefly from his own words, adding extracts from Philochorus. This tract of Dionysius is an excellent specimen of his researches and makes one hesitate to question his judgments in matters of literary history. See also the section in the Introduction on Dionysius' role as a literary historian.

[11]Dionysius omits the name of Pherecydes of Athens, for whom he expresses admiration in *AR* 1.13.1.

[12] The basic study for the meaning of ἡλικία, "the flower of one's eye," remains R. Bentley, *Dissertation upon Phalaris* (1697), in his section "The Age of Pythagoras."

[13] In book 1 of the *AR* (22.3, 28.3, 35.2, 49.1, 72.2), Dionysius quotes from the writings of Hellanicus.

[14] Dionysius quotes from Damastes in *AR* 1.72.2.

[15] Χῖος of the MSS. was emended to Κεῖος by Wilamowitz; see Jacoby *FGH* no. 442. This emendation was proved correct by the discovery of *Oxy. Pap.* no. 1011, line 54. K. von Fritz refers to Xenomedes as a Chian in *DGG* 1 Text 77, as a Cean in *DGG* 1 Text 96 and Anmerkungen 56. L. Pearson (*Early Ionian Historians* [Oxford 1939] 116) regards him as a Chian.

[16]The most recent detailed study of Xanthus is that of K. von Fritz *DGG* 1 Anmerkungen 348-377 (with bibliography). Dionysius quotes Xanthus in *AR* 1.28.2, characterizing him as one "who was as well acquainted with ancient history as any man and who may be regarded as an authority second to none on the history of his own country."

[17] F. Jacoby (*Atthis* [Oxford 1949] 354) comments on this passage: "Actually, the early historians Hekataeus and Akusilaos do not belong to the κατ᾽ ἔθνη καὶ πόλεις διαιροῦντες; the whole idea is wrong that Greek historiography began with local history." Jacoby believes (p. 86) that Dionysius is following a division of the early historians which was made by Theophras-

tus, primarily on the basis of style. But U. von Wilamowitz-Möllendorff (*Aristotle und Athen* [Berlin 1893] 1.277ff. and 2.17-33), H. Strasburger (*Saeculum* 5 [1954] 397-398), and C.G. Starr (*The Awakening of the Greek Historical Spirit* [New York 1968] 115-116) support the idea of early local history.

[18] Laqueur (*RE* s.v. Lokalchronik [1926] 1090) takes ταύτας and οἵας as referring only to γραφαί, but K. von Fritz (*DGG* 1 Anmerkungen 75) shows that the words μνῆμαι καὶ γραφαί are to be taken together.

[19] F. Jacoby (*Atthis* [Oxford 1949] 355 n. 15) prefers Reiske's emendations of ἱεραῖς and γραφαῖς: "records recorded in sacred and profane writings." For recent discussion of the passage, see K. von Fritz, *DGG* 1 Anmerkungen 74-75.

[20] The significance of this clause has been much discussed in the light of a re-examination of the fragments of the early historians. Gomme (*JHS* 33 [1913] 242) concludes, "It is clear, I think, that the main object of the chief writers of this class was not reproducing local records of epic legends in prose, but re-arrangement (which would of itself imply much correction) and, above all, criticism." The statement about the sources of the early logographers seems to be a stumbling-block to all students of historiography. T.S. Brown (*op. cit.* 838), in general a defender of Dionysius, writes, "It should not be accepted today as proof that the logographers used documentary evidence exclusively, or even primarily." Rather, he believes, the statement is to be interpreted anachronistically; Dionysius "assumed the motives of his own day for the Ionians." Jacoby (*Atthis* 178) states, "The μνῆμαι were epichoric, while the γραφαί are certainly not documentary." This is to ignore the mounting epigraphical evidence of the archon-list, the λευκώματα deposited in archives (see Pritchett, *CSCA* 5 [1972] 163), the records kept by demes (Bradeen, *CQ* 63 [1969] 153), the early Draconian and Solonian axones (R.S. Stroud, *Drakon's Law on Homicide* [Berkeley 1968] 28-29, 63-64), the lists of pedigrees (H.T. Wade-Gery, *The Poet of the Iliad* [Cambridge 1952] 8-9, 25), and, more importantly, the fact that the first four books of Craterus, presumably a sizeable collection embracing the period before 450 B.C., were devoted to early Athenian inscriptions which he had copied (Pritchett, *Historia* 18 [1969] 18). Similar records must have existed elsewhere. The conclusion of A.L. Boegehold (*AJA* 76 [1972] 23-30) that there was a central archive in Athens before 405 must be extended back to at least 420 (Pritchett *CSCA* 5 [1972] 163). See E. Posner, *Archives in the Ancient World* (Cambridge, Mass. 1972) 103-110. There is no reason to doubt that collections of laws, financial accounts and other documents existed in much greater abundance than the haphazard survival of stone and bronze versions suggests. The word γραφαί, therefore, may be understood in its normal meaning of written records.

[21] Lit. "the sudden reversals of the action that are characteristic of the stage." The word peripeteia is used in Sextus E (*M* III.3) in the sense of "plot" or "argument." Athenaeus (13. 606B) refers to a work of Nicander

of Chalcedon with the title of Peripeteiai ("Catastrophes") which apparently dealt with the vicissitudes in the lives of Bithynian kings (Jacoby *FGH* no. 700). K. von Fritz (*DGG* 1 Text 78) translates the phrase, "höchst melodramatische Geschichten." For peripeteia, see, for example, S.H. Butcher, *Aristotle's Theory of Poetry*[4] (London 1911) 329-331, and D.W. Lucas, *Aristotle's Poetics* (Oxford 1968) 127-134, Appendix III.

[22] F. Jacoby (*Atthis* [Oxford 1949] 136) claims that neither the label ἠλίθιον nor Dionysius' criticisms of early historical prose apply to the narratives of the fourth-century Atthidographers. The last part of Dionysius' sentence is translated by F.W. Walbank ("History and Tragedy," *Historia* 9 [1960] 222), who observes that the subject matter of tragedy and early history was the same and endorses Jacoby's thesis that the main source for the early history of the Greek people was the panhellenic epic.

[23] The word λέξις is an abstract noun derived from λέγειν, "to speak." The most detailed study of the use of the word in Dionysius is that by Grube, *AJP* 73 (1952) 257-259. The word is a generic term which can refer to style or literary expression as a whole or any department thereof, be it diction, composition, presentation of material, or any subdivision of these. Its meaning must therefore be determined by the context. The most common use is "diction." For other studies of the meaning of the word, see Roberts, *DHTLL* 195, *DS* 290, *DHLC* 308; Grube, *GCDS* 33, 140-141; D. A. Russell, *G&R* 14 (1967) 138. Cf. infra on chap. 22.1

[24] The word dialektos usually means "language" in Dionysius; but in *De Comp.* chaps. 3 (12.19) and 4 (18.9) the phrase τῆς διαλέκτου χαρακτήρ refers to a dialect of the Greek language. It is clear from chap. 23 that the reference here is to the Ionian dialect.

[25] For σαφήνεια, "perspicuity, lucidity, clearness," see Roberts *DHTLL* 204, *DS* 301, *DHLC* 321, and the Introduction to *DHLC* 15-17. Geigenmüller (*Quaestiones* 23) lists six Latin words used to render the Greek, and notes that the word is applied by Dionysius to diction and ideas alike.

[26] Purity (καθαρός) of style, which Dionysius designated as one of the "necessary virtues," is discussed in chapter 2 of C.N. Smiley's "Latinitas and Ellenismos" (*Bulletin of the University of Wisconsin* 3:3 [1906]). Smiley collects examples where Dionysius uses καθαρά in connection with ἑρμηνεία and other words having to do with style. Smiley's thesis, based on the earlier studies of G.L. Hendrickson and directed against the views of Radermacher, is that Dionysius' theory of style, in contrast with that of Cicero, was based on Stoic ideals of ἑλληνισμός and σαφήνεια. Cf. infra on chap. 42.5.

[27] For συντομία (conciseness) as a virtue, see, for example, Demetrius 137. Aristotle (*Rhet.* 3.16.1416b.4) scorns the injunction of brevity in favor of the "proper mean." See Cope's commentary on the passage. The basic study of brevity in ancient rhetoric is by J. Stroux, *De Theophrasti virtutibus dicendi* (Leipzig 1912). Isocrates seems to have demanded συντομία

in the narrative of speeches, but neither Aristotle nor Theophrastus in ana-
lyzing diction considered brevity a virtue *per se*. The Stoics characteristically did, since they considered talk "good" when it expressed what was necessary, and promoted it to a virtue of style. "Dionysius has taken over συντομία but has extended its limits by combining the Peripatetic μεσότης and
the Stoic συντομία and interpreting it as meaning the right length. ...This
conciseness, then, is in reality nothing more than an aspect of τὸ πρέπον":
D.M. Schenkeveld, *Studies in Demetrius on Style* (Amsterdam 1964) 73. See
also 23.360.4 and 36.384.5.

[28] R.C. Jebb (in E. Abbott, *Hellenica* [London 1880] 268) says that
the phrase τοῖς πράγμασι προσφυῆ "seems to mean, not merely 'adapted to
the subject,' but *closely adhering to the facts of the story* (whether mythical
or not), without attempt at verbal embellishment. It is illustrated by the
dry and absolutely matter-of-fact style of the extant fragments." Dionysius
uses the adjective prosphyes again in 26.366.5.

[29] In *De Thuc.* 34.381.19, the word "technikos" is contrasted with "to
physikon;" in *De Isae.* 4.96.14-15, with ἁπλότης.

[30] For the use of the word σκευωρία (lit. "care of baggage") for technical finesse, see J.F. Lockwood, *CQ* 31 (1937) 202. Cf. Roberts, *DHLC*
321. The word often has a pejorative meaning which is lacking in κατασκευή;
cf. chap. 29.374.19, σκευωρία διθυραμβική. F. Jacoby (*Atthis* [Oxford
1949] 147) concurs in this appraisal by Dionysius of the style of the earliest
Ionic local historians, "The fragments show a plain but cultivated and strictly
factual style."

[31] For Dionysius' frequent use of ἐπιτρέχειν, "to be spread upon," see
Roberts, *DHTLL* 192.

[32] The word ὥρα, not used in a rhetorical sense in Aristotle or Demetrius, is applied by Dionysius to the beginning of Plato's *Phaedrus* (*De Dem.*
7.139.21) and to a passage of Agathon (*De Dem.* 26.186.4 = Nauck *TGF*²
769.31). Cf. L. Voit, *Deinotes* (Leipzig 1934) 45.

[33] On the evidence of Aulus Gellius, *NA* 15.23, and Apollodorus, the
birth of Herodotus is usually assigned to the year 484, or very near it.
Hence, some wish to emend ὀλίγῳ πρότερον to ὀλίγῳ ὕστερον. But Dionysius may have meant by τὰ Περσικά nothing more than the expedition of
Xerxes into Greece.

[34] Or the sentence may possibly mean, Herodotus "expanded the scope
of his material and adopted a more ambitious plan designed to shed greater
luster upon the writer."

[35] Merely local history made little appeal to Dionysius. In *Ep. ad
Pomp.* 3, he prefers the sort of subject treated by Herodotus, the story of
a struggle that was epic in its character and afforded the fullest scope for
the historian's power, over that of Thucydides. In chap. 4 of the same letter, Dionysius commends Xenophon for his choice of subjects. Cf. *AR* 1.1.2:
"first of all to choose noble and lofty subjects." Ancient testimonia on the

subject are collected by P. Scheller, *De hellenistica historiae conscribendae arte* (Diss. Leipzig 1911) 38-41. See also H. Liers, *Die Theorie der Geschichts-schreibung des Dionys von Halikarnass* (Progr. Waldenburg 1886) 4.

[36]The manuscripts read 240 years. Usener-Radermacher follow Sylburg and Scaliger in believing that there was confusion in the archetype in the transmission of the numeral κ′ as μ′, and that the figure for the interval is correctly given in *Ep. ad Pomp.* 3.774. E. Rohde (*RM* 33 [1878] 195 n. 2) believes that Dionysius was following different chronologies in different places. H. Strasburger (*Historia* 5 [1956] 150) supports the figure for 240 years.

Commentary on Chapter 6

[1]For the use of the word καθιδρύειν, meaning to settle a history in (i.e. restrict it to) a single region, cf. *AR* 1.2.

[2]The word εὐτελής (lit. "cheap," hence "trifling," "mean," or "slight") is contrasted with εὔογκος (lit. "bulky," hence "dignified") in Aristotle *Rhet.* 3.7.1408a.2. Dionysius frequently couples it, as here, with ταπεινός ("low," "mean," "vulgar") and similar words: *De Comp.* 3.11.15, etc. Aristotle (*Poetics* 22.1) gives the two excellences of style as (1) perspicuity and (2) not to be "low": λέξεως δὲ ἀρετὴ σαφῆ καὶ μὴ ταπεινὴν εἶναι. A style which aims only at clarity is in danger of being commonplace and undistinguished.

[3]The word μονόκωλος is defined by Aristotle (*Rhet.* 3.9.1409b.5) as a sentence consisting of a single member without the complication or elaborate construction of the period. In Aristotle *Pol.* 1327b.35, μονόκωλος appears in the sense, "one-sided, ill-balanced, like a man with one arm or leg."

Commentary on Chapter 7

[1]In his history of Rome from the earliest times down to 264 B.C., *The Roman Antiquities,* Dionysius writes near the outset (1.8.1), "I am beginning my history with the oldest myths." He proceeds to take aetiological myths and expound them as genuine history. For example, his account of Romulus and Remus is substantially the same as that in the first book of Livy.

[2]Here and throughout the treatise, Dionysius uses the word ἱστορία for the work of Thucydides, following in this respect the Laurentianus manuscript. Most of the better manuscripts use the title συγγραφή. Marcellinus (*Vita* 18, 34, 46, 48) usually has συγγραφή, but in one place (58) adopts πραγματεία.

[3]The manuscripts of Dionysius omit ἴσως after ἀκρόασιν and read φαίνεται for the φανεῖται of the Thucydidean manuscripts.

[4]In spite of the criticism of G.E.M. de Ste. Croix (*The Origins of the*

Peloponnesian War [London 1972] 32), I believe that Gomme (*HCT* 1.149) is right in regarding the events as "future to Thucydides, but past or contemporary to the reader," because τὸ σαφὲς σκοπεῖν cannot, strictly speaking, apply to future events.

[5] The word κτῆμα carries no connotation of memorial or monument. Thucydides is contrasting his work, meant to be read over and over again, with a composition intended for a specific audience on one occasion only. These well-known words of Thucydides are also quoted in *De Comp.* 22.108.11-12. The passage is well elucidated by Lucian *How to Write History* 42. A.D. Leeman (*Orationis Ratio* 1 [Amsterdam 1963] 336) observes that in Pliny's day Thucydides' ἀγώνισμα was understood as "forensic battle," not as "show-piece."

Commentary on Chapter 8

[1] Although Dionysius pays homage to truth as the deity to whom history should be consecrated, we find him censuring Thucydides in *Ep. ad Pomp.* 3 for revealing the misdeeds of Athens and neglecting her magnificent achievements. In this earlier and less mature letter, he assumes (3.232.19ff.) that the prime object of history is to please and to instruct rather than to tell the truth. Lucian (*How to Write History* 38-39) evidently protested against such a view. T.C. Burgess, *Univ. of Chicago Studies in Classical Philology* 3 (1902) 195-197, collects testimonia on early ideals of historical writing. Passages of Dionysius relating to his theories of historical writing have been collected by P. Scheller, *De hellenistica historiae conscribendae arte* (Diss. Leipzig 1911). In the preface to the *AR* (1.1.2), Dionysius lays down two principles as fundamental for historians: "first of all, to make choice of noble and lofty subjects and such as will be of great utility to their readers, and then, with great care and pains, to provide themselves with the proper equipment for the treatment of their subject." See also F. Halbfas, *Theorie und Praxis in der Geschichtsschreibung bei Dionys von Halikarnass* (Diss. Münster 1911). The *AR* is replete with various protestations of devotion to the truth.

[2] For ἐνεξουσιάζων "showing his independence," cf. *De Comp.* 19.86. 4-5, where Roberts translates the phrase κατὰ πολλὴν ἄδειαν ἐ. as "showed the boldest independence," and compares Horace *Carm.* 4.2.10.

[3] I.138.

[4] II.65.

[5] Usener states: "de Demosthene Dionysius errat." H.D. Westlake (*Individuals in Thucydides* [Cambridge 1968] 97) comments, "Thucydides nowhere specifically assesses the ability of Demosthenes or the value of his services to Athens, and the general impression given by the narrative is equivocal." Dionysius may have had in mind the Pylos campaign where the tactical plan was the creation of Demosthenes.

⁶VII.86.

⁷ VI.15.

Commentary on Chapter 9

¹The word οἰκονομία (lit. "management of a household") is used in rhetoric for "arrangement of material, order." In Aristotle's *Rhet.* it is a synonym for τάξις. See also Longinus 1.4. The metaphorical origin of the term is explained by Quintilian 3.3.9: "economy, a Greek word meaning the management of domestic affairs which is applied metaphorically to oratory and has no Latin equivalent" (Loeb). For bibliography on οἰκονομία as a rhetorical term, see D. Matthes, *Lustrum* 3 (1959) 111-114, to which add J. Martin, *Antike Rhetorik* (Munich 1974) 217 (for our passage).

² The artistry of Thucydides' arrangement of material in jumping from one subject to another and telling the facts in their due order is well brought out by A.W. Gomme (*The Greek Attitude to Poetry and History* [Berkeley 1954] esp. 134-136) in the light of the criticisms of Dionysius and Wilamowitz.

³ The word διαίρεσις is used sometimes technically as a figure of thought in the sense of distribution: *Rhetorica ad Herennium* 4.35.47, 60.52. Cf. 3.13.23: *Distributio est in contentione oratio frequens cum raris et brevibus intervallis, acri vociferatione* ("The Broken Tone of Debate is punctuated repeatedly with short, intermittent pauses, and is vociferated sharply" [transl. of Caplan]).

⁴ The word τάξις (usually "the order or disposition of troops or of an army") is used in Aristotle for the ordering of topics which are to be handled in a speech: cf. E.M. Cope, *Introduction to Aristotle's Rhetoric* (London 1867) 331-337. See also Roberts, *DHLC* 328. Quintilian (2.13) gives an elaborate comparison between the disposition of an army and that of a discourse, as well as the analogous duties of general and orator. H. Caplan (Loeb ed. of *Rhetorica ad Herennium*, 184-185) notes that a distinction developed between τάξις, "natural arrangement," and οἰκονομία, "artistic arrangement."

⁵ In *De Isae.* 3.95.16-17, Dionysius distinguishes between the order and the elaboration of arguments (τάξις and ἐξεργασία [= *tractatio*] τῶν ἐνθυμημάτων).

⁶H. Richards (*CR* 19 [1905] 254), comparing 37.390.5, would substitute the adverb εὐπαρακολουθήτως for εὐπαρακολουθήτους. The adjective, however, modifies ἀναγραφάς, not χρόνους, as in some translations.

⁷ Dionysius' criticisms of Thucydides in chaps. 9-20 were discussed by an anonymous author of the famous *Oxyrhynchus Commentary on Thucydides* (*Oxy. Pap.* 6 [1908] no. 853). A translation of the better preserved part by Grenfell and Hunt is contained on their pp. 137-138 and is reproduced with permission as Appendix A. The commentator had a much

sounder understanding of the difficulties of Greek chronology than did Dionysius; cf., for example, Pritchett and van der Waerden, *BCH* 85 (1961) 17-20; *Historia* 13 (1964) 27-29.

[8]The date of the publications of Hellanicus is a matter of dispute. Here Dionysius regards Herodotus and Hellanicus as contemporary predecessors of Thucydides. In *Ep. ad Pomp.* chap. 3 (234.12), he groups Charon and Hellanicus as contemporaries and predecessors of Herodotus. Jacoby (*RE* s.v. Hellanikos [1912] 110) is prepared to believe that Hellanicus' first publications date from about 440 B.C. L. Pearson (*Early Ionian Historians* [Oxford 1939] 153-155) concludes that he must have written some of his work before 429. R. Meiggs (*Athenian Empire* [Oxford 1972] 44) conjectures that nothing of the *Atthis* was published before the end of the Peloponnesian War.

[9]Lucian is of a different opinion. He writes of the historian (*How to Write History* 49): "Let him call a halt here and move over there, if necessary, then free himself and return if events there summon him; let him hurry everywhere, follow a chronological arrangement as far as he can, and fly from Armenia to Media, from there with a single scurry of wings to Iberia, then to Italy, to avoid missing any critical situation" (Loeb transl.).

[10]Unidentified quotations from some lyric poets. Usener compares Pindar *Pyth.* 3.75 (τηλαυγέστερον κείνῳ φάος). The adjective τηλαυγής is used again in 30.376.11. The Greek noun φῶς, like the Latin *lux*, is used of style in the meaning "clearness, perspicuity." The reference, van Hook thinks (*Terminology* 14), is to the brightness of the day. Cf. *Ep. ad Pomp.* 2.228.2: certain faults "obscure what is clear and make it like unto darkness."

[11]The verb κατακερματίζω properly means "to change into small coin." The metaphorical use occurs as early as Plato *Rep.* 3.395b. See also Longinus 42.1. The passage is cited and Dionysius' criticism of the narrative of III.2-114 is discussed by W.R.M. Lamb, *Clio Enthroned* (Cambridge 1914) 10-11.

[12] Thuc. III.2-14.

[13] III.15ff.

[14] III.20ff.

[15] III.35ff.

[16] III.70ff.

[17] III.86-90.

[18] III.91-92.

[19] III.94ff.

[20] III.102.

[21] III.103.

[22] III.104.

[23] III.105ff.

[24] The verb διασπάω is used by Dionysius (*De Comp.* 22.105.1, 110.4; *De Dem.* 214.43, 225.20; etc.) "of a rent in the smoothness of composition or in the sequence of facts in a historical work:" J.F. Lockwood, *CQ* 31 (1937) 196.

[25] R. Laqueur, *Hermes* 46 (1911) 341, notes the striking similarity of this passage to that in Diodorus 16.1-2 (Ephorus).

[26] The stress on συνέχεια (continuity) is characteristic of Hellenistic rhetorical theory; cf. E. Burck, *Die Erzählungskunst des T. Livius* (Berlin 1934) 186. C.O. Brink (*Horace on Poetry: Prolegomena* [Cambridge 1963] 56) defines the word as "a technical term of the rhetoricians for continuity, coherence, or 'close-fitting' of words or clauses."

[27] If we examine Dionysius' own practice with regard to chronology in his *Roman Antiquities*, we find that at first he uses Olympiads to date events. Later, when he reaches the time when the consulship had been introduced, he uses both systems. He takes one year after another, first giving the consuls for the year in question, then the date according to Olympiad reckoning. In spite of his criticisms of Thucydides' chronological arrangement, Dionysius found it impracticable to avoid the annalistic method in vogue among the Romans.

[28] The writer of the *Hellenica Oxyrhynchia* adhered strictly to the Thucydidean scheme of narrative by "summers and winters." Therefore, we may infer that Dionysius did not know this history: H. Bloch, *HSCP* Supp. vol. 1 (1940) 312.

[29] For σαφήνεια as one of the "necessary virtues," see infra on chap. 22.8 and supra on 5.25.

Commentary on Chapter 10

[1] It has long been a subject of comment that Dionysius makes no distinction between the words πρόφασις and αἰτία used in Thuc. I.23.6. In the *Ep. II ad Amm.* 6.427.10, Dionysius quotes the phrase τὴν ἀληθεστάτην πρόφασιν apparently from memory, and unconsciously substitutes the word αἰτία. G.F. Abbott (*Thucydides* [London 1925] 58 n. 1) quotes several passages in Hippocrates where both terms are employed indifferently to denote the cause of a disease. G.E.M. de Ste. Croix (*The Origins of the Peloponnesian War* [London 1972] 51-58) maintains that Dionysius stands almost alone in correctly brushing aside any differences between the two words: "In fact, Thucydides does not try to distinguish, either here or anywhere else in his work, between immediate or superficial and underlying or profound causes, and it is extraordinary that such an intention should so often have been foisted upon him." Whatever may have been the meaning of the two words for Dionysius, it seems foreign to Thucydides' practice of careful dis-

crimination of similar terms (αἰτία and κατηγορία in I.69.6, αὔχημα and καταφρόνησις in II.62.4, ἀπόστασις in IV.39.2, etc.) to suppose that the words were identical. The teaching of Prodicus of Ceos about precision in speech is said by Antyllus to have influenced Thucydides (Marcellinus *Vita* 36: ἐζήλωσε δὲ ἐπ᾽ ὀλίγον, ὡς φησιν ᾿Αντυλλος, ... καὶ μέντοι καὶ Προδίκου τοῦ Κείου τὴν ἐπὶ τοῖς ὀνόμασιν ἀκριβολογίαν). Probably the best study of Thucydides' attempt to make a marked distinction between synonyms and words of similar meaning is that of H. Mayer, *Prodikos von Keos und die Anfänge der Synonymik bei den Griechen* (Diss. Munich 1913) 60-79. Some of the bibliography on "causes" in Thucydides can be found in Ste. Croix's notes, to which add L. Pearson, *TAPA* 102 (1972) 381-394. Long ago (1829), S.T. Bloomfield in his commentary on the passage, claimed that in the vocabulary of Dionysius, the word πρόφασις signified "true cause." The word is rare and in the only two occurrences noted in the *AR* (3.23.2 and 3.32.1) the Loeb translation would not seem to be in agreement. The word αἰτία is common in the *De Thuc.* as well as in the *AR*; and I translate it simply as "cause;" following the practice of E. Cary in the Loeb edition of the *AR*; see, however, F. Halbfas, *Theorie und Praxis in der Geschichts-schreibung bei Dionys von Halikarnass* (Diss. Münster 1910) 43.

[2] The MSS. of Dionysius here read τινας, whereas when the passage is repeated at 357.19 they have τινα in accord with the Thucydidean manu-scripts and all modern editors.

[3] Dionysius omits the concluding half of the sentence (ἑκατέρων, ἀφ᾽ ὧν λύσαντες τὰς σπονδὰς ἐς τὸν πόλεμον κατέστησαν).

[4] Usener's text has εἰς δεξιά, where the Thucydidean texts have ἐν δεξιᾷ.

[5] Dionysius is wont to define particular portions of the work by the numbers of their lines or στίχοι:

Chapter reference in *De Thuc.*	No. of Stoichoi	Pagination of modern text of Thuc.	Lines of Oxford Text	Approx. Ratio
10	2000	I.1-87	1564	4 : 3
19	500	I.1-23	419	5 : 4
33	100	III.82-83	79	5 : 4

Dionysius is speaking in round numbers and the three ratios would be about the same as if Book I.1-87 contained 1950 lines. The lines of his manuscript contained somewhat fewer letters than those of the modern Oxford edition. Writing on ancient stichometry for prose, F.W. Hall (*A Companion to Classical Texts* [Oxford 1913] 9) says that the average line was 16 syllables or 34-38 letters. E.G. Turner (*Greek Manuscripts of the Ancient World* [Oxford 1971]), however, reports (p. 8) that history was written in wider columns than oratory, averaging 15-22 letters per line. Similarly, C.H. Roberts (*The Classical World*, ed. by D. Daiches and A. Thorlby [London 1972] 448) states, "the length of lines (in prose) and the number of lines to a column varied widely, though an average roll would carry between 30 and 40 lines to a column, with about 20 letters to a line. The influence of reading aloud may be seen in that the rules of word-division at the ends of the lines were strictly observed." The payment of scribes was calculated and the market price of MSS. arranged by counting the number of lines: E.M. Thompson, *A Handbook of Greek and Latin Palaeography* (London 1893) 80. The edict of Diocletian set the tariff for scribes by the hundred lines. The practice of measuring works in terms of lines is at least as early as Theopompus (Photius *Bibl.* 176.120).

[6]Dionysius reads πολεμεῖν ᾿Αθηναίοις where the Thucydidean manuscripts have πολεμητέα εἶναι ("that they must go to war").

[7] Dionysius uses ἐπιτροχάδην (lit. "trippingly, running easily") three times (*De Thuc.* 14.345.8; *Ep. II ad Amm.* 2.422.9) of a cursory, summary account.

[8] In this sentence the Dionysian MSS. have πάντα (for ξύμπαντα of the Thucydidean manuscripts and all modern editors), καὶ πρὸς (for καὶ) and ἐγένοντο (for ἐγένετο). On the other hand, editors accept Dionysius' τῆς τε (for τῆς).

[9]The MSS. of Dionysius omit ἰέναι after ταχεῖς, read ἢν ἀναγκάζωνται (for εἰ ἀναγκάζοιντο) and τότε δέ (for τὸ δέ). Modern editors, with the exception of Classen, follow Dionysius (with manuscript C) in reading the subjunctive.

[10]The Dionysian MSS. (MP) read πλήν, Thucydides πρὶν δή. B. Keil (*Hermes* 48 [1913] 131 n. 1) argues on palaeographical grounds that πρὶν δή was probably in the archetype of MP. Cf. Lehnert, *JAW* 246 (1935) 81.

[11]Dionysius reads the singular ἥπτετο, which allows δύναμις to be the subject. The Thucydidean manuscripts have ἥπτοντο, for which οἱ ᾿Αθηναῖοι must be supplied.

Commentary on Chapter 11

[1]For this meaning of εἰσβολή, cf. *De Lys.* 17.27.17.

[2] Dionysius reads διότι where the Thucydidean manuscripts have διὰ τόδε ὅτι.

Commentary on Chapter 12

[1]In this long quotation from V.26, there is only one substantive difference between Dionysius' text, as established by Usener, and that of the Thucydidean manuscripts. Dionysius reads ἀκριβῶς for ἀκριβές·

[2] L. Canfora ("Tucidide Continuato," *Proagones* 10 [1970] 123-126) regards the phrase ἐς ᾿Αμφίπολιν as an interpolation to an autographical passage (V.26.5) which applies to Xenophon, not Thucydides, the στρατηγία being Xenophon's command of the Ten Thousand. Whatever one may think about Canfora's thesis (cf. Dover *CR* 87 [1973] 143-144), he offers a detailed

exegesis (123-149) of every phrase in our passage.

[3] I take διὰ τὴν φυγήν with αἰσθέσθαι. The punctuation is not clear from the text of Thucydides.

Commentary on Chapter 13

[1]G.F. Abbott (*Thucydides* [London 1925] 179 n. 1) writes: "With his usual acumen, Dionysius of Halicarnassus is at a loss to understand why Thucydides does not describe similar events at similar length: the only reason he can think of is ῥαθυμία—slackness."

[2]Dionysius' text of this passage differs from the received version in two minor details: the omission of the article ἡ before ἐπ᾽ Εὐρυμέδοντι ποταμῷ and of the preposition ἐς before διακοσίας.

[3]In the final sentence, Dionysius omits the preposition περί before the numeral and reverses the order of the genitive and the numeral. The manuscript text of Thucydides is here confirmed by *Oxy. Pap.* 16 (first century).

Commentary on Chapter 14

[1]MSS. M and P of Dionysius read 200 instead of 2,000.

[2]In his study of "Herodotisms" in Dionysius, S. Ek (*Herodotismen in der Archäologie des Dionys von Halikarnass* [Lund 1942] 153) notes this phrase as being modeled on Herodotus 1.196.5 and 8.142.3.

[3]Dionysius' text of IV.54.2 and 57.3 shows no substantive difference from that of the Thucydidean manuscripts. In II.59, Dionysius omits a μὲν before Περικλέα and reads the preposition πρὸς instead of ὡς.

[4]Dionysius is careless. The embassy for which Thucydides records the speeches of Lacedaemonian envoys (IV.17-20) was dispatched after the Spartans stationed on the island Sphacteria were cut off. A later embassy was sent (IV.41) in an effort to recover the three hundred who were captured on Sphacteria (IV.38); but Thucydides does not record their speeches. Cf. J. Wichmann, *Dionysii Halicarnassensis de Thucydide iudicia componuntur et examinantur* (Diss. Halle 1878) 11. On Dionysius' complaint that Thucydides omitted speeches on the occasion of the Athenian embassy in 430 (II.59) and yet composed a speech for the Spartans in 425, Gomme (*HCT* 3.460) comments, "Dionysius means little more than that there were two occasions for fine writing and that Thucydides missed one of them, one indeed that might have led up to Perikles' last speech."

Commentary on Chapter 15

[1]Krüger feels that the ἀντί is inappropriate. Possibly it was used instead of πρό for reasons of euphony before the following προτέρας. On the

other hand, Dionysius' love of μεταβολή has always to be remembered.

[2] The sentence is quoted as the first of a collection of testimonia on "tragic historians" by P. Scheller, *De hellenistica historiae conscribendae arte* (Diss. Leipzig 1911) 57-61. Cf. the passage in Plutarch *Mor.* 347a-c, characterising Thucydides' power of "pictorial vividness" (γραφικὴ ἐναργεία). F. W. Walbank ("History and Tragedy," *Historia* 9 [1960] 230) translates Dionysius' sentence and comments, "The examples he quotes are Plataea, Mytilene, and Melos; in all three a modern critic would be inclined to regard Thucydides' treatment as vivid, but emotionally restrained." Walbank explains the high degree of Greek sensibility to narrative descriptions to the fact that "history like other compositions would normally be read aloud, often in public gatherings, with the additional attractions with which the skilful declaimer can invest a narrative."

[3] Usener's emendation of δεινῶν for ἡμῶν of the MSS. and *editio princeps* seems attractive; but it may be noted that there is a similar diversity of cases (ἡμῶν...τοῖς ἀναγινώσκουσι) in the manuscript text of Thucydides VI.82.2, where, however, modern editors follow Herwerden in deleting αὐτῶν. W. Jaeger, *Paideia* 1[2] (tr. by G. Highet, Oxford 1945) 400, comments about this passage, "The occasion he <Thucydides> chooses for discussing them are selected with the greatest care, and are certainly not always suggested by the normal flow of events. He treats similar facts in very different ways—sometimes deliberately placing the cruelties and agonies of war in the foreground, and sometimes passing over even greater horrors with a dispassionate mention, because it is enough to illustrate this side of war by a few examples."

[4] As Krüger notes in his edition, Dionysius is in error. For example, the fate of the Melians, as narrated at the close of Book V, is given in one sentence, "The Athenians thereupon slew all the adult males whom they had taken and made slaves of the children and women" (V.116.4). Similarly, the emphasis in the account of the fall of Plataeae in the summer of 427 B.C. (III.68) is not so much on the sufferings of the besieged who received their normal fate at the hand of a victor as on the construction of an inn and the lease of the conquered territory to the Thebans. Polybius (2.56.9) characterized descriptions of the sufferings of the vanquished, such as were to be found in the historian Phylarchus, as ἀγεννεῖς καὶ γυναικώδεις.

[5] The MSS. read αὐτῇ = "her," but the *editio princeps* has αὐτῶν and this is followed by Krüger. Usener in his notes suggests αὐτῇ <τῇ βραχυλογίᾳ χρώμενος>.

[6] Of the three examples (Scione, Euboea, Aegina) which Luschnat (*Thukydides* col. 1290 l. 66), following Zoepffel, refers to as a "Typ einer blossen Stoffsammlung," the second comes from the Pentekontaetia which is marked by brevity throughout. Since Thucydides thought of the war "not as a complex political event having its financial, economic, commercial, and other such facets, but as a great catastrophe" (H.D.F. Kitto, *Poesis* [Berkeley 1966] 273-274), many of his descriptive passages have to do with

the destruction of human life. However, the seizure of women and children and the slaughter of defeated military men were the normal fate of a conquered Greek city-state: see Pritchett *Ancient Greek Military Practices* 1 (Berkeley 1971) 81. The calm reporting of disasters is also seen in Herodotus, who tells us, for example, of the falling of a roof which killed a hundred and nineteen children in Chios without a sigh for their fate (6.27), whereas Thucydides, after the slaughter at Mycallessus (VII.29.5), actually deigns to add: καὶ ξυμφορὰ τῇ πόλει πάσῃ οὐδεμιᾶς ἥσσων μᾶλλον ἑτέρας ἀδόκητός τε ἐπέπεσεν αὕτη καὶ δεινή.

[7] *Oxy. Pap.* 880 (second century) agrees with Dionysius in omitting the words τοῦ θέρους of the Thucydidean manuscripts. Dionysius also omits μέν and with some Thucydidean manuscripts uses the form ἔδωκαν instead of ἔδοσαν.

[8] Dionysius again omits a μέν and reads the active κατέστησαν instead of κατεστήσαντο.

[9] The MSS. of Dionysius omit the first καί, read χρόνῳ for θέρει ("summer"), reverse the order of "children and wives," and have the genitive plural Πελοποννησίων instead of the dative singular. With manuscripts C and F, Dionysius reads πέμψαντες (cf. M. Pehle, *Thucydidis exemplar Dionysianum cum nostrum codicum memoria confertur* [Diss. Greifswald 1908] 32) instead of πέμψαντας (*ceteri codices*). Krüger reads ἂν ἐφαίνοντο πέμψαντες.

Commentary on Chapter 16

[1] The word ἔμφασις in Dionysius bears the sense of "hint, suggestion, soupçon": Roberts, *DHLC* 18, who continues, "In our sense of emphasis due to position, the word ἔμφασις is perhaps hardly used even in the scholiasts; and it is possible that Greek has no single term to express the idea." Cf. Quintilian 8.3.83-86; van Hook, *Terminology* 15; Grube, *GCDS* 137 (for the present passage); and L. Voit, *Deinotes* (Leipzig 1934) 20. For the general meaning of the word, see D.M. Schenkeveld, *Studies in Demetrius on Style* (Amsterdam 1964) 129-130.

[2] For the word ῥητορεία, "pieces of oratory," see Roberts *DS* 301.

[3] F. Jacoby (*CQ* 44 [1950] 7 n. 1), in accord with Schwartz's hypothesis that Cratippus was a late writer, attributes the words ὧν προνοούμενος ... ἐπράχθη (as far as "harangues" in the English translation) to a "marginal note made by a late writer." But see Gomme, "Who was 'Kratippos'?" *CQ* 48 (1954) 53-55.

[4] Cf. *De Imit.* 3.208.17, where it is said of Philistius: ἐζήλωκεν δὲ πρῶτον μὲν τὸ τὴν ὑπόθεσιν ἀτελῆ καταλιπεῖν τὸν αὐτὸν ἐκείνῳ τρόπον. "Admirers of Thucydides were supposed by the later Greek critics to have been so carried away by fanaticism that they left their histories unfinished in imitation of him": Roberts, *CR* 14 (1900) 454.

⁵ This passage is cited by G.F. Unger (*NJPhP* 133 [1886] 171) in his collection of testimonia relating to the life of Thucydides.

⁶W. Schmid (*Philologus* 49 [1890] 17-25) clinches his argument that the absence of speeches in Book VIII is not due to a "stupid editor" (according to Wilamowitz) but are original, by declaring for Cratippus as the editor of the work and emending τὰ παραλειφθέντα to τὰ καταλειφθέντα. Schmid's view brought forth a quick response from J.M. Stahl (*Philologus* 50 [1891] 31-42).

⁷ Plutarch *Mor.* 345d gives a list of notable events treated by Cratippus which date from 411 to 390. The argument of E. Schwartz (*Hermes* 44 [1909] 496-502) that Cratippus was an historian of the third century who claimed to be a contemporary of Thucydides is refuted by Gomme, *HCT* 1.50 n., *CQ* 48 (1954) 53-55 (against Jacoby); and H. Bloch, *HSCP* Suppl. vol. 1 (1940) 317 n. The date of Cratippus is discussed by P. Pédech, *REA* 72 (1970) 31-45. The value to be given to the statement preserved in Dionysius that Thucydides had abandoned the use of speeches in Book VIII has been much debated. A sample of opinions can be found in J. Brandis, *RM* Ser. 3, 10 (1856) 443-445; B. Jowett, *Thucydides* (Oxford 1881) 2.211-213; G.F. Unger, *NJPhP* 133 (1886) 167-168; H. Weil, *REG* 13 (1900) 6-7; A. von Mess, *RM* 63 (1908) 389 n. 2; E. Schwartz, *Das Geschichtswerk des Thukydides* (Bonn 1919) 26; M. Untersteiner, *AFC* 7.1 (1959) 86; G.T. Griffith, *PCPS* 187 (1961) 32; L. Canfora, "Tucidide Continuato," *Proagones* 10 (1970) Appendix 1A; Luschnat, *Thukydides* 1114, 1271-1272. Wade-Gery (*Oxford Class. Dict.* 903 = 2nd ed. 1068) writes of the speeches in Book VIII: "Cratippos (a younger contemporary) says Thucydides had decided to drop their use. Modern critics treat their absence as a symptom of incompleteness; they would have been added had he lived. But it is possible that these parts without speeches are experiments in new techniques. ... was Cratippos perhaps right about Thucydides' intention?" F.E. Adcock (*Thucydides and his History* [Cambridge 1963] 35): "Some scholars have stressed a pronouncement attributed to Cratippus that the historians decided to abandon the use of set speeches because they hampered the pace of the narrative and presented difficulties to the reader. There is no agreement whether Cratippus was a younger contemporary of Thucydides and so might have been in his counsels, or whether he was a later writer who was just giving his own deduction from the absence of set speeches, a deduction which is no more than his own." Since Dionysius was a learned and, on the whole, a careful scholar, the crux of the issue is the credibility of Cratippus, whom the weight of scholarly authority now regards, not as a late-Hellenistic practical joker, but as a younger contemporary of Thucydides. Gomme (p. 55) concludes that Cratippus "knew apparently very little about the great man." For Jacoby (*CQ* 44 [1950] 6) the decisive point is his premise that "the most important speeches were added by Thucydides in the last years of his life." W. Schmid (*Geschichte der griechischen Literatur* 7.1.5 [Munich 1948] 165-166) accepts the idea that Thucydides had decided not to use speeches; K. von Fritz (*DGG* 1 Text 765) is of a differing opinion.—Wilamowitz

("Thukydides VIII," *Hermes* 43 [1908] 578-618) reaches the conclusion
that Thucydides inserted from a Spartan source the treaties in VIII.18, 37,
and 58 as well as chapters 29, 43, 52, and 57 into the already completed
history of the year 412 B.C., which had been based on a Chian source and
information touching Phrynichus and Alcibiades, obtained from Athenian
emigrants. The inconsistencies were never smoothed out. Possibly the most
important part of the passage in Dionysius is the phrase τοῖς ἀκούουσιν which
G.F. Abbott (*Thucydides* [London 1925] 192) interprets as saying that
Cratippus meant that Thucydides read his manuscript to his friends and
found that the speeches bored them. The same use of ἀκούω occurs, for
example, in *Ep. ad Pomp.* 3.236.3, where Dionysius tacitly assumes that
Thucydides' audience consisted of "hearers." Many similar passages show
how totally it was taken for granted in the ancient world that if a man were
reading a book he would not do it silently. The implication of this for the
understanding of the ancient languages is far-reaching. "It means that in-
stinctively to a Roman a poem was not a series of marks on a page but the
actual voice of the poet speaking": G. Williams, *Tradition and Originality
in Roman Poetry* (Oxford 1968) 683. See also J.H. Kells, *CR* 83 (1969)
67. B.M.W. Knox has stated the case for silent reading in *GRBS* 9 (1968)
421-435. H. Thesleff (*Arctos* 4 [1966] 89-113) conjectures that a written
style did not develop until Plato, concluding (p. 97) that "the usual way of
publishing one's opinions in the 5th century was reading them aloud to an
audience." The most interesting chapter of W.R.M. Lamb's *Clio Enthroned:
A Study of Prose-Form in Thucydides* (Cambridge 1914) is "Intonation,"
wherein the author collects striking examples of formal resonance and rhythm—
"deliberate appeals to the ear" through trochaic, iambic, paeonic, and especially heroic endings.

[8]Our modern division of Thucydides' work into eight books was already known to Dionysius. There were other ancient divisions of the work,
into nine or thirteen books. Dionysius employed the system which Marcellinus (*Vit. Thuc.* 58), quoting Asclepius, calls ἡ πλείστη καὶ ἡ κοινή. The
division was probably not made by Thucydides himself, for, if it had been,
it is not likely that any others would have obtained currency. Divisions of
other works were introduced in Alexandria. See R.J. Bonner, "The Book
Divisions of Thucydides," *CP* 15 (1920) 73-82. W.K. Prentice ("How Thucydides Wrote his History," *CP* 25 [1930] 117-127) maintains that 1) Thucydides wrote on flat sheets of papyrus, 2) his original manuscript consisted
of a pile of loose sheets with many alterations and insertions, 3) these
sheets of texts were transferred to rolls after the author's death. Prentice's
hypothesis forms the basis of the work of L. Canfora ("Tucidide Continuato,"
Proagones 10 [1970] esp. p. 9), in which he argues that V.1-83 was put together by Xenophon from notes left by Thucydides. Furthermore, Canfora
believes that Dionysius' eight books were not divided in the same way as in
modern times. He concludes that I.1-23 was a proem (p. 39, citing 41.395.
21; cf. Herodotus), Book I began at I.24, Book VI comprised V.84-VII.18.
See infra on chap. 20.1 and chap. 41.8. For earlier reconstructions of the

history into eight and thirteen books, see J. Steup in the *Einleitung* (xxxv-xxxvii) to Classen's *Thukydides* (1[7] [Berlin 1966 reprint edition]).

Commentary on Chapter 17

[1]O. Luschnat ("Die Thukydidesscholien," *Philologus* 98 [1954] 20) quotes this and similar passages in the *De Thuc.*, all of which recur in the Thucydidean scholia, as probable remains of Alexandrian exegesis. Luschnat's thesis that work was done on Thucydides in Alexandria is supported by R. Stark, *AUS* 8 (1959) 40-41. See infra on chap. 51.2.

[2]The two speeches were by Cleon and Diodotus.

Commentary on Chapter 18

[1]Synesius (Migne, *Patr. Gr.*, 66.1117 = p.237 Terzaghi) states expressly that the composition of an epitaphios was a common rhetorical exercise. The most detailed rhetorical treatment of the epitaphios is the work of V. Buchheit (*Untersuchungen zur Theorie des genos epideiktikon von Gorgias bis Aristoteles* [Munich 1960]; see the review of G. Wille, *Gnomon* 34 [1962] 757-763). Lucian (*How to Write History* 25-26) parodies an imitation of Thucydides. References to the epitaphios are frequent in Dionysius (18. 350ff., *Ep. II ad Amm.* 4.426.5, 12.431.17ff., 16.436.3), and Pseudo-Dionysius has a lengthy section (*Rh.* 6.277-283) on μέθοδος ἐπιταφίων in which he enumerates the subjects to be dealt with as πατρίς, γένος, φύσις, ἀγωγή, πρᾶξις. Then he shows how the subjects should be treated. Cf. *Rh.* 8.9.306, and H. Homeyer, *Lukian* (Munich 1965) 229. T.C. Burgess ("Epideictic Literature," *Univ. of Chicago Studies in Class. Phil.* 3 [1902] 146-157) has assembled the evidence for preserved public orations; cf. J. Martin, *Antike Rhetorik* (Munich 1974) 179-182.

[2]On this point, Dionysius is well refuted by "Dionysius" in the *Rh.* 8.9.306.17: ὁ γὰρ λέγων ἐστὶ τὸν ἐπιτάφιον Περικλῆς, ἀνὴρ τοῦ πολέμου αἴτιος. κτλ. That Thucydides could record the Funeral Speech "shows that he appreciated the idea of democratic Athens that Perikles stood for and longed to instill into his fellow citizens": A.W. Gomme, *The Greek Attitude to Poetry and History* (Berkeley 1954) 152.

[3]Dionysius reads ἱππέας τινὰς for ἱππέας of the Thucydidean manuscripts.

[4]Usener's text of Dionysius differs from the accepted version in a single detail: the order of "Athenians" and "Thessalians" is reversed.

[5] Thucydides (II.34.3) says that one coffin (λάρναξ) sufficed for the dead of each phyle. He does not use the phrase ἀνοίγειν τὰς ταφάς, an act for which there is no known parallel in Greek obsequies. However, the emendation of Henri Weil (*REG* 12 [1899] 319-320) is surely correct: τὰς ταφὰς ἀνάγει (for ἀνοίγει of MSS.), "he celebrated the funeral-rites." Cf.

examples of ἀνάγω with ὀρτήν, θυσίαν, χορόν in LSJ. See also M. Egger, *Denys d'Halicarnasse* (Paris 1902) 206.

[6]Grube (*AJP* 78 [1957] 356 n. 2) quotes this use of ὑψηλός in support of his contention that ὕψος refers to the grand manner (or style) in diction *or* composition.

[7] Jacoby (*JHS* 64 [1944] 57 n. 92), in his article on "Patrios Nomos," states, "Thucydides probably would not have mentioned the custom at all were it not for the belated addition of Perikles' speech; he did not even mention it in the description of the Sicilian catastrophe, and is duly blamed for it by Dionysios."

[8] For this information, Dionysius must have had some source not available to us. Cf. Krüger: *Unde, hoc factum esse, resciverit Dionysius, me quidem fugit.* In view of Dionysius' praise elsewhere, one might guess that it was Antiphon.

[9]For the meaning of ἐκ καταλόγου, see Aristotle *Ath. Pol.* 26.1.

Commentary on Chapter 19

[1]For a similar sentiment, see *Ep. ad Pomp.* 3.234.4ff. Thucydides' statement that the Peloponnesian war was the greatest in Greek history (I.1.1) has been defended by A.W. Gomme, *Essays in Greek History and Literature* (Oxford 1937) 116-124, who demonstrates that the whole argument of the introduction, the so-called "Archaeology" (cc. 1-23), was written in support of this statement. Thucydides was thinking of the amount of destruction.

[2] "Denys oppose à cet exposé les règles de la rhétorique, qui prescrivent dans l'introduction historique une αὔξησις du sujet, une amplification qui le mette en valeur, et des κεφάλαια, qui en donnent le sommaire préliminaire": P. Pédech, *La méthode historique de Polybe* (Paris 1964) 47. Similarly E. Täubler, *Die Archaeologie des Thukydides* (Leipzig 1927) 96-97. S.F. Bonner *LTDH* 87 defends Thucydides against Dionysius' application of the mechanical rules of rhetorical manuals. For αὔξησις, see also Roberts, *LS* 195; G. Saintsbury, *A History of Criticism*[2] 1 (New York 1902) 164-165; D.A. Russell, *'Longinus' on the Sublime* (Oxford 1964) 107-109; J. Martin, *Antike Rhetorik* (Munich 1974) 153-158; and W. Plöbst, *Die Auxesis* (Diss. Munich 1911), although Plöbst quotes only one passage of Dionysius (*De Isae.* 16.115.1: p. 39). The purpose of amplification is δείνωσις. Cicero (*De part. orat.* 15.52) says, "The right place for amplification is in the peroration; but also in the actual course of the speech opportunities occur, when something has been proved or refuted, for turning aside to amplify. Amplification, therefore, is a sort of weightier affirmation, designed to win credence in the course of speaking by arousing emotion."

[3] Cf. Aristotle *Rhet.* 3.14.1415a.6: <τὸ προοίμιον> ἐν τοῖς λόγοις καὶ ἔπεσι δεῖγμά ἐστι τοῦ λόγου ἵνα προειδῶσι περὶ οὗ ἦν ὁ λόγος.

⁴Conze's view of κρωβύλος as a method of tying long hair into a kind of "bun" at the back, on the nape of the neck, not on the crown of the head (as LSJ), has been proved correct from vase paintings. See Gomme *HCT*, 1.102.

⁵Grube, *GCDS* 52 n. 72, writes that the meaning of καιρός "in criticism comes very close to that of πρέπον, that is, appropriateness to the occasion." Roberts (*DHLC* 304) refers to Butcher "for καιρός as a word without any single or precise equivalent in any other language," and in one footnote (*DHTLL* 46 n. 2) suggests that the true meaning is "tact." C. Neumeister, *Gründsätze der forensischen Rhetorik* (Munich 1964) 56-59, maintains that the rhetorical use of the word originated with Isocrates. See also A. Hellwig, "Untersuchungen zur Theorie der Rhetorik" (*Hypomnemata* 38 [1973]) 231; W.M.A. Grimaldi, "Studies in the Philosophy of Aristotle's Rhetoric," (*Hermes Einzelschriften* 25 [1972]) 120.

⁶For διήγησις (Latin *narratio*), see *Rhet. ad Her.* 1.8.12 and Cicero *De inv.* 1.19.27. Cf. J. Martin, *Antike Rhetorik* (Munich 1974) 75-89.

Commentary on Chapter 20

¹For a similar phrase, see Dionysius *AR* 9.13.4.

²Dionysius' use of the word προοίμιον here suggests to L. Canfora ("Tucidide Continuato," *Proagones* 10 [1970] 39) that in Dionysius' text of Thucydides chaps. 1-23 of our Book I constituted the proem and that Thucydides' Book I, and hence the actual "beginning" of the *History*, started with chap. 24 ('Επίδαμνός ἐστι πόλις...). Many other scholars, the most recent of whom is H.R. Immerwahr (*The Speeches in Thucydides*, ed. by P.A. Stadter [Chapel Hill 1973] 16-31, with bibliography on p. 17 n. 2), have independently regarded I.1-23 as a proem having a unity of conception comparable to the proem of Herodotus. Cf. H. Erbse, *RhM* 113 (1970) 43-69. Testimonia for the use of the word in ancient rhetorical writers is collected in J. Martin, *Antike Rhetorik* (Munich 1974) 60-75.

³For πρόθεσις, see Roberts *DHTLL* 204, and *DHLC* 319. See also E.M. Cope in his commentary on Aristotle's *Rhetoric* 3.13.1414a.2, with references to the *Rhetorica ad Alexandrum*.

⁴The translation is that of Dionysius' text, which differs in several cases from what is regarded by most modern editors as the received text of Thucydides. The chief differences are the following (I give Dionysius' text first): I.1.1: ἦσαν (preferred by Poppo, Bloomfield and almost all editors before W.J. Alexander, *AJP* 4 [1883] 291-308) for ἦσαν; 1.2: αὕτη δὴ μεγίστη (adopted by de Romilly) for αὕτη μεγίστη δή; 1.3: ἀδύνατον (adopted by de Romilly) for ἀδύνατα; πιστεύειν for πιστεῦσαι; 22.2: ἠξίωσα for πυνθανόμενος ἠξίωσα; δοκεῖ for ἐδόκει; παρῇ (Luschnat) for παρῆν; 22.3: ἐκατέρων (adopted by many scholars) for ἐκατέρῳ; 22.4: γεγονότων for γενομένων; ἀνθρώπινον (adopted by many) for ἀνθρώπειον (Luschnat); 23.1: τὴν for ταχεῖαν τὴν; 23.3: τὰς ... μνημονευομένας for

τὰ ... μνημονευόμενα; ἡ οὐχ (adopted by all) for οὐχ. In I.22.1, de Romilly
adopts μοι for ἐμοί on the authority of C and Dionysius; but Usener reports
ἐμοί.–Dionysius incorporates all of chap. I, then goes to chap. 21.1, line 3
and continues through 23.5.

[5] Thucydides often places a pronoun subject, as αὕτη here, after a
predicate substantive and before a superlative adjective which belongs to it.
Hammond's translation of the sentence (*CQ* 46 [1952] 131) is, therefore,
incorrect. See also H. Erbse, *RM* 113 (1970) 45 n. 7.

[6]The most recent discussion of the meaning of the word τεκμήριον is
by W.M.A. Grimaldi, "Studies in the Philosophy of Aristotle's Rhetoric"
(*Hermes Einzelschriften* 25 [1972]) esp. 113-115.

[7] Dionysius' sentence is not grammatical, since he omits the main verb,
ἁμαρτάνοι ἄν, to which the participles πιστεύων and ἡγησάμενος in the
οὔτε ... οὔτε clauses are subordinate. The main verb is found in the opening
lines of the chapter which were not included by Dionysius.

[8]For the collective use of ξύμπας in the attributive position, see B.L.
Gildersleeve, *SCG* 649. The phrase τῆς ξυμπάσης means "taken as a whole."
The sentence has been discussed most recently by G.E.M. de Ste. Croix,
The Origins of the Peloponnesian War (London 1972) 7-11 (with bibliography). To those who impute to Thucydides the fabrication of his speeches,
it may be noted that such was the interpretation of Dionysius (41.395.17-
20) and that the scholiast paraphrases the phrase as ὡς ἔδοξα δὲ ὅτι εἶπον
ἂν ἀληθῶς, οὕτως εἴρηκα, εἰ καὶ μὴ αὐτὰ ἐκεῖνα τὰ λεχθέντα ῥήματα,
explaining that the historian for his own purpose "pretends ignorance that
he might bring forward his own sentiments."

[9]This passage has been pronounced very difficult by all editors. Krüger, one of the most acute editors whom Thucydides has had, abandons the
passage in his latest edition as hopeless. The difficulty lies in two facts, at
least. Where Thucydides has already employed words which would subsequently be suitable to express something else, rather than fall into tautology,
he avoids their repetition without supplying substitutes. In the present sentence, most modern scholars make either μελλόντων or ἔσεσθαι do double
duty, and thereby get quite different meanings. The second difficulty is the
matter of punctuation, which is essentially a modern device. Now our passage is also quoted by Dionysius, or pseudo-Dionysius (see Roberts, *DHTLL*
5), in the *Ars Rhetorica* 376, as evidence for the sentiment that Thucydides
believed "History is philosophy teaching by example" (ἱστορία φιλοσοφία
ἐστὶν ἐκ παραδειγμάτων). The eminent grammarian, W.W. Goodwin, in a
neglected article (*Proceedings of the American Academy of Arts and Sci-
ences* 6 [1866] 329-330), maintains that Dionysius "makes the word ὠφέλιμα
a part of the relative clause introduced by ὅσοι βουλήσονται." The resulting
change of punctuation in the common text of Thucydides permits the meaning which Dionysius finds in the passage. Goodwin translates, "it <my his-
tory> will be satisfactory as it is for all who shall wish not merely to have a
clear view of the past, but also to draw useful inferences in regard to events

which will hereafter in all human probability be like or analogous <to the past>." Goodwin takes ὠφέλιμα as a "kindred accusative after κρίνειν," the phrase being equivalent to κρίσιν ὠφέλιμον κρίνειν. The genitive μελλόντων is taken with ὠφέλιμα for the sake of parallelism with τῶν γενομένων τὸ σαφές. The Harvard grammarian has parallels throughout to support his interpretation, which, as I have indicated, results from one change of punctuation. Certainly, Goodwin has made a strong case for his theory of how Dionysius understood the passage. The sentence itself is one of the most annotated in Thucydides, because it is a statement of his so-called philosophy of history. No single scholar's interpretation has to the present time won universal support; and it seems that the correct method for the recovery of the historian's purpose is not to hypothesize an interpretation of this sentence and deduce Thucydides' thought from the premise, but to adduce his sentiment from the history as a whole and then to explain how chap. 23 accords. This is essentially the method of Paul Shorey in what remains one of the ablest articles written on Thucydides, "The Implicit Ethics and Psychology of Thucydides," *TAPA* 24 (1893) 66-88. For recent discussions of the phrase κατὰ τὸ ἀνθρώπινον see E. Toptisch, " Ἀνθρωπεία φύσις und Ethik bei Thukydides," *WS* 61/62 (1943/47) 50-67, and A. Rivier, "Pronostic et prévision chez Thucydide," *MH* 26 (1969) 129-145.

Commentary on Chapter 21

[1] Dionysius has now completed his criticism of the πραγματικὸς τόπος and turns in the second half of his treatise to the λεκτικὸς τόπος (chaps. 21-49).

[2] For λεκτικός, see Roberts, *DHTLL* 195, *DHLC* 308: = "the province of expression," as distinguished from the province of subject-matter. F.H. Colson (*CR* 25 [1961] 46) would restrict the meaning to *elocutio*. This passage is cited by J. Martin, *Antike Rhetorik* (Munich 1974) 249.

[3] The word ἰδέα is not used in Dionysius as a technical term, as it was in later rhetoric; so D. Hagedorn, *Zur Ideenlehre des Hermogenes* (Göttingen 1964) 10 n. 4.

[4] For the meaning of λέξις, see the commentary on chap. 5.23.

[5] A. Parry, "Thucydides' Use of Abstract Language," *Yale French Studies* 45 (1970) 3-20, states that an as yet inadequately examined method of the study of Thucydides would be of "the means of expression which <he> had at his disposal." He finds "abstract antitheses" as the most prominent feature of his style, and counts some four hundred and twenty examples in the eight books. He writes (p. 11), "This distinction between thought and actuality, between logos and ergon or more or less obvious equivalents, is the real idiosyncracy in Thucydides' style."

Commentary on Chapter 22

[1]The study of λέξις is divided into three parts: ἐκλογή, σύνθεσις, and σχήματα. The first is subdivided into κυρία and τροπικὴ φράσις, the second into κόμματα, κῶλα and περίοδοι and the third into σχήματα ἁπλῶν καὶ ἀτόμων ὀνομάτων and σχήματα συνθέτων ὀνομάτων. The term ἐκλογή embraces the correct choice of words. Dionysius' treatise ἡ ἐκλογὴ τῶν ὀνομάτων (*De Comp.* 1.5.15) is not preserved. According to Dionysius *De Isocr.* 3, Theophrastus posited that the source of ornateness and distinction in style lay in the choice of words, in composition, and in the employment of figurative speech, and his doctrine was substantially reproduced by later theorists.

[2]The word σύνθεσις (Latin *compositio*) covers word-order and considerations of rhythm and emphony, including hiatus and the effective quality of certain sounds—important stylistic elements in an inflected language. One special treatise on the subject survives, that of Dionysius; difficult as it is, this is one of the most rewarding books of Greek criticism. For the term, see D.A. Russell, *'Longinus' on the Sublime* (Oxford 1964) 172, and *G&R* 14 (1967) 137.

[3]The meaning of κύριος as "literal," "proper," "recognized" is well illustrated in *De Comp.* 21.95.14, where the word is opposed to μεταφορικός. E.M. Cope (on Aristotle *Rhet.* 3.2.1404b.6) writes, "The word derives its special meaning from the original signification of κύριος, 'carrying authority,' 'authoritative'; whence 'authorized, established, fixed (by authority), settled,' as ... κυρία ἐκκλησία, opposed to the *irregular* ἐκκλησία σύγκλητος, convoked at uncertain times on special occasions: and hence applied to the established, settled, regular name of a thing." For a more detailed analysis of the meaning of the word, see Cope, *An Introduction to Aristotle's Rhetoric* (London 1867) 282-283. Rhys Roberts discusses the word in *DHTLL* 195, *DS* 289, and *DHLC* 307; Geigenmüller in *Quaestiones* 15. See also R. G. Austin in his note on Quintilian 10.16, where he points out that the critic Caecilius of Calacte, a contemporary of Dionysius, compiled a dictionary of κυρίαι λέξεις for the use of students of rhetoric. See U. von Wilamowitz-Möllendorff, "Asianismus und Atticismus," *Hermes* 35 (1900) 38.

[4]For the division of words into κυρία as opposed to figurative expressions, a division which according to the scholiast on Plato *Phaedrus* 267c may be traced to Plato, see E.M. Cope (*A Journal of Classical and Sacred Philology* 3 [1857] 257) who refers to our passage.

[5]For the meaning of κόμμα (lit. "that which is cut off"), see Roberts, *DS* 288, *DHLC* 306. Cf. Grube, *GCDS* 60. Cicero *Orator* 62.211, translates the word as *incisum*. The word is discussed by E.M. Cope, *Introduction to Aristotle's Rhetoric* (London 1867) 312-313. Demetrius (*On Style* 5.241) asserted that the forcible style (χαρακτὴρ δεινός) required commata, rather than cola, because length destroys vehemence and a more forceful effect is attained when much is said in a few words.

⁶The word κῶλον means "limb." The concept originated in comparison with the human body; it came into rhetoric from music. The doctrine of colon, comma and period is Peripatetic (Aristotle *Rhet.* 3.9.1409a; see A. du Mesnil, "Begriff der drei Kunstformen der Rede: Komma, Kolon, Periode, nach der Lehre der Alten," *Zum zweihundertjährigen Jubiläum des königl. Friedrichs-Gymnas.* [Frankfurt 1894] 32-121). Demetrius at the beginning of *On Style* says that the function of κῶλα is to mark the conclusion of a thought. See Roberts, *DS* 289 and *DHLC* 307. Cicero (*Or.* 211) suggests *incisa* and *membra* as translations of κόμματα and κῶλα; see A.D. Leeman, *Orationis Ratio* (Amsterdam 1963) 1.153; J. Martin, *Antike Rhetorik* (Munich 1974) 317-320.

⁷ The word περίοδος is a compound of the words ὁδός, "road," and the preposition περί, "round." It implies a circular course. Aristotle *Rhet.* 3.9.1409a.3 defines a period as a sentence (or composition) that has a beginning and end and a magnitude that can be easily grasped. The length of the period was limited by the Greek rhetoricians. Aristotle (*Rhet.* 3.9.1409b. 5) did not recognize a period of more than two cola. Demetrius (*On Style* 16) limited the cola to four. Roman theorists enlarged the number: see Quintilian 9.4.125. Demetrius (252) says of the style he calls δεινόν that it requires a succession of short periods, since periods formed of many members produce κάλλος rather than δεινότης. The Greek orators and writers, however, seem not to have troubled themselves with any of these limitations, but wrote as freely as do modern authors. The reason for the refusal of the rhetoricians to use the term "period" for a large group of cola lay in the feeling that the unity which is the foundation of the period was marred when too much was demanded of the breath of the speaker or the attention of the hearer. See B.L. Gildersleeve, *AJP* 24 (1903) 102-103. The periodic writing of Thucydides has been characterized by R.C. Jebb (*Attic Orators* 1 [London 1876] 35-36) as follows: "It may perhaps be said that, while Antiphon has more technical skill in periodic writing, Thucydides has infinitely more of its spirit. He is always at high pressure, always nervous, intense. He struggles to bring a large, complex idea into a framework in which the whole can be seen at once. Aristotle says that a period must be of 'a size to be taken in at a glance' <μέγεθος εὐσύνοπτον>; and this is what Thucydides wishes the *thought* of each sentence to be, though he is sometimes clumsy in the mechanism of the sentence itself. Dionysios mentions among the excellences which Demosthenes borrowed from the historian, 'his rapid movement, his terseness, his intensity, his sting;' excellences, he adds, which neither Antiphon nor Lysias nor Isokrates possessed. This intensity, due primarily to genius, next to the absorbing interest of a great subject, does, in truth, place Thucydides, with all his roughness, far nearer than Antiphon to the ideal of a compact and masterly prose. Technically speaking, Thucydides as well as Antiphon must be placed on the border-land between the old running style and finished periodic writing." Ancient views on the nature of the period are discussed in L.P. Wilkinson's chapter "Periodic Prose" (pp.167-188) in *Golden Latin Artistry* (Cambridge 1963)

and D.M. Schenkeveld, *Studies in Demetrius on Style* (Amsterdam diss. 1964) 23-50. H.C. Gotoff (*HSCP* 77 [1973] 220) observes that Dionysius does not define the word periodos and that his use of the term is ambiguous. Roberts gives many references and equivalents: *DHTLL* 201; *LS* 205; *DS* 298; *DHLC* 316. The analysis of periodic structure in the introduction of L. Dissen's edition of Demosthenes' *De Corona* (Göttingen 1837) has not been superceded.–One need hardly observe that our names for the "stops" in punctuation (comma, colon, period) are borrowed from these Greek terms.

[8] In *De Thuc.* 23.360.3, 36.384.4; *Ep. ad Pomp.* 3.239; *De Imit.* VI. 2.207.2, the necessary virtues are indicated by the adjectives καθαρός, σαφής, σύντομος in that order. On additions to the list (e.g. κοινός), see P. Geigenmüller, *Quaestiones* 13. The "virtues of style" is a much-vented topic of which a judicious survey is given by G. Kennedy, *The Art of Persuasion in Greece* (London 1963) 273ff. and his bibliography in notes 16 and 25. The history of the development of ἀναγκαῖαι ἀρεταί has been sketched by S.F. Bonner, *LTDH* 15-20. Bonner follows J. Stroux (*De Theophrasti virtutibus dicendi* [Leipzig 1912] 29-43) in maintaining that Aristotle had one ἀρετή, lucidity (sapheneia), whereas F. Solmsen (*AJP* 62 [1941] 43) finds three, lucidity, ornateness, and appropriateness. Theophrastus in his work *On Style*, now lost, is thought by all to have had four "necessary virtues:" purity (hellenismos), lucidity (sapheneia), appropriateness (prepon), and ornateness (kataskeue). The Stoic theorist, Diogenes of Babylon, added brevity (syntomia), and many scholars believe that Dionysius was writing under Stoic influence: see H.G. Strebel, *Wertung und Wirkung des Thukydideischen Geschichtswerkes in der griechisch-römischen Literatur* (Diss. Munich 1935) 44 n. 157; and C.N. Smiley, "The Influence of the Stoic Theory on Dionysius of Halicarnassus," chap. 2 of "Latinitas and Ellenismos" (*Bulletin of the Univ. of Wisconsin* 3.3 [Madison 1906]) 219-231. This five-fold Stoic division was not accepted by Cicero (*Brutus* 50; *De Oratore* 1.44, 3.37; *Orator* 79), who expressly excludes brevity. Meanwhile, the subject of the virtues of style received the most detailed treatment in the rhetorical schools, resulting in a process of subdivision which degenerated into a mere list of attributes. The division of the virtues in Dionysius is studied by D.M. Schenkeveld, *Studies in Demetrius On Style* (Amsterdam diss. 1964) 74-76. In his historical sketch of ancient rhetoric (*RE* s.v. Rhetorik, Suppl. 7 [1940] 1039-1138), W. Kroll discusses the virtues in cols. 1072-1073. See also Roberts *DHTLL* 172.

[9] The "accessory virtues" for Dionysius (*Ep. ad Pomp.* 3.239.14ff.) include vividness (enargeia), the imitation of ἦθη and πάθη, grandeur (τὸ μέγα καὶ θαυμαστόν), strength (ischus), vigor (tonos), charm (hedone), and propriety (prepon). See Bonner *LTDH* 19, and Roberts *DHTLL* 172. Essential virtues were directed towards a clear exposition and were demanded of every writer. Accessory virtues impart to style beauty and vigor, and hence serve to reveal the rhetorician's power. Bonner characterizes the system of Dionysius as "a compromise in the age-old quarrel of philosopher and rhetorician."

In the *Ep. ad Pomp.*, the famous comparison between Herodotus and Thucydides is conducted by a comparison of these qualities. It was fatally easy for a would-be critic to count the number of virtues instead of assessing their quality and appeal.—Aristaeus is quoted by Herodotus (4.13).

[10]S.F. Bonner (*LTDH* 19) observes that the words εἴρηται πολλοῖς πρότερον establish that the twofold grouping of virtues, although not found in any earlier Greek rhetorician, was not original with Dionysius but must have appeared between the third and first centuries B.C.

Commentary on Chapter 23

[1]Dionysius had dealt with the beginnings of historiography in chap. 5, but he made no statement promising a return to the subject.

[2]E.M. Cope (on Aristotle *Rhet.* 3.16.1416b.3) cites passages in which λιτός is used of a smooth, easily travelled road; but the metaphor seems to come from weaving. The word λίς in Homer means smooth cloth; in the Athenian poletai records of 413 B.C. (Pritchett, *Hesperia* 22 [1953] 244) the adjective is applied to parapetasma, "curtain." For other examples where the word is applied to textiles, see T. Linders, *Skrifter Utgivna Av Svenska Institutet I Athen* 19 (1972) 62. In an inscription from Samos (*CIG* 2258), the editor of the *editio princeps* (*Museum Criticum* 1 [1814] 349) interprets λιτὴ πέτρη as "rude stone," but other meanings are possible. In the rhetorical writers, λιτός "smooth, plain," applied by Dionysius to the style of Lysias (*De Dem.* 2), is opposed to ποικίλος, "varied, embellished." See Roberts, *DS* 290, *DHLC* 308.

[3]The adjective ἀκόσμητος (from κόσμος, lit. "ornament, dress, embellishment") is one of a group of words which the rhetoricians borrowed from the vocabulary of the dress and toilet of persons. Style was likened to the elaborate garb worn by a person who is decked out in seemly or unseemly attire. Isocrates (9 *Evagoras* 8-9) writes, "To the poets is granted the use of many ornaments of language ... and they can treat of their subjects in words exotic, newly-coined, and in figures of speech." In Aristotle *Rhet.* 3.2, the λέξις κεκοσμένη is opposed to λέξις ταπεινή.

[4]See note on chap. 54.5.

[5] The adjective πομπικός (from πομπή, "parade, pomp") seems always to be used in a favorable connotation by Dionysius, "stately, impressive, ceremonial." It seems not to have the modern meaning "pompous." Dionysius (*De Isae.* 19.121.20; *Ep. ad Pomp.* 6.247.7) says that the diction of the historian Theopompus was characterized by this quality. In the epitome of the work on Imitation (*De Imit.* 5.212.3 and 19), the styles of Isocrates and Aeschines are said to be πομπικός and ἐναργής, the first-named quality being peculiar to each as compared with other Attic orators and serving as a basis for associating the two men. Cf. R.H. Tukey, *CP* 4 (1909) 392-393.

[6]In Hermog. *Id.* 9 (Sp. 2.304), lamprotes, "brilliancy," is said to assist

in producing μέγεθος, "grandeur" and ἀξίωμα, "dignity." For numerous examples of ἀξιωματικός in Dionysius, see Geigenmüller, *Quaestiones* 57.

[7] The adjective ἐγκατάσκευος, "elaborate, embellished, studied" is derived from the verb κατασκευάζω, "to build, equip," which is frequently used in literary criticism, just as ὕλη, "timber for building," was used for literary subject matter. Elaborate comparisons between literary composition and architecture are to be found in Longinus 10.7, 39.3; Quintilian 7.1 (proem.); Cicero *De Or.* 3.171; and, particularly, Dionysius *De Comp.* 6.28. 5ff. For ἐγκατάσκευος, see Roberts, *DHTLL* 189; *DS* 276; *DHLC* 297; and D.M. Schenkeveld, *Studies in Demetrius On Style* (Amsterdam 1964) 62 n. 1.

[8] In Aristotle *Rhetoric* 3.1.1404a.9 and Isocrates 9 *Evagoras* 9, κόσμος and κεκοσμημένη include all poetical and abnormal use of language; similarly, κοσμέω is used of metaphor in *Rhetoric* 3.2.1405a.10. See E.M. Cope's note on 3.7.1408a.2. Cope defines κόσμος as a "poetical or ornamental word."

[9] Strabo (1.2.6) places Cadmus first among the three authors whom he calls the earliest prose writers among the Greeks. The others are Pherecydes and Hecataeus. Pliny (*N.H.* 5.112) calls Cadmus the first that ever wrote (Greek) prose. Josephus (*Ap.* 1.13) lists Cadmus and Acusilaus as the earliest writers of history and dates them shortly before the Persian invasion of Greece. According to the Suda, Cadmus wrote a work on the foundation of Miletus and the early history of Ionia in four books. Its authenticity is suspect: see K. von Fritz, *DGG* 1 Anmerkungen 54-55.

[10] Herodotus confirms his view about the Scythians by reference (4.13) to Aristeas' *Arimaspea*. This epic poet is placed by Herodotus in the first quarter of the seventh century; but the Suda makes him a contemporary of Croesus. The floruit of Aristeas is placed by J.D.P. Bolton (*Aristeas of Proconnesus* [Oxford 1962] 179) in the third quarter of the seventh century, by K. von Fritz (*DGG* 1 Anmerkungen 21) before the middle of the century. —Opinion is divided as to whether the antecedent of ἐν αἷς is the γραφαί which have perished or those of doubtful authenticity. Most scholars seem to follow Jacoby (*RE* s.v. Kadmos (6) 1474) in taking the reference to be to forgeries of Cadmus and Aristeas. But T.S. Brown (*AHR* 59 [1954] 834-835) argues that Dionysius is contrasting in this chapter logographers whose works "have not come down to my day" with logographers named in chapter 5 whose works had survived. One might assume that because of the geographical context of the *Arimaspea*, a poem in which the author related how he had travelled Φοιβόλαμπτος γενόμενος in Siberia, Dionysius chose to regard the author as a logographer. If the reference in Dionysius is to a forgery, Bolton (p. 32) conjectures that it was a *Theogony* in prose which had been ascribed to Aristeas. But D.A. Russell (*'Longinus' On the Sublime* [Oxford 1964] 103) makes a strong case for accepting it as genuine.

[11] This sentence is quoted by W. Speyer in his study of literary forgeries (*Die literarische Fälschung in heidnischen und christlichen Altertum*

[Munich 1971] 137). T.S. Brown (*AHR* 59 [1954] 835) rightly empha-
sizes the fact, overlooked by Jacoby and W. Schmid (*Geschichte des griech.
Lit.* 7.1.1 [Munich 1929] 691), that Dionysius makes a distinction between
the "very ancient writers" such as Cadmus whose works had not survived,
and the historians whom he had named in chap. 5 as living before the Peloponnesian war and whose works had survived because of their charm.

¹² The words κύριος and τροπικός are frequently used by Dionysius as
opposites; see, in addition to the present passage, *De Lys.* 13.22.17; *De Imit.*
6.2.206.4; and *De Thuc.* 22.358.14. Cf. supra on chap. 22.3.

¹³ Greek literary criticism used expressive terms taken from such things
as the seasoning of food. The word ἥδυσμα was used in cookery for "relish,
seasoning;" hence metaphorically of style, "embellishment, flavor." Aristotle
(*Poetics* 6.27.1450b) says that μελοποιία, "song-making," is the most important of the embellishments. The "Attic salt" was proverbial. A later parallel
is Dryden speaking of Horace: "His wit is faint and his salt ... almost in-
sipid." For the verb ἡδύνειν, see van Hook, *Terminology* 29; Roberts, *DHLC*
302; J.F. Lockwood *CQ* 31 (1937) 199.

¹⁴ ἀφελής is "plain" as opposed to mountainous, literally and metaphorically. Lysias is the chief example of the "plain, simple style": *De Dem.*
2; "Longinus" 34.2. Aristotle in *Rhet.* 3.9.1409b.5 uses the word for the
simple one-clause period. Dionysius uses the word in opposition to τεχνικός
(*De Isae.* 11.107.10) and ῥητορικός (*De Isae.* 8.101.20). See Geigenmüller,
Quaestiones 107; D.A. Russell, *'Longinus' On the Sublime* (Oxford 1964)
160.

¹⁵ The verb σχηματίζειν may mean in rhetoric either "to use figures of
speech" or "to construe," "to give a certain shape" to one's expressions.
See Grube, *GCDS* 143, and W.G. Rutherford, *A Chapter in the History of
Annotation* (London 1905) 192-193.

¹⁶ The word τετριμμένος is used of "worn out" clothes and a "ravaged"
country. In rhetoric it is applied to words "used constantly" and is combined by Dionysius with κοινός and κύριος: Geigenmüller, *Quaestiones* 15-16.
Roberts (*DHLC* 329) renders, "homely, ordinary."

¹⁷ Dionysius is fond of coupling a positive expression with a negative
locution of the same meaning, as here ἀφελής and ἀνεπιτήδευτος.

¹⁸ Grube (*AJP* 73 [1952] 263) writes of the use of λέξις and διάλεκτος
in Dionysius: "When λέξις is thus used to signify diction, it is synonymous
with διάλεκτος, which is always, and φράσις which is also very frequently,
used in this sense." The two words are clearly synonymous here. Cf. supra
on chap. 5.24. See also on chap. 51.3. For the Ciceronian equivalents of
διαλεκτική, see J.S. Reid on *Acad.* 1.32.

¹⁹ The three necessary virtues are also listed by Dionysius in *Ep. ad
Pomp.* 3.239.5ff. and *De Lys.* 22.15ff.

²⁰ This view that it is the accessory virtues which best reveal the

orator's power is paralleled in Quintilian (8.3.1): "I now come to the subject of ornament, in which, more than in any other department, the orator undoubtedly allows himself the greatest indulgence. For a speaker wins but trifling praise if he does no more than speak with correctness and lucidity" (Loeb tr.). Roberts (*DHLC* 27) suggests that because clearness and emphasis were so easily achieved in the highly inflected Greek and Latin languages, their attainment called for no special recognition.

[21]ὕψος is one of at least five words normally used of "height" found in the Greek rhetoricians. The others are διηρμένος, "lofty, elevated," μετέωρος, "raised above the ground, inflated," εὐκόρυφος, "with beautiful top, ending well," and βάθος, "profound, lofty." Roberts says that the term ὕψος goes back at least to Caecilius and may be defined as "anything which raises composition above the usual level, or infuses into it uncommon strength, beauty, or vivacity": *LS* 209. For discussion of the word, see D. A. Russell, *'Longinus' On the Sublime* (Oxford 1964) xxx-xlii, who observes that ὕψος words do not commonly occur in literary criticism until the second half of the first century B.C. The development of the word is treated by J.H. Kühn, "Υψος (Stuttgart 1941).

[22]This is the only occurrence of the noun καλλιρημοσύνη (lit. "beauty or elegance of phrase") in Dionysius, although the adjective καλλιρήμων is not uncommon, occurring, for example, in *De Dem.* 18.166.4, which Russell (*ALC* 316) translates as "pretty."

[23]Cope (*ad* Aristotle *Rhet.* 3.3.1406b.3) writes of σεμνός, "contracted from σεβόμενος, *lit.* an object of worship: applied again to the *heroic measure* or rhythm, III.8.4." The adjective was used of the disposition or trait of character in the sense "august, reverend, devoted to the gods." Roberts renders σεμνολογία as "solemnity": *DHLC* 321.

[24]Megaloprepeia (lit. "magnificence as befits a great man") is not known as a technical term until Dionysius: van Hook, *Terminology* 32. The word is used side by side, as here, with ὕψος in *Ep. ad Pomp.* 2.231.22; *De Lys.* 13.23.5. In Demetrius' *On Style*, Thucydides is cited eight times as an example *par excellence* of μεγαλοπρέπεια. This he is said to achieve by rhythmic qualities, e.g. long syllables and hiatus, long κῶλα and periods (39, 40, 44, 45, 72). Such passages are part of the evidence used by A.D. Leeman (*Orationis Ratio* [Amsterdam 1963] 1. 180, 187, 351-352, etc.) to support his thesis that there was a strong Thucydidean revival in the first century, which influenced, in particular, the style of Sallust.

[25] Dionysius also uses the word τόνος, "intensity, energy, tension" in chaps. 24, 48 and 53. The word is listed by van Hook, *Terminology* 20 with other words which were originally applied to the physical constitution and bodily condition. The rhetoricians opposed words for slender and weak persons to those for the robust. Cf. [Plutarch] *Mor.* 7B: "As the body ought to be not merely healthy but also sturdy, so speech should be not only free from disease but robust too." English has similar terms. Ben Jonson's section "Of Language in Oratory" in *Timber* is replete with com-

parisons between speech and the human body: "[Speech] is likened to a man, and as we consider features and composition in a man, so words in language, in the greatness, aptness, sound, structure, and harmony of it. Some men are tall and big, so some language is high and great," etc.

²⁶βάρος (lit. "weight, heaviness") is applied to language in the meaning of "gravity, dignity, impressiveness." In *De Comp.* 11.37.16, it is named as one of the qualities which lend hedone ("charm") to language. Thucydides shared this virtue with Demosthenes: *De Dem.* 34.204.14.

²⁷ For an examination of the meanings of πάθος, see E.M. Cope, *Introduction to Aristotle's Rhetoric* (London 1867) 113-118. One of the more distinctive features of ancient literary criticism is the antithesis between ἦθος (*mores*, character as in "character part") and πάθος (*animi motus*, emotion). Good accounts of the contrast are to be found in Cicero *Orator* 37. 128 and Quintilian 6.2.8-24. See J. Martin, *Antike Rhetorik* (Munich 1974) 158-160.

²⁸The verb διεγείρειν, "to wake up," is used of the rousing effect of the style of Isocrates (*De Lys.* 28.45.19) or of a passage from a speech of Thucydides (*Ep. ad Pomp.* 4.24.8) or of πάθος, as here.

²⁹Although ἐρρωμένος occurs in only one other passage (*De Lys.* 19. 31.24) in Dionysius in a rhetorical sense (in *De Thuc.* 6.332.18 it has a literal meaning), ἐναγώνιος is very common: Geigenmüller, *Quaestiones* 59-60. The latter is derived from ἀγών "contest in assembly or court." The ἀγωνιστικὴ λέξις is the style used in such contests, and the ἐναγώνιος λόγος is a "speech in a contest of a controversial character." Russell renders the phrase as "real-life oratory." R.C. Jebb, *Attic Orators* 2.304 translates τὸ ἐναγώνιον as "the art of grappling." Roman rhetoricians made a distinction between *contentio*, the address of formal debate, and *sermo*, the informal language of conversation: Cicero *De off.* 1.37.132. Cicero says, "Rules for *contentio* we have from the rhetoricians. There are none for *sermo.*"

³⁰For δεινότης, see infra on chap. 27.4. For an attempt at the reconciliation of this list of accessory virtues with the one given in *Ep. ad Pomp.* 239.14ff., see D.M. Schenkeveld, *Studies in Demetrius On Style* (Diss. Amsterdam 1964) 74. In essence, the necessary virtues must be present in each speech or narrative. They make clear what one wishes to say, but nothing more. The accessory virtues have a wider significance; they show the δύναμις of the orator and they lend him his glory and fame. Cf. supra on chap. 22.9.

³¹For a list of the figures in Herodotus, see P. Kleber, *De genere dicendi Herodoteo quaestiones selectae* (Löwenberg Progr. 1890) 21-25.

³²πειθώ, "persuasiveness," is attributed to the language of Lysias (*De Dem.* 13.156.8; *De Lys.* 18.30.7) and Herodotus (*Ep. ad Pomp.* 3.240.6; *De Imit.* 6.3.207.19; *De Comp.* 3.14.20). Roberts sometimes translates the word as "fascination." For πειθώ as a quality of the accessory virtues, see

Geigenmüller, *Quaestiones* 34.

[33] Dionysius (*De Lys.* 10.18.9; *De Din.* 3.308.7) and the author of
On the Sublime (34.2) both affirm that χάρις ("grace, charm") was characteristic of Lysias and Hyperides. See Tukey, *CP* 4 (1909) 392. In *De Lys.*
10, Dionysius notes that χάρις is something different from, and less defin-
able than, the other ἀρεταί: ῥᾷστον μὲν γάρ ἐστιν ὀφθῆναι ... χαλεπώτατον
δὲ λόγῳ δηλωθῆναι. Grube (*GCDS* 92 n. 128) writes: "For purposes of
translation we may render χάριτες in the over-all sense as 'charm and wit'."
Cf. his pages 30-32. Roberts (*DS* 308) says, "No one English word will
quite cover the same ground as χάρις"; he uses, "charm, wit, pleasantry,
cleverness, smartness," etc. as translations. χάρις and related words are
found about eighty times in Demetrius *On Style*: D.M. Schenkeveld, *Studies
in Demetrius on Style* 19.

[34] ἡδονή (lit. "pleasure, delight"), a word frequently applied to pleasure
in eating and drinking, is used of style possessing "charm, the agreeable."
It is a comprehensive term defined by Dionysius (*De Comp.* 11.37.12-14)
as including "freshness, grace, euphony, sweetness, and persuasiveness." See
Roberts, *DHTLL* 193; *DS* 284; and infra on chap. 27.5.–G. Mestwerdt, *De
Dionysii Halicarnassensis et Hermogenis in aestimandis veterum scriptoribus
inter se ratione* (Progr. Cleve 1872) 7 notes that the sentiment of this sentence, as with many other ideas of Dionysius, is repeated in Hermogenes of
Tarsus (*Id.* p. 411.12ff. [Rabe]).

[35] Ancient critics praised the sweetness and beauty of Herodotus, but
found him lacking in emotional power: Cicero *Or.* 39, Quintilian 10.1.73;
Athenaeus 3.78e. J.D. Denniston (*Oxford Class. Dict.*[2] 509) observes that
Herodotus has suffered the fate which befell Mozart: his charm and effort-
less ease have diverted attention from his emotional powers. Grube (*GRC*
209-211) summarizes the well-known comparison of Herodotus and Thucydides in the *Ep. ad Pomp.*, chap. 3, but does not consider our passage.

[36] The examples listed in the Greek *Thesaurus* (col. 972) show that the
words ἐναγώνιον and δικανικόν were at times used by Dionysius as synonyms
for forensic oratory, the speeches of the law-courts. The δημηγορικοὶ λόγοι,
on the other hand, were deliberative speeches in the popular assembly.
Aristotle, *Rhet.* 1.3.1358b, makes a triple division of oratory based upon the
attitude of the hearer: συμβουλευτικόν ("deliberative"), δικανικόν ("forensic"),
ἐπιδεικτικόν ("epideictic"). R.C. Jebb (in E. Abbott, *Hellenica* [London
1880] 279) notes that there is only one epideictic speech in Thucydides,
the Funeral Oration, and one forensic, the pleading of the Plataeans and
Thebans before the Spartan Commissioners. The earliest extant treatise on
rhetoric is that of Anaximenes who admitted two *genera* with seven *species*.
For true division of rhetoric into deliberative, judicial, and epideictic, see,
for example, D.A.G. Hinds, "Tria genera causarum," *CQ* 30 (1936) 170-176.
In the Stoic scheme, 'encomiastic' was used instead of 'epideictic'; see Diogenes Laertius 7.42. The author's emphasis on the judicial kind is characteristically Hellenistic (e.g. Hermagorean), and this was by far the most often

employed in Hellenistic times. The same emphasis is found in the first two books of the *Rhetorica ad Herennium.*–Herodotus has many speeches and dialogues (see the partial list in W. Schmid, *Geschichte der gr. Litt.* 7.1.2 [Munich 1934] 648); but Dionysius is here concerned only with the parliamentary and judicial branches of the art.

[37] Ἀλκή, "strength," is used here metaphorically for an author's strong point. Cf. ῥώμη, "bodily strength" (*De Imit.* 3.207.17 [used of Thucydides]) and στιβαρός, "virile" (chap. 24.361.9).

[38] The point is emphasized by many scholars, in particular by Grube (*GCDS* 25-26), that the ancient rhetoricians were not merely concerned with writing but with the expression of emotion as well. This was not the case only because the emotions needed to be and could be aroused by rhetors. It was also because ancient rhetoricians did not consider writing to be merely a form of thinking, nor did they believe that thinking and feeling were mutually exclusive or that they were separate processes. R.C. Jebb (in E. Abbott's *Hellenica* [London 1880] 270-271) quotes this final sentence of chap. 23, adding, "Dionysius says most truly of Herodotus that he has almost all the excellences of style except the ἐναγώνιοι ἀρεταί–the combative excellences,–such as were afterwards developed by strenuous controversy, political or forensic."

Commentary on Chapter 24

[1] As a result of the objections of Ammaeus (*Ep. II ad Amm.* 1) that Dionysius had not given concrete examples of his criticism of Thucydides, Dionysius wrote the *Second Letter*, which is in the nature of a supplement to chap. 24 of the *De Thucydide.* The distinguishing features of Thucydidean idiom are repeated and then illustrated point by point. Text and translation of the *Second Letter to Ammaeus* are published by W.R. Roberts, *DHTLL* 131-159.

[2] The inferior MSS. of the *De Thuc.* contain a gloss at this point, explaining that Thucydides' style was neither completely prose nor poetry, but a mixture of the two elements. Cf. *Ep. II ad Amm.* 2.422.15.

[3] The Greeks of the first century B.C. distinguished "tropes" (τρόποι) and "figures" (σχήματα): "The Greeks consider that language is embellished if such changes in the use of words are employed as they call τρόπους and such figures of language and thought as they call σχήματα" (Cicero *Brutus* 69). Tropes, then, in the rhetorical sense, are a matter of diction, the use of individual words in other than their normal sense. See Roberts *DHTLL* 206-207. F.H. Colson (*CR* 25 [1911] 46) shows that "trope" included metaphor, hypallage, catachresis, and the like, and recommends that the word be translated in inverted commas. The history of the two words is outlined by D.A. Russell, *'Longinus' On the Sublime* (Oxford 1964) 126-128. See also H. Caplan in his Loeb edition of the *Rhetorica ad Herennium*, p. 332; and D.M. Schenkeveld, *Studies in Demetrius on Style* (Diss.

Amsterdam 1964) 147.–J. Steup (*Einleitung* to the first volume of the Classen-Steup *Thukydides* [Seventh reprint ed. Berlin 1966] lxxix) cites the phrase τροπικὴ λέξις of Dionysius, noting on the evidence of H. Blümner (*NJPhP* 143 [1891] 9-52) that metaphors are much less frequent in Thucydides than in Herodotus: "Es ist auch leicht einzusehen, dass ein bilderreicher Stil mit dem von Th. erstrebten höchsten Grade von Genauigkeit der Darstellung schwer vereinbar gewesen wäre." Marcellinus (*Vita* 41) seems to refer to the scarcity of metaphors when he uses the phrase μεταφοραῖς τισι. J.F. Corstens, *De translationibus quibus usus est Thucydides* (Diss. Leiden 1894), has classified the metaphorical vocabulary of Thucydides under twenty-one headings (family, clothing, education, palaestra, military, etc.). Especially frequent is the image of blooming (ἀκμή, ἀκμάζω: I.19, II.42.4, IV.133.1, etc.). See also F. Rittelmeyer, *Thukydides und die Sophistik* (Diss. Erlangen 1915) 70-72, and infra on chap. 31.2.

[4] The word γλωττηματικός is four times (35.383.9; 50.409.19; 52.412.8) applied by Dionysius to Thucydides as a quality of diction to be eschewed. Isocrates (*De Dem.* 4.135.7) is praised for his avoidance of such words. For definitions of the word as given by Aristotle and Galen, see Roberts, *DHTLL* 187. For the term γλῶτται in rhetoric, see E.M. Cope, *Journal of Classical and Sacred Philology* 2 (1856) 141, 3 (1857) 74; P. Chantraine, "La stylistique grecque," *Actes du premier congrès de la Fédération internationale des associations d'études classiques* (Paris 1951) 346-347; and W.-D. Lebek, *Hermes* 97 (1969) 64-66.

[5] ἀπηρχαιωμένος, "archaic, antiquated, obsolete," is three times combined in the *De Thuc.* with γλωττηματικός (50.409.19; 52.412.8). J.D. Denniston, *Greek Prose Style*[2] (Oxford 1960) 17, writes, "Thucydides definitely adopts a uniform archaic colour for large portions of his work."

[6] J.H. Freeze, in a note to Aristotle *Rhet.* 3.2.1404b.3, writes, "It is impossible to find a satisfactory English equivalent for the terms ξένος, ξενικός, τὸ ξενίζον, as applied to style. 'Foreign' does not really convey the idea, which is rather that of something opposed to 'home-like,'—out-of-the-way, as if from 'abroad.' Jebb suggests 'distinctive'." Roberts translates as "strange." W.B. Stanford uses "exotic." Geigenmüller (*Quaestiones* 104) comments: Ξένον *non esse peregrinum, sed inusitatum, admirabile, eximum apparet ex locis.* D.A. Russell (*ALC* 314) renders the phrase περιττὸν καὶ ξένον in *De Dem.* 15.161.6 as "special elegance." D.W. Lucas (*Aristotle's Poetics* [Oxford 1968] 208) explains that Plato and Isocrates use the word in the sense of "non-Attic," but that it usually means "out of the ordinary," adding that an ordinary word acquires τὸ ξενικόν by an unusual formation or by its application. E.M. Cope (*Introduction to Aristotle's Rhetoric* [London 1867] 283) notes that in Quintilian 8.2.1-11 the word κύριον is opposed to ξενικόν, any term that is not "proper" and "usual," any foreign or strange word that strikes one as singular and unusual. Diodorus (12.53) applies the phrase τὸ ξενίζον τῆς λέξεως to the exaggerated style of Gorgias and its "foreign" ornaments.

⁷ Dionysius in the *Ep. II ad Amm.* illustrates his criticism of Thucydides' choice of words by citing from two groups, the one obscure and archaic, the other poietika, a word taken by some to mean "poetical," but by Ernesti as "artificial" or "elaborate." Of the first group, Dionysius cites from Thucydides the words τὸ ἀκραιφνές (I.19.1; I.52.2), ὁ ἐπιλογισμός, ἡ περιωπή (IV.87.1); ἡ ἀνακωχή (I.40.4, etc.). The word ἐπιλογισμός presents a difficulty, since it does not occur in our text of Thucydides, nor is it likely to be considered obscure. (Parenthetically, the word should be added to the collection of *Testimonia Pseudothucydidea* in Appendix III of Hude's *editio maior.*) Usener suggests that the word actually written by Dionysius was ἐπηλύτης (I.9.2), an unusual form (but see Xenophon *Oec.* 11.4) found in all Thucydidean manuscripts, but generally emended to ἔπηλυς. Although censuring Thucydides for using ἀκραιφνές, Dionysius uses it himself frequently (*AR* 3.20.2, 6.14.3, 8.63.3, 8.65.3). As examples of artificial or poetical words, Dionysius cites ἡ κωλύμη (I.92.1; IV.27.3, 63.1), ἡ πρέσβευσις (I.73.1); ἡ καταβοή (for καταβολή of Diony. MSS.) (I.73.1; VIII.85.2, 87.3); ἡ ἀχθηδών (II.37.2; IV.40.2); ἡ δικαίωσις (I.141.1; III.82.4; IV.86.6; V.17.2; VIII.66.2). The first three words are annotated by the scholiasts on the historian as peculiar to the diction of Thucydides (παρὰ Θουκυδίδῃ ἰδίως: Rutherford says that ἰδίως means "in a peculiar sense"). C.F. Smith has written three papers on the poetic vocabulary of Thucydides. The first ("Traces of Tragic Usage in Thucydides," *PAPA* 22 [1891] xvi-xxi) is confined to the vocabulary of the third book and comprises an investigation of 38 words or phrases "probably borrowed from Tragedy." The second ("Poetic Words in Thucydides," *PAPA* 23 [1892] xlviii-li) enumerates 77 words. Smith observes that half of these occur in speeches and elevated passages, but hardly any in Book VIII. He concludes that "Thucydides's poetic vocabulary was largely a matter of choice, and not owing mainly to the undeveloped state of Greek prose." The third paper ("Traces of Epic Usage in Thucydides," *TAPA* 31 [1900] 69-81) is an analysis of certain words (27) taken directly from the epic, and others (32) taken indirectly through Tragedy or the Lyric. Smith believes that Thucydides "consciously avoids at ... times the language of daily life and creates for himself a great literary dialect. He uses rare terms and unusual forms of expressions because ordinary words have traditional associations that may detract from the dignity of the subject at such a time. He uses poetical terms, because poetry alone can adequately express deep human passion and pathos, and because such words have been, in a measure, sacred to his readers from their earliest use of the great national text-book in poetry. ... The effect was like borrowing great biblical words." R.C. Jebb (in E. Abbott's *Hellenica* [London 1880] 308) gives as samples of poetic diction: ναυβάτης (I.121.3; cf. Pollux 1.95), ἀχθηδών (II.37.2), ἐσθήματα (III.58.4), ἐσσαμένων (= ἰδρυσαμένων, III.58.5), κεκμηῶτες (III.59.2), περίρρυτος (IV.64.3), περιωπή (IV.87.1), φυλοκρινεῖν (VI.18.2), ἐπηλυγάζεσθαι (VI.36.2). L.A.L. Cyranka, *De orationum Thucydidearum elocutione cum tragicis comparata* (Diss. Breslau 1875) devotes three chapters to collections of words (47 verbs, 27 substantives, 40 adjectives), phrases (*ca.* 65) and syntactical constructions found

only in Thucydides and the tragic poets. Cyranka's examples, he says, are
compiled largely from the notes in the editions of Bloomfield, Krüger, and
Classen. He argues against the position of Poppo (see the Introduction, pp.
xxxiii-xxxiv). Almost simultaneously, C.E. Hesse (*Dionysii Halicarnassensis
de Thucydide judicia examinantur* [Progr. Leipzig 1877] 17) and J. Wichmann, *Dionysii Halicarnassensis de Thucydide iudicia componuntur et examinantur* (Diss. Halle Sax. 1878) 16ff. presented collections of poetic words;
and J.D. Wolcott (*TAPA* 29 [1898] 104-157) collected words "which make
their earliest appearance in Thucydides" (Substantives: 430 [Wolcott's figure
of 330 on p. 145 is an error of addition] ; Verbs: 383; Adjectives: 159; Adverbs: 85; Total: 1057). A large percentage of his new words consists of
verbal substantives in -μα (common in tragedy and Ionic; P. Chantraine, *La
formation des noms en grec ancien* [Paris 1933] 175-190), and in -σις (see
E.G. Sihler, "On the Verbal Abstract Nouns in -σις in Thucydides," *TAPA*
12 [1881] 96-104, an article to be used with caution because the author
repeatedly states that the purpose of these verbals was to produce "condensation," whereas they are most frequently found in periphrastic constructions
that constitute expansion. Thucydides was striving after logical precision,
and nouns admit of more concise modification than verbs. For the frequency
of -σις nouns in Greek, see P. Chantraine, *op. cit.* 276-286. T.B.L. Webster,
Acta Congressus Madvigiani 2 [1958] 31, observes that the word ἀπόδοσις
appears on thirteenth century tablets from Pylos in the sense of 'repayment,'
and suggests that the -σις noun was in origin a sort of participle.), and -της,
nouns in -ία, compounds with ἐπί, ἀντί, πρό and ξύν, and formations with
παν-, ὁμο-, φιλο-, and κακο-. Finally, in a lengthy dissertation written under
E. Norden, J. Ehlert (*De verborum copia Thucydidea quaestiones selectae*
[Berlin 1910]) has given a full bibliography on the subject, with long lists
of so-called Ionic (including Herodotean), poetic (including Homeric and
tragic) and neoteric words. The salient point about these collections of neo-
terisms and poetical words is their uniform distribution throughout the history, a fact to be borne in mind when examining theories about the manner
of composition. Although unaware of Ehlert's work, H.W. Litchfield ("The
Attic Alphabet in Thucydides," *HSCP* 23 [1912] 129-154) has compared
the orthography of Thucydides with early inscriptions, concluding that
Thucydides showed "a greater aloofness from the Ionic usage than is generally conceded." See also R. Herzog, *Die Umschrift der älteren gr. Literatur
in das ion. Alphabet* (Progr. Basel 1912) 95, 99.—Just as B. Rosenkranz
(*Indogermanische Forschungen* 48 [1930] 127-178) has argued that Ionic
words, which O. Diener (*De sermone Thucydidis quatenus cum Herodoto
congruens differat a scriptoribus atticis* [Diss. Leipzig 1889]) and A. Thumb
had thought were borrowed from Herodotus, were a part of the (epigraphical) language of Athens in the fifth century and that dialectical Euboean
and Boeotian forms were used in the spoken language, so K.J. Dover
("Thucydides," *G&R*, Survey no. 7 [1973] 12) suggests that words which
were poetic and archaic to Demosthenes and later writers were used in
ordinary parlance by the contemporaries of Thucydides. But a real difficulty
lies in any assumption that the language of decrees before the development

of a formulaic legal style at the close of the fifth century represents common parlance; all that we can be sure of is that the words of one particular speaker were inscribed on stone. In the early Athenian decree which preserves regulations about the Eleusinian mysteries (*IG* I^2 6), the following phrase is found at the top of the preserved right side (in Attic script): τὰ μὲν ἀκόσια ἁπλεῖ, τὰ δὲ ἑκόσια διπλεῖ, thus providing examples of ἀντίθεσις, ἰσόκωλον and ὁμοιοτέλευτον, a quarter of a century before Gorgias' arrival in Athens. *Pace* Rosenkranz, the language of official inscriptions showed traces of literary influence. The Athenian ekklesia included the highly educated as well as those not so articulate. On the sequence of clauses in early Attic inscriptions, see Pritchett, *CSCA* 5 (1972) 178 n. 83.–L. Campbell in his "Introductory Essay" to his *Sophocles*^{2} (Oxford 1879) writes of the wide diversities and peculiarities of language at the time of Sophocles, and the first chapter of W.G. Rutherford's *New Phrynichus* (London 1881) is devoted to a study of the "Growth of the Attic Dialect." One laments the loss of Dionysius' treatise ἡ ἐκλογὴ τῶν ὀνομάτων (*De Comp.* 1), which might enable us to sharpen our sense of the differences of diction among Attic writers. Gordon Williams (*Tradition and Originality in Roman Poetry* [Oxford 1968] 743-750) has very interesting observations on the problem of what constitutes a poetic vocabulary. The vocabulary of Thucydides has been analyzed by P. Huart, *Le vocabulaire de l'analyse psychologique dans l'oeuvre de Thucydide* (Paris 1968), in particular in the Introduction, 1-32. Huart endorses Chantraine's thesis that Thucydides developed a vocabulary, not for *variatio*, but one which provided the Greeks with "l'équipement nécessaire à une langue philosophique et scientifique" (p. 26). We must realize that Thucydides was writing at a time when there was not only no dictionary to explain the meaning of words, but the very idea that it was possible to define the meaning of a word was a new conception which was used by Socrates to the utter discomfort of all who came into argument with him. Furthermore, our modern linguistic conscience permits us to take a word wherever we find it; from opposite sides of the world we have taken the terms "palaver" and "taboo," as readily as we manufacture technical terms from "dead" languages. And the lack of a vocabulary was not the only difficulty with which Thucydides had to contend; the language had as yet no settled or recognized grammar. By this is meant not merely that there was no body of rules such as that formulated later by the Stoics and Dionysius Thrax, but Attic was in a plastic condition in which people did not systematically follow the same grammatical principles under similar circumstances.

[8] For ἀξιωματικός, see Geigenmüller, *Quaestiones* 57, and Roberts, *DHLC* 288.

[9] The word αὐστηρός (lit. "bitter, harsh" to the tongue, as of water, wine) is a rhetorical term suggested by the sense of taste ("austere, stern, severe"). It is a favorite term with Dionysius and chap. 22 of the *De Comp.* is devoted to this style of word-arrangement. See Grube *GCDS* 17; H.F. North, *CP* 43 (1948) 1.

[10]For στιβαρός "sturdy, robust, virile," one of numerous rhetorical words drawn from the vocabulary of words describing physical condition, see van Hook, *Terminology* 20, and Roberts, *DHLC* 322. The meaning does not differ much from that of ἰσχυρός, with which it is joined in *De Comp.* 100.10.

[11]The participle βεβηκώς, always applied to the austere style of composition (Geigenmüller, *Quaestiones* 76), is said by Roberts (*DHLC* 292) to be "used of a firm, regular tread." LSJ renders as "stately."

[12]In *De Comp.* 20.91.15, Dionysius refers to "rough letters," and from the lines quoted in this passage Roberts (*DHLC* 329) deduces that the letters σ, φ, γ, χ, στ, ξ, πτ, σχ, σκ are meant. In 14.54.12, Dionysius says that the rho is rough (τραχύς).

[13]In *De Dem.* 7 and *Ep. ad Pomp.* 2, Dionysius analyzes the style of Plato with regard to its clearness (τὸ λιγυρόν). Elsewhere in the *De Dem.*, he writes of λιγυρὰν ἁρμονίαν (36.209.6), λιγυρὰν λέξιν (40.216.12), and λιγυρὰ σχήματα (43.227.14). Plutarch (*Mor.* 974A) records Democritus' remark that with regard to τὸ λιγυρόν men imitate the swan and nightingale.

[14]μαλακός, like Latin *mollis*, as a habit of life, means "soft, languid, pleasant, lazy." As used by Dionysius, the word sometimes suggests the idea of "lacking in backbone, unmanly, effeminate": Roberts, *DHLC* 309. When applied to sound, the word is sometimes combined with εὐεπής, "euphonious." For a metaphorical use applied to reasoning, see E.M. Cope on Aristotle's *Rhetoric* 2.22.1396a.10.

[15]Dionysius frequently uses the verb συγξεῖν (lit. "to smooth by scraping or planing") and its compounds. See van Hook, *Terminology* 38; and Roberts, *DHLC* 324.

[16]As an example of Thucydides' austere and rugged diction, Dionysius had already (*De Comp.* 22) devoted the better half of a chapter to an analysis of Thuc. I.1.1-2.2. He, therefore, did not illustrate this point in the *Ep. II ad Amm.* In his analysis in the *De Comp.*, he concerned himself with euphony, substantiating his views in detail "and in so doing gives us some of the most valuable information we have about Greek pronunciation and euphony" (W.B. Stanford, *The Sound of Greek* [Berkeley 1967] 16). Dionysius' chapter can be understood only if one recognizes that "reading aloud was entrenched in ancient education and usage as the only recognized means of gaining the full meaning of the written page" (G.L. Hendrickson, *CJ* 25 [1929] 193). Dionysius objects to the combination of sounds (σ-ξ, ν-τ, ν-π, ν-κ, hiatus) at the opening of the History (Θουκυδίδης Ἀθηναῖος ξυνέγραψε τὸν πόλεμον τῶν Πελοποννησίων καὶ Ἀθηναίων) and those (hiatus thrice repeated, ν-τ, ν-πρ) in the following phrase (καὶ ἐλπίσας ...) as causing an interruption of the voice in pronunciation, the glottal stop, as it is now called. "In our present state of insensitivity to the sound of Greek it would take many years of teaching and training before we could experience it aurally as fully as Dionysios could" (Stanford, *op. cit.* 80). An anonymous

author of an article on "Panegyrical Oratory of Greece" (*Quarterly Review* 27 [1822] 383) aptly wrote of Dionysius' criticism "which gives less pleasure perhaps from the information it imparts, than it does mortification from showing us, how much there is in antiquity which we can never thoroughly appreciate." Fascinating as the analysis of the inner mechanism of the craft may be, we can be sure that Thucydides and Demosthenes were not solicitous to count their longs and shorts nor did they consciously play the game of hide-and-seek with the letters of the alphabet. The method of procedure is one thing, and the method of analysis another.—A.W. de Groot, *A Handbook of Antique Prose-Rhythm* 1 (Groningen 1919) finds no metrical tendency in the sentences of Thucydides. He concludes (p. 20), "I venture to say that it is Thucydides who appears to be entirely or almost entirely careless of the arrangement of long and short syllables in the sentence."

[17] A. Greilich (*Dionysius Halicarnassensis quibus potissimum vocabulis ex artibus metaphorice ductis in scriptis rhetoricis usus sit* [Diss. Breslau 1886] 43) devotes a section to the expression στρέφειν ἄνω καὶ κάτω, concluding from the examples cited in H. Blümner's *Technologie* that it is borrowed from weaving, i.e., "to twist, to plait." Van Hook (*Terminology* 36) believes that the meaning rather is "to turn upside down, up and down;" but the examples cited from Plato (*Gorgias* 511a, *Phaedr.* 278c) have to do with the art of eristic, twisting this way and that of words and ideas so that their sense is reversed. Verbs (ὑφαίνειν, ποικίλλειν, πλέκειν, etc.) indicating the skilful interweaving of the threads of discourse are common in Dionysius.

[18] Dionysius uses many words for metal-working. The verbs τορεύειν (lit. to work metal in relief) and ῥωᾶν (lit. to file, fine down) are here used of the literary industry and accuracy of Thucydides. For ῥωᾶν cf. Aristophanes *Ran.* 901. The two words are discussed at length by A. Greilich, *op. cit.* (supra, 24.17) 5-8.

[19] The word λόγος, here rendered by "phrase," is the verbal noun from a verb whose meanings are "count, tell, say, speak." Logos is any meaningful combination of words. As Aristotle defines it in the *De Interp.* chap. 4, it covers both sentences and phrases, but "sentence-or-phrase" is, as Ackrill notes, a cumbrous expression; so a choice must be made between sentence and phrase according to the context. See J.L. Ackrill, *Aristotle's Categories and De Interpretatione* (Oxford 1963) 124. Dionysius Thrax (p. 22.5: Uhlig) gives the definition: λόγος ἐστὶ πεζῆς λέξεως σύνθεσις διάνοιαν αὐτοτελῆ ἔχουσα. Definitions of a sentence, ancient as well as modern, are given in J. Ries, *Was ist ein Satz?* (Prague 1931) 208-224. It seems that the ancients never developed a single word equivalent to our "sentence": W.R. Johnson, "Luxuriance and Economy: Cicero and the Alien Style," *University of California Publications in Classical Studies* 6 (1971) 15. T.B.L. Webster in his study of Greek sentence construction (*AJP* 62 [1941] 385-415) finds that Thucydides, in sentence length and in degree of subordination, was no archaiser, but was ahead of his time, anticipating to a large extent the structure of the fourth century.

[20]Ackrill (p. 115) writes of ὄνομα, "In some contexts it is tempting to write 'word' or 'noun,' but only 'name' can do duty in all contexts." The word is discussed by P.B.R. Forbes in an interesting article, "Greek Pioneers in Philology and Grammar," *CR* 47 (1933) 105-112. We do not have a lexicon of Greek grammatical terminology comparable to the work of J.C.T. Ernesti on Greek rhetorical terms.

[21]Demetrius (*On Style,* 92-93) says that the use of one word for an entire phrase is a practice which adds grandeur to the style. He gives as an example the word σιτοπομπία ("corn-convoy") for ἡ τοῦ σίτου κομίδη and then quotes from Xenophon *Anab.* 1.5.2, οὐκ ἦν λαβεῖν ὄνον ἄγριον, εἰ μὴ οἱ ἱππεῖς διαστάντες θηρῷεν διαδεχόμενοι, where the single word διαδεχόμενοι "is equivalent to saying that those in the rear were pursuing, while the others rode forward to meet them, so that the wild ass was intercepted."

[22]In *Ep. II ad Amm.* 5, Dionysius gives as examples the nouns παραίνεσις, "exhortation" and ἀξίωσις "claim" instead of τὸ παραινεῖν and τὸ ἀξιοῦν which Dionysius would substitute in the sentence (I.41.1): δικαιώματα μὲν οὖν τάδε πρὸς ὑμᾶς ἔχομεν, παραίνεσιν δὲ καὶ ἀξίωσιν χάριτος τοιάνδε. Thucydides' reasons for preferring the nominal to the verbal construction are discussed by J.D. Wolcott, *TAPA* 29 (1898) 143, 157. See also J.G.A. Ros, *Metabole* 57 n. 19. Dionysius ascribes the tendency to mere wilfulness. Hermogenes (p. 249.12ff. edition of H. Rabe: ἔτι δὲ σεμνὴ λέξις ἥ τε ὀνοματικὴ καὶ αὐτὰ τὰ ὀνόματα ... ὡς ἐλάχιστα γὰρ ἐν σεμνότητι δεῖ χρῆσθαι τοῖς ῥήμασιν, ὥσπερ ὁ Θουκυδίδης ...) shows keener perception when he attributes the frequent employment of nominal instead of verbal forms to an effort to give to the expression of the thought greater dignity and elevation than could be secured by the use of the corresponding verbs. Hermogenes cites as an example III.82.4 (τόλμα μὲν γὰρ ἀλόγιστος ...). Thucydides may have seen, as Hermogenes and Sallust clearly did, that a nominal style can achieve a compression that verbal styles cannot. Thus, in Latin and French aphorisms, nouns tend to count for everything; most of the verbs are forms of the verb "to be." Thucydides, as noted in chap. 24.7, coined many verbal substantives in -μα, -της and -σις.

[23]Dionysius (*Ep. II ad Amm.* chap. 6) illustrates this point by substituting the nouns ἀνάγκη and πόλεμος for the verbs ἀναγκάσαι and τὸ πολεμεῖν in the sentence (I.23.6) τὴν μὲν οὖν ἀληθεστάτην αἰτίαν, λόγῳ δὲ ἀφανεστάτην, τοὺς Ἀθηναίους οἴομαι μεγάλους γινομένους ἀναγκάσαι εἰς τὸ πολεμεῖν. Dionysius alters the text, reading οὖν for γάρ, αἰτίαν for πρόφασιν, λόγῳ δὲ ἀφανεστάτην for ἀφανεστάτην δὲ λόγῳ, οἴομαι for ἡγοῦμαι, and omitting one phrase.

[24]For the use of προσηγορία as "appellative, common noun," see Roberts *DHTLL* 204. A. Croiset, *Thucydide* (Paris 1886) 123 translates as "un adjectif." The Stoic division of nouns into ὀνόματα (proper nouns, names) and προσηγορίαι (common nouns, appellatives) is set forth in Diogenes Laertius 7.57-58, where it is said that proper nouns "signify individual qualities" like the "quality of being Diogenes" and common nouns "general

qualities" such as "being a horse." The deficiencies of this system are discussed by R.H. Robins, *Ancient and Mediaeval Grammatical Theory* (London 1951) 27-28.

[25] Dionysius gives no examples of these. W. Warren (*AJP* 20 [1899] 318) has shown that there must be a lacuna between chapters 6 and 7 of the *Second Letter*; this observation has escaped the notice of Usener, Roberts and others. Roberts (*DHTLL* 135) translates the two words as "common nouns" and "proper nouns."

[26]Dionysius at times uses quite different terminology from that of Dionysius Thrax, who in the second century B.C. wrote an epitome of grammar as developed by the Stoics and Alexandrians. In Dionysius Thrax, ἐνέργεια is the word for active "voice" (διάθεσις).

[27] As an illustration of an active verb (κωλύει) used in place of a passive (κωλύεται), Dionysius (chap. 7) cites (I.144.2): οὔτε γὰρ ἐκεῖνο κωλύει ταῖς σπονδαῖς οὔτε τόδε. But the manuscripts of Thucydides give ἐν ταῖς σπονδαῖς, which is the reading of all editors except Stahl. With or without ἐν, κωλύει is used impersonally "there is no hindrance to;" cf. Aristophanes *Aves* 463 (quoted first by Krüger). R. Rauchenstein (*Philol.* 37 [1877] 64) would emend to the passive κωλύεται, which would mean that Dionysius' Thucydidean text was indeed defective. According to Poppo, Valla had the same reading as Dionysius. The second example cited by Dionysius is I.2.2: τῆς γὰρ ἐμπορίας οὐκ οὔσης οὐδ᾽ ἐπιμιγνύντες ἀδεῶς ἀλλήλοις, where Dionysius would have the passive ἐπιμιγνύμενοι. Cf. J.G.A. Ros, *Metabole* 57.

[28] For illustrations of the active used for the passive, Dionysius cites two phrases in I.120.2: ἡμῶν δὲ ὅσοι μὲν Ἀθηναίοις ἤδη ἐνηλλάγησαν, where Dionysius would substitute συνήλλαξαν, and τοὺς δ᾽ ἐν τῇ μεσογείᾳ (τὴν μεσόγειαν = Thucydidean MSS.) μᾶλλον κατῳκημένους, where Dionysius wants κατῳκηκότας.

[29]Dionysius (chap. 9) gives illustrations from VI.78, IV.10, II.35 (*bis*). The first reads: καὶ εἴ τῳ ἄρα παρέστηκεν τὸν μὲν Συρακόσιον, ἑαυτὸν δ᾽ οὐ πολέμιον εἶναι τῷ Ἀθηναίῳ. Dionysius says that Thucydides means τοὺς Συρακοσίους and τοὺς Ἀθηναίους, respectively. Kühner-Gerth (*Griech. Gram.* 1³ [Leipzig 1898] 14) cite this and other examples of the use of the singular in prose authors and find its origin in a manner of referring to despotisms, like Herodotus' τὸν Πέρσην (8.108).

[30]It is quite clear from chap. 10 of the *Ep. II ad Amm.* that what Dionysius has in mind is interchange of gender (ἀντιμετάταξις), and the meaning of συνάπτω must be interpreted accordingly not as "to join with" but as "to attribute to." As illustrations of nouns, Dionysius gives τάραχος for the feminine ταραχή, and ὄχλος for ὄχλησις. The former word is not found in our texts of Thucydides, where ταραχή occurs eleven times, but may have been the reading in Dionysius' text of Thucydides for one of the passages. The noun ὄχλος is used in Thucydides I.73.2, not in its usual sense of "crowd" (twenty-six times in Thucydides), but of "annoyance,

trouble." Moeris (289 P) says that this latter meaning is an old Attic use of ὄχλος.–Dionysius also says that in place of τὴν βούλησιν Thucydides uses τὸ βουλόμενον in VI.24.2. However, the Thucydidean manuscripts read τὸ ἐπιθυμοῦν τοῦ πλοῦ. Cf. J.G.A. Ros, *Metabole* 59 n. 25. – Finally, as an example of the neuter used for the feminine, Dionysius quotes (IV.78.3) ὥστε εἰ μὴ δυναστείᾳ μᾶλλον ἢ ἰσονομίᾳ ἐχρῶντο τῷ ἐπιχωρίῳ οἱ Θεσσαλοί, proposing the change of τῷ to τῇ. However, the Thucydidean manuscripts here read an adverbial accusative τὸ ἐγχώριον, glossed by the scholiast as ἐγχωρίως. Cf. J.G.A. Ros, *Metabole* 59.

[31] In his translation of this word in the *Ep. II ad Amm.*, W.R. Roberts (pp. 135, 184) renders akolouthia as "sequence, agreement of gender." Dionysius repeats much of chapter 24 in his letter to Ammaeus.

[32] Thucydides uses probably oftener than any other writer the neuter singular of participles as abstract substantives. M. Nietzki (*De Thucydideae elocutionis proprietate quadam* ... [Diss. Königsberg 1881] 37ff.) collects examples such as VI.24.2: οἱ Ἀθηναῖοι τὸ ἐπιθυμοῦν τοῦ πλοῦ οὐκ ἐξῃρέθησαν (for τὴν ἐπιθυμίαν), I.90.2: τὸ μὲν βουλόμενον καὶ ὕποπτον τῆς γνώμης οὐ δηλοῦντες (for τὴν βούλησιν καὶ τὴν ὑποψίαν), etc. He observes that this use was not common in tragedy. Classen (*Einleitung* p. lxxx) says that this is no capricious mannerism; Thucydides is striving to clothe the abstract idea in a dress which may render it in the particular case more easy of apprehension, while at the same time the neuter secures the maintenance of that indefiniteness which pertains to the notion itself. – L. Schlachter (*IF* 24 [1909] 189-221) examines 22,121 (Indicative: 43.5%, Participle: 35.8%, Infinitive: 16.3%, Subjunctive: 2.2%, Optative: 2.%, Imperative: 0.1%) verbal forms in the narrative portion which disclose in his judgment remarkable differences in "modal structure" between the first three books and the last five, and, following F.W. Ullrich (*Beiträge zur Erklärung des Thukydides* [Hamburg 1846]), concludes that this change indicates different periods of composition for the two groups. He claims, for example, that the participle is relatively much more frequent in the later books. By the use of a computer, G. Maloney ("La fréquence et l'ordre des formes verbales dans l'oeuvre de Thucydide," *RELO* 1970.3. 87-109) has charted the dispersement of verbal forms in different sections of the history. Verbal forms are more frequent in speeches, the genitive absolute in the narrative, and so on.

[33] "τὸ σημαῖνον = the expression: τὸ σημαινόμενον = the thing signified, the sense": Roberts, *DHTLL* 204. It was among the Stoics that grammatical studies were accorded a definite place in the philosophical discipline. They attempted to frame a theory of language, making it largely a symbolic reflection of psychological processes. This led them to a distinction in language between "the signifier" and "the signified." See Diogenes Laertius 7.43-44, 62-63, and Sextus Empiricus *Adv. Math.* 8.264, 279. For an outline of their grammatical theory, see R.H. Robins, *Ancient and Mediaeval Grammatical Theory in Europe* (London 1951), esp. 25-26. For the doctrine of "le signe," see F. de Saussure, *Cours de linguistique générale* (Paris 1922) 97ff. Diony-

sius illustrates Thucydidean transfer of form to meaning in chap. 13 of the
Ep. II ad Amm., citing (VI.35.1) τῶν δὲ Συρακοσίων ὁ δῆμος ἐν πολλῇ
πρὸς ἀλλήλους ἔριδι ἦσαν where Dionysius says that the singular noun δῆμος
is assimilated to the expression of the sense which is plural. But the use of
a collective noun with a plural verb was a not uncommon practice in the
Greek language. See B.L. Gildersleeve *SCG* 120. For collections of many
examples of the σχῆμα κατὰ τὸ σημαινόμενον in Thucydides, see W. Roscher,
Leben, Werk und Zeitalter des Thukydides (Göttingen 1842) 344ff.; K.W.
Krüger - W. Pöhel, *Griechische Sprachlehre*[5] (Leipzig 1875) 58.4; J.G.A.
Ros, *Metabole* 62, 196-223.

[34] D.W. Lucas (*Aristotle Poetics* [Oxford 1968] 201) defines σύνδεσμος
as "a connective, a word joining other words, phrases, or clauses, i.e. certain
particles and conjunctions." Roberts (*DHTLL* 206) defines συνδετικός as
"conjunction." There is difficulty in the exact rendition of the term. Sometimes it includes particles such as μέν and δή (Demetrius *On Style* 55, 56),
sometimes prepositions (*De Comp.* 22.102.16 and among the Stoics in general [K. Barwick, *Abh. der sächs. Akad. zu Leipzig* 49.3 (1957) 35]). P.B.R.
Forbes (*CR* 47 [1933] 111) notes that the Stoics used the phrase προθετικοὶ
σύνδεσμοι ("prepositive conjunctions") for prepositions, whereas in our passage the two words are separated. The word is discussed in E.M. Cope's
Introduction to Aristotle's Rhetoric (London 1867) 371-374, 392-397.

[35] J.G.A. Ros, *Metabole* 131 n. 20, cites six authors who devoted
special monographs to Thucydidean prepositions: J. Golisch (ἐς, ἐν, ἀπό, ἐκ,
etc.), T. Wisén (ὡς), A.R. Alvin (παρά), Z. Grundström (πρός), K.K.G.
Kümmell (ἐπί), and P. Debbert (περί, ἀμφί). Possibly more informative
than these dissertations and *programmschriften*, written between 1859 and
1883, is the work of R. Helbing *Die Präpositionen bei Herodot und anderen
Historiken* (Würzburg 1904). Helbing presents a whole mass of statistics
dealing with the entire range of historical literature. Of the three historians
Herodotus, Thucydides and Xenophon, Thucydides is the polyprothetic,
Xenophon the oligoprothetic (p. 6). In Thucydides, ἐς, ἐν, ἐπί, lead; but
this is not surprising, since these prepositions are used largely in describing
campaigns, and Thucydides' history is one of war. By contrast, κατά stands
first in Polybius and πρός comes second. Helbing notes the diminution of
εἰς and the intrusion of πρός to avoid hiatus, which Polybius wanted to
avoid at all costs. Of the three so-called poetic prepositions σύν, ἀνά, and
ἀμφί, Helbing comments about σύν (p. 30): "Thucydides aber drängt die
mehr poetische Präposition sehr in den Hintergrund." Moreover, ἀνά and
ἀμφί have short shrift in Thucydides, each occurring only twice (ἀνά: III.22.1,
IV.72.2; ἀμφί: VII.40.2, VIII.65.1. H.W. Smyth, *Greek Grammar* [Cam-
bridge 1956] 372, is incorrect in writing that Plato *Th.* 170c "contains the
only use of ἀμφί in Attic prose outside of Xenophon"). Thucydidean usage
contrasts with that of Herodotus (σύν: 73 [72: Powell] examples, ἀνά: 64
[66: Powell], ἀμφί: 34 [35: Powell]), who consciously hyper-epicized.
For the stylistic effect of the preposition and the need for research on this
subject, see B.L. Gildersleeve, *AJP* 23 (1902) 15-16. There has been no

follow-up on the thesis of L.L. Forman (*On the Difference between the Genitive and Dative used with ἐπί to denote Superposition* [Baltimore 1894]) that the distinction between cases with prepositions is sometimes one of imagery, picturesqueness and representation rather than of logical coherence: cf. Gildersleeve, *AJP* 18 (1897) 119-120.

[36]In *De Comp.* 2, Dionysius sketches the development of the division of the Greek language into στοιχεῖα, "elements," or μέρη, "parts," of speech. The early Stoics conceived of four parts (noun, verb, conjunction, and article); but later Stoics divided nouns into proper and common: Diogenes Laertius 7.57-58. Dionysius says, "the subject would afford scope for a long discussion." The only collection of testimonia on the subject is that of L. Lersch, *Die Sprachphilosophie der Alten* (Bonn 1838) 2.25-46. For the difficulty in rendering the word μόριον, see Roberts, *DHLC* 311.

[37] In other words, the article and particles. Ὀνόματα is here translated as "words" rather than as "nouns." The phrase ἐν τοῖς διαρθροῦσι τὰς τῶν ὀνομάτων δυνάμεις is repeated in the *Ep. II ad Amm.* (2.424.1) with the substitution of νοημάτων for ὀνομάτων in the four preserved manuscripts. Reiske understood the reference in our text as it stands to be to the article, and proposed emendation to ῥημάτων; but Krüger defends ὀνομάτων as being used in its broader sense. F. Blass (*Attische Beredsamkeit* 2[2] [Leipzig 1887] 222-223) reads ὀνομάτων, construing the passage as a reference to anarthrous composition. C.E. Hesse (*Dionysii Halicarnassensis de Thucydide judicia examinantur* [Progr. Leipzig 1877] 19 n. 72) and W.R. Roberts (p. 134) also retain ὀνομάτων but understand a reference to particles. Roberts here translates ὀνομάτων as "individual words." Unfortunately, Dionysius gives no examples to illustrate his point. Writing of the austere style, of which Thucydides is a prime representative, Dionysius (*De Comp.* 22.98.2) says that it lacks articles. This characterization might apply for Thucydides, first to his omission of the article with such words as βουλή (III.70.3, 4), δῆμος (I.107.3, VI.27.2), διαπολέμησις (VII.42.5), ναυμαχία (VIII.61.3), νεκροί (I.54.2, III.109.1, IV.14.4, V.10.11, VII.5.2, VIII.106.3), ὅπλα (VII.82.2), πολιορκία (I.102.3, II.70.2), πόλις (II.72.4); second, to the frequent omission in the case of nouns joined to αὐτός and the demonstrative pronouns (I.27.3, 51.1, 87.1, 140.4; III.59.2, 85.4, 95.3; VI.12.1; VIII.80.2, 100.4, 102.1); and third, the omission when a dependent genitive precedes (I.1.2 [διὰ χρόνου πλῆθος], 3.1, 11.1, 12.2, 36.2; II.72.1; IV.12.2; VI.34.4, 86.2). — As to the article with proper nouns in Thucydides, there have been four substantial contributions: L. Herbst, *Philol.* 40 (1881) 369-382 (summarized in English in *AJP* 2 [1881] 541); Carolus Schmidt, *De articulo in nominibus propriis apud Atticos scriptores pedestres* (Kiel 1890); B.L. Gildersleeve, *AJP* 11 (1890) 483-487; and A. Pfeifauf, *Der Artikel vor Personnennamen bei Thukydides und Herodot* (Innsbruck 1908). See also J.G.A. Ros, *Metabole,* 455 n. 3. Dialogue and narrative show marked divergences. The first book is comparatively oligarthrous, the sixth and seventh comparatively polyarthrous. As to the position of the article, Gildersleeve has written (*AJP* 17 [1896] 126): "Indeed, one might learn

more from the contrasted handling of article, adjective and substantive in
Herodotos and Thukydides than from many pages of rhetoric about the
chasm that divides the two authors. He who should be at pains to watch
what Aristotle calls the ὄγκος position and the συντομία position, and the
easy grace of the slipshod position—substantive, article and adjective—would
have an insight that might save him from phrase-making." The passage in
question in Aristotle is *Rhet.* 3.6.1407b.26-37. — As to particles, J.D. Denniston (*Greek Particles*[2] [Oxford 1954]), offers the following comments on
Thucydidean usage: ἀλλά (p. 4: "Thucydides sometimes inserts a comparative adverb in the negative clause, and it has been said that in such cases
ἀλλά has the force of ἤ. It seems more natural to regard οὐκ ... ἀλλά as
the primary construction, and the comparative as secondary and redundant,"
p. 21: "When the particle marks assent or complaisance, it corresponds
roughly to the English 'Well,' and has the same vague and colloquial tone:
hence its absence in the more formal speeches of Thucydides"); ἄρα (p. 38:
"in Thucydides it <the use in a conditional protasis> predominates strongly
over the other uses"); the colloquial particle ἀτάρ (p. 51: "In Prose, ἀτάρ
is common in Hippocrates, fairly common in Herodotus, Plato, and Xenophon, unknown in the orators, Thucydides, and Aristotle"); γάρ (p. 73:
"Fusion of clauses is, as Sernatinger remarks, an idiom characteristic of
Herodotus and [in a less degree] Thucydides, who no doubt adopted it
from Herodotus"); δέ (p. 177: "Only in Homer and Herodotus is apodotic
δέ really at home. Among other authors, Sophocles uses it, though rarely,
more often than Aeschylus and Euripides, who eschew it almost entirely.
Thucydides, Plato, and Xenophon use it occasionally"); δή (p. 207: "With
superlative adjectives and adverbs. This is a favorite use of Thucydides: I
have counted about thirty-six instances in him," p. 213: "Δή τις is mainly
found in the poets, and in Herodotus, Hippocrates, and Plato. In Thucydides I can find only III 104.1," p. 214: "With verbs. δή is freely used by
the tragedians to emphasize verbs ... In the austerer style of Thucydides ...
this usage is hardly to be found;" p. 238: "In Thucydides connective δή
is still proportionately rare, including less than ten per cent. of the examples
of the particle"); δῆθεν (p. 264: "Apart from Thucydides, who uses it
five times, it is almost entirely absent from Attic prose"); δήπου (p. 267:
"... is rare in tragedy, frequent in comedy and prose [though in Thucydides
only in VII 87.4: 87.5]"); μέντοι (p. 404: "Already in Herodotus, adver-
sative μέντοι predominates over other uses: and this predominance is even
more strongly marked in Thucydides"); οὖν (p. 425: "The tendency to use
οὖν <as a connecting particle> particularly in questions ... perhaps survives
into the fourth century ... But there is no trace of this tendency in Herodotus or Thucydides"); τε (p. 497: "In prose, single connective τε is much
rarer. Mainly confined to the historians [more than 400 times in Thucydides,
according to Hammer ...]" p. 500: "Often in Thucydides τε introduces
a clinching or summing up of what precedes." <This use is called by Classen
"das überleitende τε," by American syntacticians the "postscript" or "infer-
ential" τε, translating "and consequently,">); τοι (p. 556: "There is
usually a certain combative tone in καίτοι. For this reason it is not common

in unimpassioned, cold-blooded exposition. It is significant that out of 24 Thucydidean examples all except I 10.2 are from speeches [VIII 72.1 reported speech] .") On the three Thucydidean τοι's, termed the confidential particle, see B.L. Gildersleeve, *AJP* 33 (1912) 240. D.P. Tompkins (*YClS* 22 [1972] 198-199) discusses the particles τοι, δή and που. The following publications are concerned with Thucydidean particles: E.L. Green, "Πέρ in Thucydides, Xenophon, and the Attic Orators," *PAPA* 32 (1901) cxxxv-vi. B. Hammar, *De τε particulae usu Herodoteo, Thucydideo, Xenophonteo* (Diss. Leipzig 1904). L. Herbst, "Thukydides" (notes on particles, *passim*), *Phil.* 24 (1867) 610-730. C.W.E. Miller, "On τὸ δέ = 'Whereas,' " *TAPA* 39 (1908) esp. 125-127 (Thucydides). O. Oeltze, *De particularum μέν et δέ apud Thucydidem usu* (Diss. Halis Sax. 1887). H. Saeve, *Quaestiones de dicendi usu Thucydides. I. De vi et usu particulae γάρ* (Upsala 1864).

[38] For the line drawn between verse and prose in the Greek rhetorical writers, see Roberts *DHLC* 33-39 and supra on 24.7.

[39] The term ἀποστροφή is discussed by Quintilian 9.2.38-39.

[40] My translation is that of the Teubner text, which adopts Krüger's emendation of τροπικῶν for τοπικῶν. W. Warren (*AJP* 20 [1899] 317) says of the same reading in *Ep. II ad Amm.* 2.424.4: "This <τοπικῶν> is the reading of the manuscripts here and in the *De Thucyd. Iudicum*. Krüger wrote τροπικῶν, and has been followed by van Herwerden and Usener. It seems possible, however, to keep the manuscript reading and understand a reference to Thucydides' proleptic use of prepositions and adverbs of place, e.g. II.5,92; V.52,11. This is favoured by the coupling with χρόνων." W.R. Roberts follows Warren, translating "and by the strained use of expressions denoting place." Pavano does not seem to be aware of the problem, but reads τροπικῶν. Dionysius' treatment of the subject has been lost in the lacuna between chapter 13 and 14.

[41] In *Ep. II ad Amm.* chap. 14, Dionysius illustrates the personification of things by citing Thuc. I.71.7: πρὸς τάδε βουλεύεσθε εὖ καὶ τὴν Πελοπόν-νησον πειρᾶσθε μὴ ἐλάσσω ἐξηγεῖσθαι ἢ οἱ πατέρες ὑμῖν παρέδοσαν, where Dionysius objects to the use of a word for territory with ἐξηγεῖσθαι. The notion is, do not let the power and glory of the Peloponnesus degenerate under your leadership. As an example of the use of things for persons, he cites the use of τὸ ὑμέτερον (it is your way, or your characteristic) for ὑμεῖς in I.70.3: τὸ δὲ ὑμέτερον τῆς τε δυνάμεως ἐνδεᾶ πρᾶξαι τῆς τε γνώμης μηδὲ τοῖς βεβαίοις πιστεῦσαι. R.S. Radford refers to this passage of Dionysius on page 29 of his Johns Hopkins dissertation, *Personification and the Use of Abstract Subjects in the Attic Orators and Thucydides* (Baltimore 1901). Personification of natural objects and forces, of concrete substantives belonging to the military language, and of rhetorical and political terms, is frequent in Thucydides. He uses the names of countries instead of their inhabitants with greater freedom than any other Greek writer. Especially striking are the personifications of intelligence and of abstract qualities.

[42] The enthymeme is said by Aristotle (*Rhet.* 1.2.1356b.8-9) to be to

rhetoric what the syllogism is to logic; and he explains it as an argument or proof based on the probable only. A frequently cited example from Aristotle (*Rhet.* 2.21.1394a.2) is the following: "No man who is sensible ought to have his children taught to be excessively clever, for, not to speak of the charge of idleness brought against them, they earn jealous hostility from the citizens" (Loeb tr.). Aristotle's enthymeme seems to be an argument based on probable—as opposed to certain—premises, and leading to a particular, not a general, conclusion. The effect is to emphasize that rhetoric is a technique of argument, like dialectic, rather than of ornamentation. R.C. Seaton (*CR* 28 [1914] 113-119) traces the development of the word in post-Aristotelian writers, where it finally comes to mean, 'a syllogism with one premise suppressed.' See also Cicero *Topica* 55, Demetrius *On Style* 30-33, Quintilian 5.14.4, and *Rhet. ad Her.* 4.18.25. R.C. Jebb (*Attic Orators* 1. 193) defines the term as "rhetorical syllogisms." Roberts (*DHTLL* 191) states that in the rhetorical writers "ἐνθυμήματα sometimes meant little more than *considerations, points.*" Indeed, R. Volkmann (*Die Rhetorik der Griechen und Römer*² [Leipzig 1885] 192) cites examples where ἐνθύμημα and ἐννόημα are synonymous. G.M.A. Grube (*GCDS* 139) distinguishes three meanings of the word. See also F. Solmsen, *AJP* 62 (1941) 39 n. 15, and J.H. McBurney, "The Place of the Enthymeme in Rhetorical Theory," *Speech Monographs* 3 (1936) 49-74. In connection with the enthymeme, the two-volume study of J.B. Saint-Hilaire (*Rhétorique d'Aristote* [Paris 1870]) is still valuable. I cite from his closing paragraph (2.376): "Aristote attache une immense importance à l'emploi de l'Enthymème, sans lequel l'art de la rhétorique lui semble à peu près impossible. Aujourd'hui, l'enthymème est relégué à un rang très-secondaire; et cette différence peut à elle seule nous montrer l'intervalle énorme qui sépare le point de vue des Anciens et le nôtre. L'art oratoire était pour eux l'Art par excellence; il est chez nous presque oublié." W.M.A. Grimaldi, "Studies in the Philosophy of Aristotle's Rhetoric," *Hermes Einzelschriften* 25 (1972), sees in Aristotle's use of enthymemes "the integrating structure of rhetorical discourse" (p. 16). See infra, chap. 34.4.

   [43] I adopt the translation of νοήματα ("conceptions") given by H.E. Butler in his Loeb edition of Quintilian, where the Greek term is defined in 8.5.12. The Latin equivalent is *sententia* ("maxim"): see also Ernesti s.v. νόημα. Roberts (*DHTLL* 197) defines the term as "thought, thought expressed in a sentence." — Already in antiquity Thucydides was admired for the abundance of his maxims. Plutarch (*Fabius Maximus* 1.8) writes about the conversation of the Roman leader, "It had no affectation, nor any empty, forensic grace, but an import of peculiar dignity, rendered weighty by an abundance of maxims. These, they say, most resembled those which Thucydides employs" (Loeb tr.). Plutarch quotes maxims of Thucydides in *Mor.* 540c, 548d, and 551a. Marcellinus (*Vita* 51) writes, τὸ δέ γνωμο-λογικὸν αὐτοῦ ἐπαινετόν. Stobaeus collected some forty-two maxims from Thucydides in his anthology, mostly of a political nature, a smaller number ethical. The three orations of Pericles are particularly rich in *sententiae.*

W. Schmid (*Geschichte der griechischen Litt.* 7.1.5 [Munich 1948] 199 n. 5)
has counted one hundred and twenty-two in the entire history. These have
been studied in a separate monograph: C. Meister, *Die Gnomik im Geschichtswerk des Thukydides* (Diss. Basel 1955). Some contain statements of meth-
odology, such as the maxims on archaeology, as in I.20.1, 21.1 on the un-
reliability of oral tradition. Most are concerned with personal and political
ethics and political machinations in war and peace.

⁴⁴In *Ep. II ad Amm.* chap. 15, Dionysius cites as examples of excessive parentheses two long passages from I.2.2 and I.9.2. The former passage
is redrafted by Dionysius; the latter is discussed stylistically by W.R.M.
Lamb, *Clio Enthroned* (Cambridge 1914) 95. This chapter of Dionysius is
discussed approvingly by F. Blass (*Die attische Beredsamkeit*² [Leipzig 1887]
1.225). According to J. Schmitt, *De parenthesis usu Hippocratico, Herodoteo,
Thucydideo, Xenophonteo* (Diss. Greifswald 1913), there are about three
hundred examples of παρένθεσις in the entire work, evenly distributed over
all eight books. Most of them are found in the narrative parts; comparatively
few (37) are in the speeches. These parentheses always constitute independent statements of fact and are essentially logical and factual explanations
and amplifications. They are usually introduced by γάρ or δέ, less frequently
by καί. Sometimes the parenthesis precedes that which is to be explained or
amplified: I.87.1, 104.2, 105.6, 135.3. Maxims sometimes appear in parenthesis: I.42.3, 123.1; II.45.1, 61.4, 62.3, 64.3; VI.38.4, 78.2 (cf. C. Meister,
Die Gnomik in Geschichtswerk des Thukydides [Diss. Basel 1955] 25). The
longest parenthesis seems to be VI.64.1. For the parenthesis as a feature of
Greek style, see E. Schwyzer, *APAW* 1939. no. 6; on p. 21 he notes examples in early Athenian inscriptions. Whereas modern grammarians consider
the parenthesis as an offence against the laws of an orderly sequence of
thought, independent sentences taken up into the body of the main sentence
can hardly have been artistically a sin with the Greeks since they were employed freely by the most skilful of all the Attic orators—Isocrates and
Demosthenes. We have to do, not with an evidence of lack of control, but
with a conscious device of art to produce the effect of nature. It contributes
to the rejuvenation of language, which is *celare artem*.

⁴⁵As involved passages, hard to unravel, Dionysius (*Ep. II ad Amm.*
16) cites a section (II.42.4) of the Funeral Oration, and one (I.138.3) characterising Themistocles.

⁴⁶In the final chapter (17) of the *Ep. II ad Amm.*, Dionysius cites
three passages (I.2.1, I.70.2, III.82.4) without further observation. Their
antithetical and rhetorical character is apparent.

⁴⁷Parisosis is precise or approximate equality of cola as measured by
the number of syllables. See Aristotle *Rhetoric* 3.9.1410a.9. Some rhetoricians used ἰσόκωλον of precise equality, and παρίσωσις of approximate
equality: R. Volkmann, *Die Rhetorik der Griechen und Römer*² (Leipzig
1885) 482. Exact correspondence is so rare that it seems an unnecessary
refinement of terminology. The seven examples of parisosis in the narrative

part of Thucydides Book VII, the one most commonly read by students, as collected by J.C. Robertson, *The Gorgianic Figures in Early Greek Prose* (Baltimore 1891) 39-40, are the following: 5.4 (τῇ μὲν παρασκευῇ ... ἔξοντας, τῇ δὲ γνώμῃ ... ἐσόμενον); 21.3 (οὐ δυνάμει ... ἐπιχειροῦντες); 44.2 (τὴν μὲν ὄψιν ... ἀπιστεῖσθαι); 44.3 (τὸ μὲν ἄρτι ... προσανῇει); 57. 10 (Δημοσθένους ... εὐνοίᾳ); 60.2 (οὔτε ... ἔξειν); 87.5 (τοῖς τε ... δυστυχέστατον).

⁴⁸Paromoiosis is equality of cola heightened by the use of words of similar sound at the beginning (termed ὁμοιοκάταρκτον) or the end (termed ὁμοιοτέλευτον), i.e., assonance, or parallelism in sound (Roberts). Inflected languages like Greek abound in unintentional homoioteleuta, whereas in an uninflected language like English, the figure is almost certain to be intentional. Examples where the rhetorical design seems plain in the narrative of Book VII are: 25.8 (ἐμηχανῶντο ... ἐχρῶντο); 49.3 (μένειν ... μέλλειν). An example of homoiokatarkton is III.82.8 (εὐσεβείᾳ μὲν ... εὐπρεπείᾳ δέ).

⁴⁹Paronomasia and parechesis, words not mentioned by Aristotle (while Dionysius speaks only of the former), both involve play on words, or a similarity in sound between two words of dissimilar meanings. Ancient definitions are collected by E.M. Cope, *Journal of Classical and Sacred Philology* 3 (1857) 71-72. Following Blass, most scholars use the term paronomasia to denote those cases where the root is the same, and parechesis those where the root is different. It is important to note that unlike other figures, paronomasia bears no relation to the structure of the sentence. Examples of paronomasia are: VII.44.7 (φίλοι τε φίλοις καὶ πολῖται πολίταις); 49.2 (στενοχωρίᾳ ... εὐρυχωρίᾳ); of parechesis: 39.2 (αὖθις καὶ αὐθημερόν); 44.3 (ἄρτι ... ἔτι). Cicero (*Orator* 25.84) warns against the kind of paronomasia which is produced by the change of a letter because the effect is too obvious. J.D. Denniston (*Greek Prose Style*² [Oxford 1960]) notes that in early Greek prose effects were obtained by assonantal devices: "The early writers of Greek prose, casting about for some ἥδυσμα to compensate for the absence of metre, hit upon alliteration and other forms of assonance to fill the gap" (p. 127). S. Lilja (*Suomen Tiedeseura: Commentationes humanarum litterarum* 41:3 [1968] 35-51) has studied alliteration in the earliest Greek prose.

⁵⁰R.C. Jebb (*Attic Orators* [London 1876] 1.98 n. 1) defines antithesis as "the opposition of words, or of ideas, or of both, in the two corresponding clauses of a sentence," and this definition represents the consensus of opinion of the Greek Rhetoricians, and may be traced back to Aristotle's *Rhetoric to Alexander* 26. In Cicero *De part. orat.* 6.21, antithesis is regarded as a feature of the agreeable (*suave*) style. False antithesis (Aristotle *Rhetoric* 3.9.1410b.10; cf. E.M. Cope, *Introduction to Aristotle's Rhetoric* [Cambridge 1867] 314-315) occurs where two not antithetical thoughts are expressed in a form which would lead one to expect antithetical thoughts. Theoretically, Gorgianic figures, being σχήματα λέξεως, should be antitheses of words alone. There is a wide prevalence of antithesis in early

Greek thought (for example in Heraclitus); but Gorgias furnishes numerous instances of false antithesis (Διὸς μὲν ἀγάλματα, αὐτῶν δὲ ἀναθήματα). The question of whether rhetorical design is present can probably best be determined by asking whether the author could have expressed himself naturally without the use of the figure. A complete example of antithesis is IV.61.7: οἵ τ᾽ ἐπίκλητοι εὐπρεπῶς ἄδικοι ἐλθόντες εὐλόγως ἄπρακτοι ἀπίασιν. J.C. Robertson (*op. cit.* [supra, 24.47] 39) lists the following examples of false antitheses in the narrative of Book VII: 5.4 (τῇ μὲν παρασκευῇ ... ἔξοντας, τῇ δὲ γνώμῃ ... ἐσόμενον); 21.3 (οὐ δυνάμει ... ἐπιχειροῦντες); 44.2 (τὴν μὲν ὄψιν ... ἀπιστεῖσθαι); 57.7 (ἀνάγκῃ ... ἔχθος); 69.2 (ἔργῳ ... εἰρῆσθαι). The most detailed study of antithesis in Thucydides is the work of F. Stein, *De figurarum apud Thucydidem usu* (Cologne 1881). See also J.E. Hollingsworth, *Antithesis in the Attic Orators* (Diss. Chicago 1915) 25-26; and G.C. Kenyan, *Antithesis in the Speeches of the Greek Historians* (Diss. Chicago 1941) 44-85. Kenyan observes that antithesis is more frequent in the fifteen speeches delivered before Gorgias reached Athens than in the twenty-five delivered afterwards.

    [5] [1]J.C. Robertson (*The Gorgianic Figures in Early Greek Prose* [Baltimore 1893]) has assembled the sometimes conflicting data from the ancient rhetoricians and deduced (p. 7) that the "Gorgianic figures" are antithesis, parison, paromoion, and paronomasia. E. Norden (*Die antike Kunstprosa*[5] [Stuttgart 1958] 1, 25-29) shows that "Gorgianic" figures were in use both in verse and in prose before Gorgias. He offers examples taken from the study of A. Nieschke, *De figurarum quae vocantur σχήματα Γοργίεια apud Herodotum usu* (Progr. Münden 1891). The same author had earlier published a programm (*De Thucydide Antiphontis discipulo et Homeri imitatore* [Münden 1885]) in which he adduced many alleged Gorgianic figures from the Iliad, Odyssey, Solon, Theognis, and other early poets. Robertson (p. 10) objects that design is absent and that the poetic form is the cause of the parallelisms. In any case, the antithetical period was characteristic of sophistical rhetoric in general; and F. Zucker ("Der Stil des Gorgias nach seiner inneren Form," *Sitz. der deutschen Akad. der Wissens. zu Berlin*, Klasse für Sprachen, 1956:1) shows (16-19) that Herodotus' style abounded in logical ensembles of antithetical groups. D. Fehling, *Die Wiederholungsfiguren und ihr Gebrauch bei den Griechen vor Gorgias* (Berlin 1969), gives very full lists of figures of repetition before Gorgias, demonstrating the antiquity of many figures which we tend to assign to the age of formal rhetoric. All possible combinations of repetition are considered. S. Usher in his review (*JHS* 90 [1970] 232) of this admirable book acutely observes that it was particularly in respect to parison, i.e. as an imitation of poetry, that parallelism based on numbers of approximately equal length was made the distinguishing feature of a new rhetorical style, one which outlasted the figures of assonance. L. Radermacher (*SAWW* 227.3 [1951] 52-60) stresses the fact that the evidence that Gorgias produced a formal written τέχνη is late and doubtful; he taught by oral instruction and example. The most important ancient testimonia about Gorgias are Aristotle *Rhet.* 3.1.1404a.9;

Diodorus 12.53; and Dionysius *De Lys.* chap. 3. J.H. Finley regards Gorgias not as the begetter of the antithetical style, but as one who embellished it, "seeking in every detail and by every means a symmetry and balance of expression which his predecessors had used with greater moderation" (*HSCP* 50 [1939] 80). Good diagrammatic analyses of Gorgias' periods are presented by V. Pisani, *Enciclopedia Classica* 2.5.1 (Turin 1960) 107-109. Of the collections of Gorgianic figures in Thucydides, two may be noted: that of P. Leske, *Über die verschiedene Abfassungszeit der Theile der Thukydideischen Geschichte* (Progr. Liegnitz 1875) 29-34, who finds that they are much more numerous in the first half of the work than in the second; and the full collection of figures in the speeches by H. Steinberg, *Beiträge zur Würdigung der Thukydidischen Reden* (Berlin 1870), who argues (23 and 30) that Thucydides used these figures with an eye to the requirements of ethos. For example, there are many figures in the speech of Hermocrates, a Sicilian speaker; but the earnest defence of the Plataeans (III.53-59) is relatively free of such artifices. Similarly, in the narrative sections, the episode (II.48-53) of the plague at Athens is rhetorically simple, whereas reflections on stasis at Corcyra (III.82-84) are filled with Gorgianic color. Finally, it is to be noted that the Gorgianic figures are far more numerous in the speeches than in the narrative part, and to this fact is to be attributed in large measure Dionysius' disapproval of the former. – E.R. Dodds (*Plato's Gorgias* [Oxford 1959] 6-10) states that Gorgias was not a "sophist" at all, but a rhetor who painfully polished every sentence that he wrote, caring passionately about its form. His style seems to us affected and boring; but his contemporaries were bewitched by it. "Men as diverse in their gifts and interests as Thucydides, Antiphon, and Isocrates succumbed in varying degrees to the fascination." K.J. Dover (*Thucydides Book VI* [Oxford 1965] xvii) comments that Thucydides "was largely immune to the very great influence which the rhetorician Gorgias exercised on prose literature in the last quarter of the fifth century ... Thucydides' assonances are conspicuous and memorable precisely because they are rare." Cf. Also J.D. Denniston, *Greek Prose Style*[2] (Oxford 1960) 12-13. Finally, Gomme (*HCT* 2.131) writes, "He was doubtless much influenced by Gorgias, especially in his younger years; but the general effect is different. Gorgias is rich and flowing; the river of Thucydides' eloquence is equally abundant, but is obstructed by rocks, and curious eddies are formed. Unlike the other he has something to say. Like the finest passage of all in this manner (iii.82-83), it was not approved by Dionysios of Halikarnassos."

[52] Licymnius of Chios and his pupil Polus of Agrigentum are referred to in Plato's *Phaedrus* 267c. Polus is one of the speakers in Plato's *Gorgias*. Licymnius is mentioned as a rhetorician and poet in Aristotle *Rhetoric* 3.12.1413b.14, 13.1414b.17. Both were the authors of textbooks of rhetoric: L. Radermacher, "Artium Scriptores," *Sitzungsb. d. Oesterr. Ak. Wien* 227 (1951), Abh. 3, 112 and 117.

[53] K. Barwick ("Probleme der stoischen Sprachlehre und Rhetorik," *Abh. der sächs. Akad. zu Leipzig* 49.3 [1957] 106) quotes this sentence,

contending that the order of the figures is a traditional Stoic one, found also in Caecilius.

⁵⁴Classen believes that the phrase τὸ ποιητικὸν τῶν ὀνομάτων means "die Freiheit zu nenen Wortschöpfungen," but earlier in this chapter Dionysius refers to Thucydides' use of conjunctions and prepositions ποιητοῦ τρόπον. Demetrius (*On Style* 112-113) refers briefly to the poetic diction of Herodotus and Thucydides. Marcellinus (*Vita* 41) writes, διὰ τὸ ὑψηλὸν καὶ ποιητικαῖς πολλάκις ἐχρήσατο λέξεσι. In *De Comp.* 25.124.12-15, Dionysius characterizes a poetical vocabulary as "consisting of rare, foreign, figurative and coined words in which poetry takes delight." F. Rittelmeyer (*Thukydides und die Sophistik* [Diss. Erlangen 1915] 52-53) gives a sampling of such words. See also supra on 24.7.

⁵⁵ For τραχύς, see supra on chap. 24.12. The word ἁρμονία was used primarily in Greek carpentry (which employed dove-tailing in preference to nails) for the "joining" of timbers. In rhetoric, the word "seems usually to connote 'harmony' in the more restricted (musical) sense of notes in fitting sequence: cf. our 'arrangement' of a song or piece of music": Roberts *DHLC* 290. R.C. Jebb (*Attic Orators* 1.21-22) notes that ἁρμονίαι refers to the putting together of words in contrast with λέξεις, the choice of words. The term is discussed at length in Cope's *Introduction to Aristotle's Rhetoric* 379-387. In the Theophrastan system, ἁρμονία was a subdivision of κατασκευή (ornamentation): J. Stroux, *De Theophrasti virtutibus dicendi* (Leipzig 1912) 22-23, 64-67; cf. H. Caplan in the Loeb edition of *Rhetorica ad Herennium*, 268-269. D.W. Lucas (*Aristotle's Poetics* [Oxford 1968] 58) translates the word as "melody;" Russell and Winterbottom (*ALC* [Oxford 1972] 321) as "verbal structure" and (p. 324) "rhythmical form."

⁵⁶This is probably the most quoted sentence in the entire treatise. Sentences which illustrate Dionysius' criticism of the τάχος τῶν σημασίων are given in F. Rittelmeyer, *Thukydides und die Sophistik* (Diss. Erlangen 1915) 66ff.

⁵⁷ The word chromata means literally "colors." Roberts (*DHLC*) translates it as "complexion" (p. 89) and "ornaments of speech" (p. 159). Ernesti (p. 384) explains it as "Colorit, Character des Ausdruks in Rüksicht auf Sinn und Gedanken." H.E. Butler in his translation of Quintilian gives the meaning of the Latin equivalent *color* as "gloss," or "varnish." Van Hook (*Terminology* 43) writes: "By a *color* here D. refers to the character or nature of the style as effected by certain forces or qualities which are found in the thought and content of his writings." S.F. Bonner (*Roman Declamation* [Berkeley 1949] 55) notes that before Seneca's day, the Latin *color* was used to represent the Greek χρῶμα; but in Seneca it takes on the meaning, "plea, excuse." Cf. R.G. Austin on Quintilian 12.33. W.B. Stanford (*Greek Metaphor* [Oxford 1936] 61 n. 1) has an interesting note on the use of words for color, but the most detailed treatment of Dionysius' vocabulary from the art of painting is the chapter by A. Greilich, *op. cit.* (supra, 24.17) 30-38.

⁵⁸Roberts (*DHTLL* 205) comments on στριφνός, "Firm, solid: the reference being to the *close texture* of the language of Thucydides."

⁵⁹πυκνός is "terse, compact, concentrated." In *De Dem.* 4.136.4, the word is combined with στρογγύλος, "compact, rounded," and opposed to πλατύς "diffuse." The noun pyknotes Roberts (*DS* 300) renders as "close succession." In *Ep. ad Pomp.* 5.243.6, Dionysius attributes the same quality to the diction of Philistus; the author of *De Imit.* (6.2.205.3) to Pindar.

⁶⁰Ernesti notes that πικρός is often the opposite of ἡδύς. Roberts (*DHTLL* 201) renders as "repellent, odious, harsh," and the noun πικρότης as "incisiveness, pungency." The word is used many times by Dionysius, in particular as characteristic of the diction of Demosthenes and Thucydides. E.M. Cope discusses the use of the word in his commentary on Aristotle's *Rhet.* 1.10.1368b.4. Cf. infra on chap. 53.5.

⁶¹Roberts (*DHLC* 291; *DHTLL* 186) gives "austere, severe, stern" as meanings of αὐστηρός. See supra on chap. 24.9.

⁶² The word ἐμβριθής (lit. "weighty") is applied by the author of *On the Sublime* (9.3) to thoughts which are grave and full of dignity. Cf. *De Dem.* 21.176.3: τόνοι ἐμβριθέστεροι.

⁶³ "δεινός *proprie significat id, quod homines terrore afficit:*" Geigenmüller, *Quaestiones* 66. This non-technical use of the word is found here and in *De Lys.* 13.23.7. The various meanings of the word are outlined by Roberts in the Loeb edition of Demetrius, p. 266. The word δεινός has a varied use, being used by Demetrius for his fourth classification of style, "powerful," and applied to Demosthenes. δείνωσις in Quintilian (6.2.24) is *rebus indignis, asperis, invidiosis addens vim oratio.* Ernesti defines deinosis as *invidiae atque odii exaggeratio.* Cope (*Aristotle's Rhetoric* 2.213-214) characterizes it as, "The art of exciting indignation or odium against any person or thing, by exaggeration or intensification; vivid description heightening the enormity or atrocity of that against which you wish to rouse the indignation of the audience." For δεινότης, see infra on chap. 27.4.

⁶⁴ For pathetikon, see Roberts, *DHTLL* 198-199. One may observe that the very qualities which Dionysius in this sentence acknowledges as characteristic of Thucydides' diction are removed by Dionysius when he recasts Thucydidean passages.

⁶⁵ For τόνος, see supra on chap. 23.25.

⁶⁶Here and in *Ep. II ad Amm.* 2.424.21 (ἀσαφὲς γίνεται τὸ βραχύ) Dionysius makes Thucydides' anxious search for brevity the cause of his obscurities. But Aristotle (*Rhet.* 3.12.1414a.6) says that verbosity is just as fatal to clearness as condensation. This fact is partly recognized by Dionysius (*Ep. II ad Amm.* 15.434.14-15) when he remarks that numerous parentheses in Thucydides make the meaning hard to follow. Quintilian (9.4.32) makes the arrangement of words the factor that contributes to lucidity on the one hand, or ambiguity on the other.

[67] For ξένος, see supra note 6 of this chapter.

[68] πεποιημένος is used by Dionysius in the sense either of "artificial" or of "coined, invented." The latter meaning, as required in our passage, is defined by Aristotle, *Poetics* 21.17.1457b: "an invented word is one not used at all by any people and coined by the poet. There seem to be such words, e.g. 'sprouters' for horns and 'pray-er' for priest" (tr. of Fyfe). For the phrase πεποιημένα ὀνόματα, "newly-made words," see Grube, *GCDS* 84 n. 95, and D.M. Schenkeveld, *Studies in Demetrius On Style* (Amsterdam 1964) 107-115. J. Martin's discussion (*Antike Rhetorik* [Munich 1974] 269) is limited to onomatopoeic words.

[69] Pavano translates, "in tutte le opere;" incorrectly *me iudice*. Dionysius assumed the existence of common critical standards for all works of art, literature, painting, sculpture, and music. See *De Comp.* 25.132-135; *De Dem.* 240-243; *De Isoc.* 3.59; *De Isaeo* 4.96; etc.

Commentary on Chapter 25

[1] For ἀπόδειξις, see M. Egger, *Denys d'Halicarnasse* (Paris 1902) 216: "exposition, démonstration." Roberts (*DHTLL* 175) suggests "demonstrations, illustrations" for this passage.

[2] I adopt the translation of Roberts (*DHLC* 11 n. 2) for the words κεφάλαια and περιοχή, although they imply a modern division of Thucydides' writings which was apparently not used in antiquity. The two words are not otherwise coupled by Dionysius. Generally, the title periochai is used for the summaries of the books of an author. H. Mutschmann ("Inhaltsangabe und Kapitelüberschrift im antiken Buch," *Hermes* 46 [1911] 93-107) shows that just as the mechanical book divisions of Alexandrian scholars resulted in the book as a literary unit, so the mechanical device of writing κεφάλαια over the columns of *volumina* developed into the organic sense divisions, i.e. chapters, as are found on both sides of papyri. Then followed the collection (συγκεφαλαίωσις) of such κεφάλαια, prefixed to each book as a table of contents, which were used by later compilers. Roberts translates κεφάλαιον in the *De Comp.* as "topic, heading." The punctuation in papyri for division into paragraphs was normally called the παράγραφος.

[3] After quoting this passage, Roberts (*DHTLL* 175-176) continues, "He [Dionysius] prefers, that is, to treat his subject in the epideictic style of an essayist, rather than in the disjointed manner of a schoolmaster who must care more for paedagogic effectiveness than for literary form."

[4] Here Dionysius defines his purpose in studying the style of Thucydides as mimesis. The sentence is discussed by R. Roberts, *CR* 14 (1900) 441. The essay was intended for a literary circle of educated friends. In *De Lys.* 20.32.17, he refers to his audience as ψυχαὶ εὐπαίδευτοι καὶ μέτριαι. G.P. Goold (*TAPA* 92 [1961] 190) has described the "professional circle" of Dionysius, as follows: "The Dionysians were not mere *grammatici*. Their

courses were not 'Greek without tears' or even Greek courses at all; their works presume in those they taught—and these must have been Romans—a complete mastery of Greek and a wide acquaintance with the Greek classics. They were Professors of Literature, which meant Greek literature, since they had not the faintest idea that Latin—and not Greek—was to become the common tongue of Western Europe and was already pregnant with the speech of modern civilization; they were Professors of Classics, like ourselves, with their attention focused on the genius of an age long since passed; and their writings contain no direct reference to the times in which they lived. To judge from their apparent ease of movement and communication, they enjoyed the privileged life of university men." Mimesis in the sense of imitation of earlier writers plays a large part in ancient criticism. Numerous studies include E. Stemplinger, *Das Plagiat in der griech. Lit.* (Leipzig 1912) 81ff.; Kroll, *RE*, Suppl. 7, 1113-1117; R. McKeon, "Literary Criticism and the Concept of Imitation in Antiquity," *Mod. Phil.* 34 (1936) 1-35; D.L. Clark, *Quart. Journ. Speech* 37 (1951) 11-22; D.W. Lucas, *Aristotle Poetics* (Oxford 1968) App. 1. Similar concepts prevailed in Renaissance literature: R.R. Bolgar, *The Classical Heritage* (Cambridge 1954) 265-275.

⁵ Dionysius repeats a quotation from Thuc. I.1.2, which he had used in chap. 20. There are variations in the two Greek texts: for τὰ ἔτι, chap. 20 reads ἔτι; σκοποῦντι μοι — σκοποῦντι; ξυνέβη πιστεῦσαι — πιστεύειν ξυμβαίνει.

⁶Dionysius' text for I.2.1-2 does not differ from the manuscript version.

⁷ Dionysius' text adds οὖν αὐτῶν after καταφρονήσαντες. L. Sadée, *Diss. phil. argent.* 2 (1879) 161, believes that the two words were inserted after the lacuna occurred. Pavano in his edition (p. 243) is of the contrary opinion.

⁸ Ἀγκύλος (from ἄγκος, "bend" lit. "crooked, curved") is opposed to ὀρθός (lit. "straight, direct"): van Hook, *Terminology* 17. Ἀγκύλως is joined with βραχέως in chap. 32 and *De Isae.* 13.110.4. Metaphorically, the word is used of style that is "involved, intricate." Geigenmüller (*Quaestiones* 25, 28) renders the word in Latin by *contortus*. LSJ, however, says of our passage, "in good sense, *terse*." Ἀγκύλως is defined by Hesychius as ἀποτόμως, "concisely;" so the word has two almost directly opposite meanings, just as *contortus* may mean "energetic, powerful" (common in Cicero) or "intricate." This two-fold meaning is brought out, as indicated in the *Thesaurus* 1.352 (*ancipiti lingua*), in a passage from Alciphron 3.28.1, where the phrase ἐριστικὸς καὶ ἀγκύλος γένηται is used of trick words for a glib debater. The Loeb renders this "captious and catchy." F.A. Wright translates simply, "become a glib debater." — See also infra on chap. 31.1.

⁹The period of Thucydides marks an effort to coordinate the circumstances of the action. Since the circumstances are subordinate to the action, the action itself (ὥρμησαν καὶ ἔβαλλον) is presented at the end. The period is impressive by its rough beauty and is not obscure. By contrast, Dionysius writes a banal and dragging sentence. He places the principal proposition

(συστραφέντας ... ὥρμησαν ... ἀθρόοι) in the middle and destroys the harmony of the ideas according to M. Egger, *Denys d'Halicarnasse* (Paris 1902) 216-218. – It may be noted that Dionysius construed ἀθρόοι with ὥρμησαν and not ἐμβοήσαντες (like Classen and most modern editors).

Commentary on Chapter 26

[1]B. Jowett (*Thucydides* 2 [Oxford 1881] 447) states that the reading of Dionysius (παραλειφθέντα) "is probably correct." De Romilly, following Arnold and Classen, prefers καταλειφθέντα ("qu'on y avait ménagée").

[2]Classen believes that the form προεξαναγόμενοι, found only in the text of Dionysius, is necessary. The manuscripts of Thucydides read προεξαγαγόμενοι; also de Romilly.

[3]Dionysius' reading of παρεβοήθει, for παραβοηθεῖ, παραβοηθῇ or παραβοηθοῖ of the Thucydidean manuscripts, is adopted by virtually all editors.

[4]Dionysius reads κατίσχυον where the manuscripts of Thucydides have κατίσχοιεν.

[5] Dionysius reads καὶ οἱ ἄλλοι with manuscript E of Thucydides. J.E. Powell (*CR* 52 [1938] 4) has shown that scribes have a tendency to insert καί after δέ and argues against the theory that E had access to a text cognate with that of Dionysius. Classen rejects the ἄλλοι, which is read by Hude and de Romilly, and Dover (*HCT* 4.447) suggests that it may be a displacement. H.A. Holden, in his note on VII.4.3, regards the substantive as an appositive to ἄλλος.

[6]Dionysius, with some Thucydidean manuscripts, has ὅτε and is followed by Classen. Others read ὁπότε.

[7] The two principal manuscripts of Dionysius read ἐν ὀλίγῳ, apparently repeated from the previous line, instead of ἐν ἐλαχίστῳ of the Thucydidean manuscripts.

[8] All editors and some Thucydidean manuscripts read ἐμβολαί, "ramming attacks," instead of Dionysius' ἐκβολαί, the reading also of the majority (ABFGM) of the medieval manuscripts of Thucydides.

[9]Dionysius' ἀφθόνοις is preferred by Hude to ἀφθόνως of the Thucydidean manuscripts.

[10]Dionysius has ἐφθέγγοντο instead of φθέγγοιντο of the Thucydidean manuscripts and all editors.

[11]Dionysius has ναυτικήν instead of αὐτίκα.

[12] Dionysius omits καὶ αὖθις from the phrase εἴ ποτε καὶ αὖθις of the Thucydidean manuscripts.

[13] Dionysius has the present infinitive ἀντιλαμβάνεσθαι instead of the aorist.

14 B reads ὑποχωροῦσιν where the other Thucydides manuscripts and Dionysius read ἀποχωροῦσιν. Classen regards ὑπο. as the proper word for retreat before a superior force.

15 The reading of Dionysius (δι᾽ ὀλίγου πόνου), supported by B and the scholiast, is preferred to that (δι᾽ ὀλίγου) given by the manuscripts generally. See W.R. Roberts, *CR* 14 (1900) 246.

16The word Ἀθηναίους, deleted in the Oxford and Budé texts, is supported by all manuscripts, and should be retained, according to W.R. Roberts, *CR* 14 (1900) 246: "Dionysius quotes at considerable length and with warm admiration the passage of which this sentence forms a part, and the fact that he gives the proper noun seems to show that he found it in his copy of Thucydides and felt it to be graphic–'these very Athenians.' There is no variant in the MSS. of Dionysius, and Usener is constrained to remark in his critical footnote, ''Αθηναίους emblema Dionysio vetustius.' An interpretation it may conceivably be; but conjectural interpolations anterior to Dionysius and the papyrus fragments open up a region into which our existing evidence does not enable us to follow."

17 Cf. Kühner-Gerth, *Gr. Gram.* 1³ 637.

18 Thucydidean manuscripts and Dionysius have the same text, which is regarded by all editors as corrupt. There is a good discussion of the problem by C.F. Smith in the appendix (189-190) of his school edition of Book VII (Boston 1888). There is a great range of emendation.

19Dionysius omits αὐτῷ, found in BCG of the Thucydidean manuscripts. See A. Kleinlogel, *Geschichte des Thukydidestextes im Mittelalter* (Berlin 1965) 147.

20All editors follow Dionysius (P) in reading παρὰ λόγον for παράλογον of the Thucydidean manuscripts, since the latter word is not used as an adjective by Thucydides.

21Dionysius reads ἀνδρῶν where the Thucydidean manuscripts have ἀνθρώπων.

Commentary on Chapter 27

1As Roberts (*DHTLL* 32) notes in his appraisal of Dionysius as a literary critic, Dionysius can pay a really fine tribute to a really great passage (VII.69-72) of Thucydides. Similarly, Bonner (*LTDH* 84) writes, "It is, however, interesting to notice that after this point (c. 25 onwards) there is comparatively little evidence of actual criticism according to stock divisions in the remaining thirty chapters, which are devoted to a thorough examination of the style of Thucydides."

2Μεγαληγορία, which was rendered into Latin (Cicero *Or.* 5.20, *Tusc.* 5.31.89; Quintilian 10.1.66) by *grandiloquus* (see Geigenmüller, *Quaestiones* 55), is coupled by Dionysius with σεμνότης (*De Dem.* 4.135.15), ἀξίωμα

(*De Dem.* 44.230.15) and in this passage καλλιλόγια and δεινότης. Both Demetrius (*De eloc.* 29) and "Longinus" (16.1) use the word. Roberts (*DS* 292) translates it as "lofty utterance, elevation"; D.A. Russell (*ALC* 308) as "solemnity."

[3] Of the qualities which contribute to "beauty" of language, Dionysius in four places associates καλλιλογία with Thucydides (here and *De imit.* 6.3. 209.5; *De Dem.* 4.135.12; *Ep. ad Pomp.* 5.243.7). Similarly, εὐστομία is the attribute of "beauty" especially characteristic of Lysias (*De Lys.* 12.20. 13; *De Dem.* 13.157.17). Roberts (*DHTLL* 143; *DHLC* 304) translates καλλιλογία as "elegant language", D.A. Russell (*ALC* 308) as "fine writing."

[4] In his interesting monograph, Δεινότης, *ein antiker Stilbegriff* (Leipzig 1934), L. Voit distinguishes two meanings of the term (3-6), (1) passionate force or intensity, and (2) rhetorical skill generally. The passages containing the word in Dionysius are assembled by Geigenmüller (*Quaestiones* 67-68), who finds that the Latin equivalents are *vehemens* and *vis*. Roberts (*LS* 196; *DHTLL* 187-188; *DS* 273-274; *DHLC* 294; Loeb *Demetrius* pp. 266-267) has a number of translations: "oratorical power, intensity, mastery, impressiveness, nervous force, skill, and resourcefulness." Grube (*GCDS* 31 n. 38, 55, 70 n. 36, 136-137) usually renders the word as "forcefulness." The quality was attributed to Demosthenes above all others and seems to be the joint result of force and clearness. Although Voit discusses many passages, I find no reference to ours.

[5] Geigenmüller, *Quaestiones* 34, refers to this sentence as the *locus gravissimus* in the treatise. Dionysius makes a major distinction between ἡδονή (lit. "pleasure, delight"), used of style as "charm, the agreeable," and καλόν, "beauty." The pertinent passages are collected by Geigenmüller, the chief one being *De Comp.* 11.37. "Charm is described by Dionysius as including ὥρα "freshness;" χάρις "grace;" εὐστομία "euphony;" γλυκύτης "sweetness;" and πιθανόν "persuasiveness." "Beauty" involves μεγαλοπρέπεια, "grandeur;" βάρος, "impressiveness;" σεμνολογία, "solemnity;" ἀξίωμα, "dignity;" πίνος, "mellowness." In the *De Comp.* a good style is regarded as resulting from the combination of ἡ ἡδονή and τὸ καλόν. For discussions of the distinction in Dionysius, see W. Kroll, *RM* 62 (1907) 92-93, and F. Quadlbauer, *WS* 71 (1958) 96.

[6] The noun κατασκευή ("ornamentation, artistic treatment") and the verb κατασκευάζω ("to equip, construct, prepare") are frequently used in Dionysius of literary composition. Ernesti records three uses of κατασκευή. The most detailed treatments of the word seem to be by A. Greilich, *Dionysius Halicarnassensis quibus potissimum vocabulis ex artibus metaphorice ductis in scriptis rhetoricis usus sit* (Diss. Breslau 1886) 10-12; C. Brandstaetter, "De vocis κατασκευή apud Dionysium Halicarnassensem ceterosque rhetores usu" (*Griechische Studien Hermann Lipsius zum sechzigsten Geburtstag dargebracht* [Leipzig 1894] 153-156); and D.C. Innes, *CR* 80 (1966) 145-146. It is well to emphasize that, like Latin *ornare*, the original sense of the verb in its rhetorical analogies is to arm, equip, *not* to decorate or embellish. So

figures seem to have been thought of as fortifications, not decorations. The word rarely has a tinge of the pejorative which σκευωρία does. In the Theophrastian system, κατασκευή embraced correct choice of words (ἐκλογὴ ὀνομάτων), artistic composition (ἁρμονία), and figures (σχήματα): H. Caplan, Loeb *Rhetorica ad Herennium*, p. 268. See also Quintilian 2.4.18; Diogenes Laertius 7.59; Roberts, *DHLC* 305. For the meaning of κατασκευάζειν as a technical term of dialectics (to 'construct' an argument), see J.M. Cope's note on Aristotle's *Rhetoric* 1.15.1376b.21, and p. 268 of his *Introduction*.

⁷ φορτικός (lit. "fit for carrying a burden, vulgar, coarse, low"), like ἄγροικος (lit. "of the country," then "boorish, rough, rude"), is one of a number of critical terms which had its origin in the social status of members of society. E.M. Cope discusses the meaning of the word in his commentary on Aristotle's *Rhetoric* 2.21.1395b.15. In *De Dem.* 29.192.11, the word is joined with διθυραμβώδης; in *De Lys.* 3.10.22, with ὑπέρογκος, "ponderous, verbose."

⁸The word σκολιός, applied to style, is translated by Roberts as "tortuous" (*DHTLL* 205), by Lockwood as "twisty" (*CQ* 31 [1937] 202). The meaning of the word is best illustrated in chap. 40 (392.25), where comparison is made with labyrinths: ποιεῖ τὸν Ἀθηναῖον ἀποκρινόμενον λαβυρίνθων σκολιώτερα.

⁹For δυσπαρακολούθητος, see infra on chap. 47.16.

¹⁰For the use of ἀγωγή in the sense of "training, education," cf. *De Comp.* 1.5.3. For its use as a rhetorical term, see Anon. Seg. 182 in Spengel-Hammer 1.384.

¹¹Dionysius says in *De Comp.* 4.19.10 that the style of the historian Hegesias especially exhibited τὸ ἀγεννές (lit. "low-born, sordid," hence in style, "ignoble, mean, degenerate"). See Roberts, *DHLC* 285.

¹²This is the only occurrence of the adjective χαμαιτυπής in Greek. Used of a grovelling style, it is derived from χαμαιτύπη, "harlot," and χαμαιτυπεῖον, "brothel." For examples in rhetoric of a similar word χαμαιπετής (lit. "falling to the ground"), see Lockwood, *CQ* 31 (1937) 203. Although terms for sex are found in rhetoricians, such as ἀνδρώδης, "virile, masculine," and παρθενωπός, "soft, charming," χαμαιτυπής is the only word I have noticed from the area of bawdry. Dionysius held that the language of literature should, where necessary, draw fearlessly on the language of ordinary life. "There is, I maintain, no part of speech (used to denote any person or thing) so low, or sordid, or coarse, or otherwise obnoxious, that it will find no fit place in literature. My advice is to bring out such words in composition with a bold and manly confidence in accordance with the practice of Homer, in whose poems the commonest words are found" (Roberts' tr. of *De Comp.* 12.46.19-47.5).

¹³Examples of ἀκατάσκευος and cognate words are collected by A. Greilich, *op. cit.* (supra 27.6) 10-12. ἁπλοῦς and ἀφελής are sometimes synonyms of ἀκατάσκευος. For the use of this word in references to arrange-

ment of subject matter, see R.C. Jebb, *Attic Orators* 1.100 n. 1. Jebb translates as "inartificial."

[14] For κριτήριον as an Epicurean term, see Roberts, *DHLC* 250-251.

[15] The ancient rhetorical schools considered it necessary for the critic to possess not only the rational but also the irrational instinct (ἄλογος αἴσθησις). Cf. supra on chap. 4.2. In *De Lys.* 11, Dionysius again uses the phrase when he forgets his rhetorical system and creates pure criticism on a high plane in expressing his overmastering enthusiasm for the charm of Lysias' style. There is need for a study of the concept of alogos aisthesis in ancient literary criticism. Bonner (*LTDH* 104) quotes this sentence from chap. 27 and continues, "An interesting recognition of the existence of these two diametrically opposed methods of criticism is given by Gibbon in his remarks on 'Longinus.' 'The ninth chapter,' he says, 'is one of the finest monuments of antiquity. Till now, I was acquainted only with two ways of criticising a beautiful passage: the one, to show, by an exact anatomy of it, the distinct beauties of it, and whence they sprung; the other, an idle examination, or a general encomium, which leaves nothing behind it. Longinus has shown me that there is a third. He tells me his own feelings upon reading it; and tells them with such energy, that he communicates them.' ... The expression of personal feeling is responsible for the lasting greatness of 'Longinus.' But for showing, by an exact anatomy, the distinct beauties, and whence they spring, there is no critic of antiquity, whose work at any rate is extant, to compare with Dionysius of Halicarnassus."

Commentary on Chapter 28

[1] The meaning of περιττός must be determined by the words with which it is coupled. Usually it is found with words denoting the grand style: see infra on chap. 54.5. Here and in *De Dem.* 25.184.6 and [Longinus] *On the Sublime* 2.3, however, the meaning is pejorative, "excessive, superfluous." See Roberts, *DHTLL* 201, *DHLC* 316, and Geigenmüller, *Quaestiones* 100-101. For περίεργος, see infra on chap. 47.16.

[2] The δυνατοί are often referred to as the "rich" (Gomme *HCT* 2.181), the "upper classes," the "nobles."

[3] Roberts (*DS* 281) notes that the verb ἐπιτραγῳδεῖν is not a common one. He renders, "to declaim in tragic tones." Words taken from the theater, such as τραγῳδεῖν and θεατρικός, are usually employed in a disparaging sense in stylistic diction.

[4] The same verb ἐξαλλάττειν is used in *De Dem.* 10.148.18, where it is said that Thucydides and Demosthenes try to do the same thing, namely to vary normal usage and achieve uncommon and extraordinary effects. Cf. infra on chap. 54.3.

[5] This passage about discord at Corcyra made such an impression upon Sallust that imitation of it has been noted in at least fourteen places: K.

Büchner, *Sallust* (Heidelberg 1960) 432. Cf. P. Perrochat, *Les modèles grecs de Salluste* (Paris 1949) 17-18.

⁶The text of Dionysius omits τε, which, as Gomme notes, certainly makes an unnecessary λάβοντες much easier. Cf., however, Ros, *Metabole* 419.

⁷ The text of Dionysius reads ἀνεχρῶντο where the Thucydidean manuscripts have ἀπεχώρησαν, which no one has made any sense of. See G. Grote, *History* 6 (12-vol. ed. 1899) 275 n. 1. What seems to be the correct reading ἀπεχρῶντο is supported by the remarks of ancient grammarians, Suidas, Zonares, and Bekker *Anec.* 1.423.

⁸Dionysius' reading of διέφθειρον is preferred by all editors to διέφθειραν, which most manuscripts of Thucydides have. In all of the rest of the description of the horrors the imperfect prevails and there is no sufficient reason for the change of tense. Dionysius omits the following αὐτοῦ, "on the spot," found in the Thucydidean manuscripts.

⁹*Pace* Gomme (*HCT* 2.372) and Smyth (*Greek Grammar* 1089), L. Herbst (*Philologus* 16 [1860] 345-347) has shown that ἐν τοῖς with a superlative suggests not absolute preeminence, but prominence among competitors. Cf. Kühner-Gerth, *Gr. Gram.*³ (Leipzig 1898) 1.29 n. 4. There may have been cases of stasis which Thucydides did not record.

¹⁰This passage from III.82 is also quoted by Dionysius at the beginning of the *De Demosthene* where he takes Thucydides as representative of the first, Lysias of the second, and Thrasymachus and Isocrates of the third or middle style. He refers to the first style as "novel, affected, and elaborately artificial, crowded with all kinds of ornamental additions."

Commentary on Chapter 29

¹In this and the following three chapters, Dionysius states his objections to individual Thucydidean sentences and then recasts the originals in order to bring home to the reader exactly what it is to which he objects. He gives here as many examples of this method of criticism as in all the previous essays taken together. These four chapters provide more sustained analysis than any other chapters which are extant. Dionysius succeeds in removing the obscurity; but he also destroys the compactness which he acknowledges as characteristic of Thucydides' style.

² Although Dionysius introduces chap. 29 with the words ἃ δὲ τούτοις ἐπιφέρει ... ἃ μέλλω νυνὶ λέγειν, his discussion passes from τοὺς Λακεδαιμονίους in III.82.1 to ἐστασίαζέ τε in 82.3. Classen conjectured that Dionysius' text of Thucydides did not contain the intervening passage. On the other hand, Steup attributed the omission to the carelessness of copyists.

³Ordinarily, "solecism" was a term applied to a fault in connected speech, while a "barbarism" was a fault in a single word; but authors were not always in agreement in their definition of these terms. See Sextus Emp.

ad Math. 1.210, and J.F. D'Alton, *Roman Literary Theory and Criticism* (London 1931) 78. There developed among the Greeks the conception of "correct Greek" (Ἑλληνισμός) as against debasements (βαρβαρισμός, σολοι- κισμός). Colloquial speech in its various forms was despised and regarded as a degradation from which grammarians and rhetoricians must save the literary style: see L. Lersch, *Die Sprachphilosophie der Alten* (Bonn 1838) 1.48-50; H. Steinthal, *Geschichte der Sprachwissenschaft bei den Griechen und Römern* (Berlin 1863) 365-374. Seneca (*Epist.* 3.95.65) uses the phrase, *grammatici, custodes Latini sermonis.* The language of literature formed the only material of grammatical study.

⁴Or, more literally, "when political art (dynamis) was in its prime." In the *De Dem.* 14.158.17, Dionysius says that Demosthenes perfected the middle style to the limit of human capacity.

⁵ Reiske supplies τέλη: τὰ <τέλη> τῶν πόλεων, "the magistrates (or parties) in the cities."

⁶The manuscripts of Thucydides are almost uniform in reading (III.82. 3), πύστει (M = ἀποπύστει) τῶν προγενομένων πολὺ ἐπέφερε τὴν ὑπερβολὴν τοῦ καινοῦσθαι τὰς διανοίας. For πύστει, the Dionysian MSS. twice (374.2 and 11) read ἐπιπύστει, a word not found in LSJ, and once a corrupt form without ἐπι- where the same passage is quoted in *De Dem.* 1.128.18. The explanatory passage in 374.14 reads ἐπιπυνθανόμενοι. Stahl, Widmann and Herweden adopt ἐπιπύστει; other editors prefer πύστει. The text is discussed by A. Kleinlogel, *Geschichte des Thukydidestextes im Mittelalter* (Berlin 1965) 151 and 160 n. 39. – Dionysius also reads προγεγενημένων instead of προγενομένων. The former is certainly acceptable, since the perfect is the more usual form, although favored only by Stahl of modern editors. – For πολύ, Cod. P of Dionysius reads πολλήν in 374.12, and the latter is preferred by Reiske and Gomme (*HCT* 2.374). The adverbial use of πολύ is undeniably harsh; Krüger, citing the scholiast, says it is equivalent to κατὰ πολύ. – For τοῦ καινοῦσθαι, the MSS. of Dionysius, both in 374.12 and in *De Dem.*, read ἐς τὸ καινοῦσθαι. This has no advantage since the construe of τοῦ καινοῦσθαι τὰς διανοίας with τὴν ὑπερβολὴν offers no difficulty. – On the whole, Stahl may be right in favoring the text of Dionysius. I follow the scholiast (τῷ ἀηθεῖ) in interpreting ἀτοπία as "strangeness" rather than "enormity" (Gomme).

⁷ P. Huart ("Le vocabulaire de l'analyse psychologique dans l'oeuvre de Thucydide" [*Études et Commentaires* 69 (1968)] 19) says that Thucyd- ides' creation of the verb ἐφυστερίζειν "seems to have offended Dionysius."

⁸For σκευωρία used of technical finesse, see supra on chap. 5.30.

⁹In each case that Dionysius uses the words διθύραμβος (*De Lys.* 3.11. 1; *De Dem.* 7.140.12, 7.141.8, 29.192.6; *Ep. ad Pomp.* 2.231.3) and διθυραμβικός (*De Thuc.* 29 and *Ep. ad Pomp.* 2.230.15), the words convey the idea of empty bombast. The dithyramb at Athens during and after the end of the fifth century became the wildest and in point of style the most extravagant of all the kinds of poetry. To use words suited to a dithyrambic

poet is therefore an exaggeration of the ordinary defect of the introduction into prose of poetical language. See Aristotle *Rhet.* 3.3.1406b.3, and E.M. Cope's note on this passage: "διθυραμβεῖν is a step beyond τραγωδεῖν in pomp and exaggeration of language."

[10]In other words, for the customary meaning of words they substituted a meaning based upon their own views. This sentence has been studied recently by W. Mueri, "Politische Metonomasie," *MH* 36 (1969) 65-79, who argues against Gomme that ἐς τὰ ἔργα goes with τὴν ἀξίωσιν. I adopt a translation suggested by Dionysius' paraphrase below. Poppo suggests a structure ἀπὸ κοινοῦ with both ἀξίωσιν and ἀντήλλαξαν. – E.M. Cope (*ad* Aristotle *Rhet.* 1.9.1367b.29) singles out this passage in which Thucydides mentions the perversion of moral terms amongst the signs of demoralization prevalent in Greece at the period of the Corcyrean sedition as a specimen of what Aristotle terms ὑποκορισμός, a special form of the misapplication of names.

[11]Dionysius alters the text of the last phrase, although he had just quoted it. Krüger in his 1823 edition states that he fails to find any poetical circumlocution here.

[12] For παρομοίωσις, see supra on chap. 24.48.

[13] For παρίσωσις, see supra on chap. 24.47.

[14] Gomme (*HCT* 2.374) criticizes Dionysius' statement that all the epithets in the sentence just quoted are nothing but ornament, observing, "This is the reverse of the truth." For example, φιλέταιρος, omitted in Dionysius' paraphrase, is a key-word.

[15] For Dionysius' frequent use of καλλωπισμός and καλλωπίζειν (lit. "to make the face beautiful") for the "embellishment of language," see Lockwood, *CQ* 31 (1937) 199, and Geigenmüller, *Quaestiones* 112.

[16]Dionysius' version of the sentence is sharply criticized by P. Huart, *op. cit.* (supra, 29.7) 23: "la disparition de πρόσχημα rend le rapport σώφρονες - ἄνανδροι incompréhensible. Et les masculins pluriels, οἱ σώφρωνες - οἱ συνετοί, restreignent fâcheusement la portée de la pensée."

Commentary on Chapter 30

[1]The use of the verb σκληραγωγεῖν affords another example of the freshness of Dionysius' language. The verb means "to bring up <a child> hardy" (LSJ). Here Dionysius speaks of "toughening-up, hardening" one's style as though a delicate child were in question. The language of Dionysius is studied in general terms in the first chapter of W. Schmid's *Die Atticismus in seinen Hauptvertretern von Dionysius von Halikarnass bis auf den zweiten Philostratus* 1 (Stuttgart 1887) 1-26.

[2] Marchant acutely observes that this sentence is so obscure that Dionysius, while commenting on what precedes and what follows, discreetly leaves it alone. Earlier editors take ἀποτροπή to have an active meaning

which it has in other passages, i.e. "for averting <hostile attack>"; but LSJ suggests a meaning from the middle ἀποτρέπεσθαι, which is adopted here (so Gomme and others). Dionysius and all the better Thucydidean manuscripts read the nominative ἀσφάλεια, where Jones, de Romilly, *et al.* adopt the dative ἀσφαλείᾳ from the scholiast's explanation. Gomme wishes to emend the passage.

³ The translation is of Dionysius' text, which reads τυχών τε (twice, here and in *De Dem.* 1.129.8). The Thucydidean manuscripts omit τε: "the plotter, if successful." Gomme (*HCT* 2.377) believes that Dionysius retains the true text. See also A. Grossmann, *NJPhP* 125 (1882) 357-358.

⁴ The Thucydidean manuscripts read αὐτῶν for αὐτῷ: "if he provided against the need for either of these," a loose reference to ἐπιβουλεύσας and ὑπονοήσας as implying ἐπιβουλή and ὑπόνοια. For αὐτῷ, see Dionysius' final sentence in this chapter.

⁵ For the construction with ἐκπεπληγμένος, see C.F. Smith, *PAPA* 22 (1891) xviii.

⁶ The adjective καθαρός, usually applied by Dionysius to "pure" language (Geigenmüller, *Quaestiones* 13-14; cf. supra on chap. 5.26), here has the sense of "clear, lucid": Lockwood, *CQ* 31 (1937) 199.

Commentary on Chapter 31

¹ For ἀγκύλως, see supra on chap. 25.8.

² Whereas metaphor is a general term for a word transferred from one meaning to another, μετάληψις is used when a partial synonym is substituted. The examples cited by Dionysius are συγγενές for συγγένεια and ἑταιρικόν for ἑταιρία. Metalepsis is studied by R. Volkmann, *Rhetorik*² 427-428. Our passage is discussed near the end (p. 215) of Ernesti's long treatment of μετάληψις. R.C. Jebb (in E. Abbott's *Hellenica* [London 1880] 308) observes that Thucydides used "metaphors rather bolder than Greek prose easily tolerated in its riper age," citing: δουλοῖ φρόνημα τὸ αἰφνίδιον (II.61.3), ἐπικλασθῆναι (III.59.1), πόλεμος βίαιος διδάσκαλος (III.82.2), τῆς πόλεως ἰατρός (VI.14), ἡ ἐπιστήμη ἐγγηράσεται (VI.18.6). See supra on chap. 24.3.

³ The harshness of the ellipsis has been the subject of comment by modern editors without acknowledgement that they had been anticipated by Dionysius.

⁴ Usener's supplement of <ἀντὶ τῆς συγγενείας καὶ τῆς ἑταιρίας> is suggested by the scholium of M and is regarded by Roberts (*CR* 14 [1900] 454) as "successful," although his reference to chap. 25 is incorrect. Pavano substitutes plural forms.

⁵ I prefer the present ἀποδιδούς of the manuscripts, although Usener adopts L. Sadée's (*De D.H. scriptis rhetoricis quaestiones criticae* [Strassburg 1878] 216) emendation to the aorist.

[6]Dionysius alters the Thucydidean text.

[7] I follow Classen's translation. The manuscripts of Thucydides and Dionysius read ὠφελίας (*vel.* -είας), which is retained by the Budé editors ("en visant à l'utilité") and Ros (*Metabole* 178). Bekker and Arnold also retain the genitive, but find a construe with μετά, thereby destroying the balance of the sentence, as it is clear that μετὰ τῶν κειμένων νόμων directly answers παρὰ τοὺς καθεστῶτας. Dionysius' paraphrase below has suggested to most editors that he read the dative ὠφελίᾳ, but the same paraphrase suggests to Vollgraff and Herwerden that he read the nominatives, ὠφελίαι and πλεονεξίαι. The dative is supported by Valla's rendering of the passage. The dative may mean "to render help" (Marchant), "for the benefit of the commonwealth" (Poppo), "for the sake of mutual aid" (Gomme), or "for the benefit of the law," i.e. "protection" (Spratt). For μετά, see Kühner-Gerth, *Gr. Gram.*[3] 1.507. The pressing need of the sentence is a verb. It is interesting that Dionysius' paraphrase is uniformly cited as the authority for so many variations.

[8] The MSS. of Dionysius read the imperfect ἐγίγνοντο where the Thucydidean manuscripts have an optative.

[9]Roberts (*DHLC* 26) draws attention to the fact that the "figure" called *hyperbaton* is almost ignored by Dionysius, although in the *De Comp.* he was writing on word order and the figure had been recognized as early as Plato (*Protag.* 343e), who probably took over the notion from the Sophists. See also Quintilian 8.6.62. When Dionysius does mention hyperbaton, as here and in chap. 52, he is clearly thinking not of desirable but of highly undesirable "inversion." For general bibliography on hyperbaton (Lat. *transgressio*), see D.A. Russell, *'Longinus' On the Sublime* (Oxford 1964) 137, to which add E. Schwyzer and A. Debrunner, *Gr. Gram.* 2 (Munich 1950) 697-698 and J. Martin, *Antike Rhetorik* (Munich 1974) 308-309. Longinus (22.3-4) describes the psychological effect of hyperbata—the impression of impromptu speech and the anxiety felt by the hearer as a result of the suspension of meaning. — There are two studies which treat the subject in Thucydides: F. Darpe, *De verborum apud Thucydidem collocatione* (Diss. Münster 1865) and H. Scheiding, *De hyperbato Thucydideo* (Progr. Jauer 1867). Darpe concludes that his unusual order of words has a twofold motive: a desire to meet the gravity of the subject by a like gravity of style (*dicta factis exaequare*: Sallust *Cat.* 3), and an attempt to express by position that which the orator effects by voice. A.W. Spratt in his edition of Book VI (Cambridge 1905) xli-xlii, writes: "Of all Thucydidean 'hyperbata' the most common is the trajection of τε, in some cases so abnormal as to suggest to editors its instant excision, as, for instance, in VI.6.2. If any principle can be laid down it would appear to be this, that the logical sequence supersedes the grammatical, and that the conjunction is appended to the particular word in the sentence which gives the most rhythmical arrangement." — The order of words in Thucydides has been a subject of study in the introductions to several editions of Thucydides. Noteworthy are those of A.W. Spratt (*Thucydides Book VI* [Cambridge

1905] xxxi-xliii), E.C. Marchant (*Thucydides* Book I [London 1905] xxxviii-xlii), J. Classen (*Einleitung* to Book I, second edition [Berlin 1873] lxxxiv-xc), and the completely rewritten *Einleitung* in J. Steup's revision of Classen (seventh reprint edition [Berlin 1966] lxxvi-lxxxiv). The beginning English student would do well to start with C.D. Morris (*Thucydides Book I* [Boston 1897] 49-52) a passage which is taken over largely from Classen. Of two dissertations on word order, that of O. Diener, *De sermone Thucydidis quatenus cum Herodoto congruens differat a scriptoribus Atticis* (Diss. Leipzig 1889) points out (pp. 75-77) the frequency in Thucydides of a dependent genitive between the preposition and the governing noun (ἀπὸ τῶν νόμων τῆς δεινότης), an order which is also discussed by Roberts (*DHLC* 337); the other of L. Lindhamer, *Zum Wortstellung im Griechischen* (Diss. Munich 1908) analyzes the position of the verb, noting that Thucydides frequently places it between words closely dependent upon it, as between a noun and its apposition (I.100.2, II.12.1, III.35.1, IV.76.4).

[10]Dionysius here wrongly interprets οὐκ ἐχόντων ἄλλοθεν δύναμιν, which means not that they lacked other means of pledging their friendship, but that they could not help themselves in any other way (i.e. by the support of other states) and so were willing to swear to a reconciliation with the intention of breaking their oaths at the first opportunity.

Commentary on Chapter 32

[1]For σκολιός, see supra on chap. 27.8.

[2]Goodwin (*GMT* 903.8) raises grave doubt about the possibility of the infinitive with φθάνω. Kühner-Gerth (*Gr. Gram.*[3] 2.76) suggests that Thucydides wished to avoid the intolerable φθάσας θαρσήσας.

[3]Dionysius is mistaken: ἐν τῷ παρατυχόντι means when chance presented the opportunity. See Classen's note on the Thucydidean passage and Thuc. V.38.1.

[4]J.G. Sheppard and L. Evans (*Notes on Thucydides* [London 1876] 354) say that the word ἄφρακτον is not, as Dionysius would have it, equivalent to ἀφύλακτον. They translate the latter as "unguarded, off his guard," the former, "without means of defense"; but examples in LSJ do not support this distinctinction. The difference in meaning is the same as that between Latin *inermis, imparatus* and *non custoditus*.

[5] The translation follows that of Gomme (*CQ* 42 [1948] 14), who, however, inserts an ἤ after οἱ πολλοί. A more common translation is that of P. Shorey (*TAPA* 24 [1893] 75): "Most men more easily submit to be called clever knaves than honest simpletons," which would be easier if ὄντες were omitted. The comments of Dionysius are condemned by Reiske, but approved by Gomme (*HCT* 2.379). As to numerous emendations, it may be noted that Dionysius had our manuscript text in front of him.

Commentary on Chapter 33

[1]E. Norden (*Die antike Kunstprosa*[5] [Stuttgart 1958] 7) notes that the phrase to charm men (θέλγειν τοὺς ἀνθρώπους) by speech was common in the philosophical literature. See Plato *Phaedr.* 276d.

[2]Some take καθισταμένων as the subjective genitive with τὸ πρόθυμον; others take it as a genitive absolute. Of the latter some construe τὸ πρόθυμον with αἴτιον, and this is perhaps the view of most modern commentators. This cannot be right. If ἀρχὴ ἡ διὰ πλεονεξίαν καὶ φιλοτιμίαν is the cause, something resulting from it cannot be a distinct (δ᾽) coordinate cause, but would have to be attached by τε or καί.

[3]Most editors follow Dionysius in reading προστιθέντες for προτιθέντες of the Thucydidean manuscripts. Dionysius also reads περιγενέσθαι instead of περιγίγνεσθαι.

[4]Classen translates γενναῖον by "nobility of mind" ("ein edler Sinn"). The Greek would permit the meaning "pure birth."

[5] Gildersleeve (*AJP* 12 [1891] 76) is surely right in changing φθάσωσι into φθάνωσι.

[6]For the meaning of διήγημα, see Grube, *GCDS* 137; Roberts *DS* 285.

[7] A good deal has been made of the fact that Dionysius does not refer to chap. 84, which is thought to offer many more targets for his attack than chaps. 82 and 83. One scholion says that 84 was not accepted by ancient commentators, and Cod. F obelizes every line of the chapter. Moreover, there is a paucity of scholia. Hence, it is generally inferred that 84 was not in Dionysius' text. On the other hand, Dionysius omits from consideration several sentences of chaps. 82-83 (τὸ δ᾽ ἐμπλήκτως ..., καὶ τὰς ἐς σφᾶς ..., etc.) which one might expect him to criticize; and indeed Steup suggests that the careless copyists of Dionysius have omitted several passages. Dionysius stopped his elaborate criticism with the words ἐπὶ δὲ τῷ ἀγάλλοντα of chap. 82.7 after finding enough material for his purposes, being content to quote III.83 without further analysis. The significance of his silence has been discussed by G. Jachmann, *Klio* 33 (1940) 242; cf. M. Untersteiner, *AFC* 7 (1959) 89-90. On the basis of the language, L. Straub (*Philologus* 70 [1911] 565-569) is certain that the passage is Thucydidean, whereas Gomme (*HCT* 2.382-383) for the same reason is convinced that the chapter is spurious. Thomas Arnold in his first edition devoted six pages of print to a defense of the chapter; in his subsequent editions he recanted, defending with much fervor the idea he had formerly scouted. For recent discussions see E. Wenzel, *WS* 81 (1968) 18-27 (for authenticity); and A. Fuks, *AJP* 92 (1971) 48-55 (against authenticity). The latter argues that the absence of an economic explanation for stasis in III.82-83 confirms the case against the authenticity of III.84, where economic causes are prominent. P. Huart ("Le vocabulaire de l'analyse psychologique dans l'oeuvre de Thucydide" [*Études et Commentaires* 69 (1968)] 484) also objects to the sentiments of the chapter.

Commentary on Chapter 34

[1]The normal practice of Dionysius is to use λόγοι δημόσιοι to cover both λόγοι δημηγορικοί ("speeches before the assembly, parliamentary speeches") and λόγοι δικανικοί ("forensic speeches, speeches belonging to trials"); but Roberts notes (*DHTLL* 188) that δημηγορία is a general word used of all Thucydidean speeches.

[2]Dionysius himself thinks otherwise, as he makes clear in chap. 55. In his study relating to the sources of Marcellinus, W. John (*De veterum rhetorum studiis Thucydideis quaestiones selectae* [Diss. Griefswald 1922] 20 n. 10) notes that the opinion that the speeches represent the acme of Thucydidean art is found in chap. 38 of the *Vita*.

[3]The theory of εὕρεσις was presented in elaborate and systematic form in the earliest Latin rhetorical treatises. "εὕρεσις is *inventio*; it is not 'invention' if by that we imply some degree of imaginative creation. It is simply the 'discovery' of what requires to be said in a given situation (τὰ δέοντα εὑρεῖν), the implied theory being that this is somehow already 'there' though latent, and does not have to be made up as a mere figment of imagination. ... The nature of ancient *inventio* and its difference from modern invention are of the first importance": D.A. Russell, *G&R* 14 (1967) 135. In Book 2 of the *Ad Herennium*, the author shows how to apply the means of invention to each type or subtype of a discourse. See H. Caplan's analysis (pp. xlviii-l) in the introduction to his Loeb edition. Cf. M.L. Clarke, *Rhetoric at Rome* (London 1953) 7. Sometimes orators were credited with a capacity for Invention alone, particularly those trained in the system of Hermagoras (D. Matthes, *Lustrum* 3 [1959] 114ff.): Cicero *Br.* 263, 271; Tacitus, *Dial.* 19.13; Quintilian 3.11.22. For this stereotyped division of rhetoric, see G. Kennedy, *The Art of Persuasion in Greece* (Princeton 1963) 265-266, 304-314.

[4]For ἐνθυμήματα, see supra on chap. 24.42.

[5] For νοήματα, see supra on chap. 24.43.

[6]For the meaning of πηγή, see R.E. Wycherley, *CR* 51 (1937) 2-3. Lockwood (*CQ* 31 [1937] 195) lists eight "stream similes" used in Dionysius.

[7] For περιττός, see supra on chap. 28.1; for ξένος, on chap. 24.6. The word παράδοξος is not listed by Geigenmüller and does not occur elsewhere in our treatise. Cicero (*De Fin.* 4.27.74; *Par. Stoic.* proem 4) translates παράδοξα by *admirabilia*, the *Rhetorica ad Herennium* (1.3.5) by *turpe*. The *ad Her.* (1.6.9) says that a cause is "discreditable" (*turpe*) "when the subject itself alienates the hearer." E.W. Bower (*CQ* 52 [1958] 225) has studied the word in rhetorical contexts, explaining the difference in meaning as depending on whether the point is the inherent characteristics of a case or the reaction of the audience. Perhaps "startling" is a better translation in our context.

[8]P. Moraux ("Thucydide et la rhétorique," *LEC* 22 [1954] 3-23) alludes to this sentence at the beginning of an article in which he maintains that the divisions and arrangement of the arguments in the speeches of Cleon and Diodotus (III.37-48) fit perfectly the categories set forth in the rhetorical theory of Aristotle's *Rhetoric* and the *Rhetorica ad Alexandrum*. Moraux concludes that the roots of this rhetorical theory go back to Thucydides' contemporaries. The thesis that Thucydides was following a rhetorical tradition is amplified by O. Luschnat, *RE* Supp. 12 (1970) 1147-1150 (with bibliography).

[9]M. Egger, *Denys d'Halicarnasse* (Paris 1902) 223, refers to this paragraph as "cette page curieuse, qui rappelle quelques beaux vers de Lucrèce [4.1141-1162] et qui donne un avant-goût d'un couplet célèbre de Molière" [Act II, Scene IV, lines 711-730]. Earlier (chap. 2) Dionysius had ridiculed those who resented any attempt to remove Thucydides from his pedestal.

Commentary on Chapter 35

[1]See chap. 15.

[2]See chaps. 6-8.

[3]This sentence is discussed in detail by F. Blass, *Die attische Beredsamkeit* 1[2] (Leipzig 1887) 237-238.

[4]Chap. 24.

[5] This is the third reference suggesting that the treatise, although addressed to Tubero, was ultimately destined for a wider public. Cf. supra chaps. 2 and 25.

[6]For φράσις, which in Dionysius is used side by side with λέξις, see Roberts, *CR* 15 (1901) 253.

Commentary on Chapter 36

[1]Dionysius now turns to the speeches of Thucydides which he divides into dialogues (chaps. 36-41) and harangues (chaps. 42-49). As in his treatment of the narratives, he first selects speeches which win his approval and then those which he considers deserving of censure. In the first sentence of chap. 36, he uses the word λόγοι, whereas, at the beginning of chap. 37 he employs διάλογος. Cf. Luschnat, *Thukydides*, 1152.

[2]Thuc. II.71.1.

[3]Lockwood (*CQ* 23 [1929] 181 n. 5) cites this passage in his study of the word ἠθικός, which he finds to have two meanings: (1) "simple, everyday, of the man in the street," as befits the simple style of the ordinary man; or (2) "in character, dramatic," as befits the style of a particular character. Although the word ἠθικός does not occur in the *De Thuc.*, Lockwood concludes that the reference to "propriety" in connection with the speeches

in Thucydides is in each case (chaps. 36, 41, 45) to "suitability of language and expressions to the characters of the speaker and the subject." For meanings of the difficult term ἦθος, see also D.A. Russell on "Longinus" 9.15 and *G&R* 14 (1967) 139; A. Hellwig, "Untersuchungen zur Theorie der Rhetorik" (*Hypomnemata* 38 [1973]) 259. D.P. Tompkins (*YClS* 22 [1972] 181-214) maintains that Thucydidean speakers do vary significantly in their manner of speaking and are differentiated by their styles. Marcellinus (57) characterized Thucydides as ἀνηθοποίητος; cf. F. Zucker, "Anethopoietos" (*Sitz. deut. Akad. der Wiss. zu Berlin* 1952.4) 4-5; and H.-M. Hagen, *Ethopoiia* (Diss. Erlangen 1966) 51-53. Gildersleeve (*AJP* 17 [1896] 126, 38 [1917] 339), as an illustration of the correspondence between style and content, observed that one might attribute the peculiar twists and turns of the speech of the Mytilenaeans in Book III to the embarrassment of the traitorous allies of the Athenians.

[4] Marcellinus (50) speaks of Thucydides' θαυμασταὶ βραχύτητες. Cf. Cicero, *De Orat.* 2.22: *sententiis magis quam verbis abundantes*, 2.13: *ita porro verbis est aptus et pressus*; Quintilian 10.1.73: *densus et brevis et semper constans sibi Thucydides.* R.C. Jebb ("The Speeches of Thucydides," in E. Abbott's *Hellenica* [London 1880] 309) illustrates the brevity (1) in such constructions as γυναικείας ἀρετῆς, ὅσαι ... ἔσονται (II.45.12) or τῶν μὲν ἤδη ἄρχειν, τῶν δὲ διανοεῖσθαι (sc. ἄρχειν, I.124.3); (2) in the suppression of a clause which can be supplied mentally, as often before a sentence introduced by γάρ (cf. I.120 *ad init.*); (3) in the pregnant use of words, as VI.11.2, ὅπερ ἡμᾶς ἐκφοβοῦσι (= ἐκφοβοῦντες λέγουσι). Jebb comments, "no ordinary hearer could have followed his meaning with full comprehension."

[5] For ἁρμονία, see supra on chap. 24.55.

[6] This is the only example of the use of the adjective ἔναυλος (lit. "on or to the flute") in the rhetorical works of Dionysius. Geigenmüller (*Quaestiones* 87 n. 1) lists it as a word of uncertain meaning. Dionysius uses the word in *AR* 9.7.3, which the Loeb editor renders "ringing in their ears," apparently a more vivid expression for "fresh in the memory." The lacuna at this point in the manuscripts makes a precise definition impossible. Hesychius defines the word as ἔμπνους, "alive, inspired."

[7] Dionysius reads πρός and is followed by Classen, Jones and Luschnat. The reading of C (παρά) is adopted by Hude and de Romilly.

[8] Dionysius reads τοῦ κινδύνου καί instead of τὸν κίνδυνον of the Thucydidean manuscripts. The verb συναίρω is generally construed with the genitive: see Schwyzer, *Gr. Gram.* 2.103-104.

[9] Dionysius has the word order ἱερὰ Διὶ ἐλευθερίῳ, which is adopted by Hude, Jones and Luschnat, instead of Διὶ ἐλευθερίῳ ἱερά, the reading of the majority of the Thucydidean manuscripts and of Classen.

[10] Dionysius' ἐκείνοις is omitted in the Thucydidean manuscripts.

[11] The reading of all modern editors (γῆν instead of τὴν γῆν) is found

in Dionysius and MS. C of Thucydides.

[12] Dionysius reads ὥσπερ where all Thucydidean manuscripts have καθάπερ.

[13] Dionysius' text of this sentence (τοιαῦτα τῶν Πλαταιέων λεγόντων Ἀρχίδαμος ἀποκρίνεται τοιάδε) differs from that of the Thucydidean manuscripts (τοσαῦτα εἰπόντων τῶν Πλαταιῶν Ἀρχίδαμος ὑπολαβὼν εἶπεν).

[14] The anarthrous form of πρότερον, read by Dionysius, is preferred by most editors (Hude, Jones, de Romilly, Luschnat).

[15] Dionysius has πᾶς in the predicate position, whereas all Thucydidean manuscripts except A have the attributive position.

[16] Dionysius reads the subjunctive where all Thucydidean manuscripts except C have the future indicative which is unsupported by any other instance in Thucydides of the future indicative after a verb of fearing. Ros' attempt (*Metabole* 367) to defend the indicative is rejected by Luschnat.

[17] Dionysius omits ἀριθμῷ ("by number") of the Thucydidean manuscripts.

[18] Dionysius reads ἀποφοράν instead of φοράν, "rent," of the Thucydidean manuscripts.

[19] Dionysius and one papyrus read ἀγγέλλοντες where the Thucydidean manuscripts have ἀπαγγέλλοντες or ἀπαγγέλοντες; cf. A. Kleinlogel, *Geschichte des Thukydidestextes im Mittelalter* (Berlin 1965) 18 n. 43.

[20] After the word Πλαταιεῖς, a long passage starting with the words ἀφ' οὗ, which follow Πλαταιεῖς of 387.6, is repeated in MS. P.

[21] Dionysius reads ἀνασχέσθαι where the Thucydidean manuscripts have ἀνέχεσθαι (all editors) or ἀντέχεσθαι.

[22] Dionysius reads the optative δέοι, where the Thucydidean manuscripts have the indicative δεῖ, "if it must be so."

[23] Dionysius and MS. C read the article and are followed by most editors.

[24] Dionysius (with Stahl, Classen, Steup and de Romilly) reads the imperative where the majority of Thucydidean manuscripts (with Jones and Luschnat) have the indicative, "Ye are my witnesses."

[25] The reading of Dionysius, προτέρων, is adopted by Teubner and Budé editors (correctly, cf. 388.5) in preference to that of the Thucydidean manuscripts, πρότερον.

Commentary on Chapter 37

[1] Dionysius applies the term διάλογος to the speeches of the Plataeans and Archidamus in Book II, where the exchange consists of two pairs of short speeches, the second Plataean speech being in indirect discourse. The

form is not parallel to the Melian "dialogue." Isidorus (*Etym.* 6.8.2) gives
the following definition: *Dialogus est conlatio duorum vel plurimorum,
quem Latini sermonem dicunt.* Cf. R. Hirzel, *Der Dialog* (Leipzig 1895)
1.44-45; H.L. Hudson-Williams, *AJP* 71 (1950) 156-169.

[2] W.R.M. Lamb, *Clio Enthroned* (Cambridge 1914) 73, translates the
latter part of the sentence, "ancient amateurs of this kind of composition."

[3] Dionysius uses the word πρόβουλοι instead of Thucydides' ξύνεδροι.

[4] Actually, the dialogue was not between an Athenian general and the
Melian commissioners. Thucydides (V.84.3) says that two Athenian generals
sent envoys to make proposals to the Melians. Dionysius' criticisms of the
Melian Dialogue form the basis of chap. X of F.M. Cornford's *Thucydides
Mythistoricus* (London 1907), where several of the passages are translated.

[5] Roberts (*DHLC* 327) notes that "form" is the proper translation for
σχῆμα in this passage.

[6] Δραματίζει is Usener's conjecture for καὶ δραματικόν of MSS. Although a compound of δραματίζω is known (Diog. L. 3.56), the simplex
does not otherwise occur in classical Greek. Thucydides changes from narrative to full dramatic form, prefixing, as in a play, the names "Athenians,
Melians" to the speeches.

[7] Dionysius has λαοί where the Thucydidean manuscripts have πολλοί.

[8] Dionysius reads ἡμῶν, an objective genitive, which is adopted in the
Oxford and Budé texts, instead of ὑμῶν (Thucydidean manuscripts), a subjective genitive.

[9] Dionysius has προκαθήμενοι where the Thucydidean manuscripts have
καθήμενοι, "who are sitting."

[10] At the beginning of the sentence, the text of Dionysius omits the
words καθ' ἕκαστον γὰρ, found in the Thucydidean manuscripts.

[11] Dionysius reads ἐν ὀλίγῳ with all Thucydidean manuscripts. Modern
editors adopt the reading of Valla, ἐνὶ λόγῳ (*perpetua oratione*).

[12] The meaning of ἐπιείκεια in Thucydides has been discussed by J. de
Romilly, *Phoenix* 28 (1974) 95-100.

[13] Quintilian (9.1.10-11) states that the term σχῆμα is used in two
senses: "In the first it is applied to any form in which thought is expressed,
just as it is to bodies which, whatever their composition, must have some
shape. In the second and special sense, in which it is called a *schema*, it
means a rational change in meaning or language from the ordinary and simple form" (Loeb tr.). The word is discussed in chap. 6 (116-134) of D.M.
Schenkeveld, *Studies in Demetrius On Style* (Amsterdam 1964). For the
distinction between 'figures' and 'tropes' and for bibliography, see H. Caplan's Loeb ed. of *Rhetorica ad Herennium*, pp. 274-275, and D.A. Russell,
'Longinus' On the Sublime (Oxford 1964) 128-130. See also supra on chap.
24.3 and infra on chap. 53.12. Cicero (*De Orat.* 3.52.200) says that the

figures of speech are almost countless: *formantur autem et verba et sententiae paene innumerabiles*; but the scholiast to Aristides (p. 373) reports that Dionysius recognized thirty-two: Διονύσιος ὁ Ἁλικαρνασσεὺς λέγει, ὅτι λβ´ εἰσὶ σχήματα τοῦ λόγου. G. Ammon (*De Dionysii Halicarnassensis librorum rhetoricum fontibus* [Diss. Munich 1889] 35) believes that σχήματα τῆς λέξεως are meant, but he does not speculate as to the reason for the number. Whereas figures of speech are common in Thucydides, figures of thought, σχήματα τῆς διανοίας (Irony, Oxymoron, ἐκ πλαγίου ῥῆσις, ἐπιτίμησις, πανουργία), are seldom or never used: καὶ ποικιλώτατος μὲν ἐν τοῖς τῆς λέξεως σχήμασι, κατὰ δὲ τὴν διάνοιαν τοὐναντίον ἀσχημάτιστος (Marcellinus *Vita* 56). Figures of thought generally involve a display of feeling and hence they ill accorded with the self-contained style of Thucydides. Although there are numerous instances of latent irony (cf. L.A. MacKay, "Latent Irony in the Melian Dialogue," *Studies Presented to D.M. Robinson* 2 [Saint Louis 1953] 570), examples of a rhetorical burst of feeling are rare: πῶς οὐ δεινὰ εἴργασθε: III.66.2 (speech of the Thebans). Basic passages for figures of thought in general are *Rhet. ad Her.* 4.13.18 and Quintilian 9.1.19-21, 2.26; cf. R. Volkmann, *Die Rhetorik der Griechen und Römer*[2], 460-461, 488-505. H. Steinberg (*Beiträge zur Würdigung der thukydideischen Reden* [Progr. Berlin 1870] 20-21) has collected examples of such figures in the speeches of Thucydides. He observes, moreover, that the evidence supports the statement of Marcellinus (*Vita* 57) that figures of thought are lacking in the speeches of Pericles, Archidamus, and Nicias, whereas Steinberg finds that they occur in the speeches of Alcibiades, Cleon and Athenagoras. The subject, which has been ignored by recent scholars who write on the stylistic characterizations of Thucydidean speakers, is one deserving of further study.

[14] In the grammar of Dionysius Thrax (16.640b), there were two ἄρθρα, the "prepositive," which we today call the article, and the "postpositive," which we call the relative pronoun. His treatment of pronouns in paragraph 17 included the personal and reflexive, but no mention is made of αὐτός. A complete codification of the grammar of the language had not been completed by the time of Dionysius. Apollodorus Dyscolus (*Pron.* 5.19) says that Apollodorus the Athenian and Dionysius Thrax called pronouns ἄρθρα δεικτικά.

[15] Literally, "neither does he preserve the concord by making this word conform to feminine singular nominative nor to plural neuter accusative." Dionysius finds fault with Thucydides for writing the pronoun αὐτοῦ when he should have written αὐτῆς referring to ἐπιείκεια ("fairness"), or αὐτά, referring to τὰ τοῦ πολέμου. Neither of these substitutions is correct. Most modern commentators of Thucydides very appropriately refer αὐτοῦ to τοῦ διδάσκειν καθ᾽ ἡσυχίαν ἀλλήλους ("the proposal to engage in quiet interchange"). Cf. J.G.A. Ros, *Metabole* 53 n. 9. F. Bücheler (*NJPhP* 109 [1874] 691) concludes that Dionysius must have written φαίνετε in 389.7 instead of the φαίνεται found in all manuscripts of both Dionysius and Thucydides, and Usener-Radermacher adopt Bücheler's reading. Bücheler draws this conclusion from the words of Dionysius that τὰ τοῦ πολέμου were neuter accusative, and φαίνεται is then incomprehensible. Steup takes φαίνετε into his

text. Classen objects that Thucydides nowhere uses the active voice, although the middle occurs more than ninety times, and, further, that the parallelism of the period is destroyed by the adoption of φαίνετε. Moreover, as Pavano points out in an appendix (p. 246), when Dionysius recasts the sentence, he uses φαίνεται. My translation follows the manuscripts.

[16]The word κατάλληλος is used for the correct grammatical construction. See Roberts, *DHTLL* 194, and Geigenmüller, *Quaestiones* 24.

[17] Dionysius has the aorist participle in accord with many Thucydidean manuscripts, instead of the future, adopted by all editors. See A. Kleinlogel, *Geschichte des Thukydidestextes im Mittelalter* (Berlin 1965) 101.

[18] Dionysius reads παυόμεθα for παυοίμεθ᾽ ἄν of Thucydidean manuscripts.

Commentary on Chapter 38

[1]The text of Dionysius attributes to the Athenian words spoken by the Melians. The error may be that of a copyist. This passage is discussed by L. Canfora, *Belfagor* 26 (1971) 411, who attributes incongruities in the dialogue to the editing of Xenophon.

[2] Dionysius has a second aorist form (τράπεσθαι) where the Thucydidean manuscripts have the present.

[3] There are enough parallels in the Greek *Thesaurus* to suggest that "an incredibly long speech" is an alternative rendition.

[4] This clause leads me to suspect that a phrase such as ἄδικον ἀρχήν was omitted after ὁμολογοῦντος.

[5] See Andrewes' note (*HCT* 4.162), and de Romilly in the "notes complémentaires" in the Budé edition.

Commentary on Chapter 39

[1]P. Huart ("Le vocabulaire de l'analyse psychologique dans l'oeuvre de Thucydide" [*Études et Commentaires* 69 (1968)] 484), referring to this sentence, explains that Dionysius fails to see that Thucydides attributes exactly the same concept of justice to Lacedaemonians and to Athenians.

[2] Dionysius reads ὥστε δέ, where the majority of the Thucydidean manuscripts, followed by Jones and de Romilly, omit the δέ. Classen believes that the δέ is more likely to have been dropped than inserted after ὥστε, and that it is frequently used in this dialogue to introduce a reply with some emphasis. So also Graves.

[3] I give Jowett's translation. As he notes, "This is a condensed sentence in which the reason of the statement is included in the statement itself, and the reason for both clauses is included in the second."

[4] Dionysius' criticisms of this example of false antithesis are endorsed

by E.M. Cope, *Journal of Classical and Sacred Philology* 3 (1857) 73.

Commentary on Chapter 40

[1] The inference from this paraphrase is that Dionysius, with nearly all Thucydidean manuscripts, read πολεμίων in his text of V.102.1 instead of πολέμων, adopted by all modern editors. An analogous confusion occurs in IV.80.3.

[2] Since παραμύθιον is commonly found with the genitive, Krüger believes that Dionysius here preserves the correct reading instead of the dative as in all Thucydidean manuscripts. As παραμύθιον is used in the meaning of "encouragement" (Plato *Euthyd.* 272b; cf. *Laws* 10.885b), good sense can be obtained by taking κινδύνου as an objective genitive and translating, "an encouragement to risk."

[3] Dionysius reads ἐπὶ σκοπῆς μιᾶς instead of ἐπὶ ῥοπῆς μιᾶς (<depend> "on a single turn of the scale") of most Thucydidean manuscripts. Cf. Kühner-Gerth, *Gr. Gram.*[3] 1.498.

[4] Dionysius, with the majority of Thucydidean manuscripts, has ἐπιλείπωσιν where AB, and apparently *Oxy. Pap.* 880, followed by all modern editors, read ἐπιλίπωσιν.

[5] Dionysius' text is here quite different from the received Thucydidean text. Usener notes that the MSS. of Dionysius show attempts at emendation. Thus, they read τῆς μὲν ἀνθρωπείας, τῆς δ᾽ for τῆς ἀνθρωπείας τῶν μὲν, and νεμέσεως τῶν τ᾽ for νομίσεως τῶν δ᾽ εἰς of the Thucydidean manuscripts and *Oxy. Pap.* 880, thereby making a very hard sentence even more difficult.

[6] Translating the phrase ἀπὸ φύσεως ἀναγκαίως where the Thucydidean manuscripts have ὑπὸ φύσεως ἀναγκαίας. It is to be noted that *Oxy. Pap.* 880 (II cent.) likewise has ἀπό.

[7] A reference to the first enthymeme in chap. 38.

Commentary on Chapter 41

[1] Dionysius reads ἰσχυρὰ ὄντα where the Thucydidean manuscripts have ἰσχυρότατα.

[2] Dionysius reads πάροντα instead of ὑπάρχοντα of the Thucydidean manuscripts.

[3] Dionysius has the aorist infinitive where the Thucydidean manuscripts have the present.

[4] Dionysius reads γε instead of τε ("and so") of Thucydidean manuscripts.

[5] Dionysius omits ἔτι.

⁶Dionysius' reading of δυνάμεις, for δυνάμει of the Thucydidean manuscripts, is defended by M. Pehle, *Thucydidis exemplar Dionysianum cum nostrorum codicum memoria confertur* (Diss. Greifswald 1907) 22.

⁷ Dionysius reads ὁρῶντας where Thucydidean manuscripts have ἑκόντας, "voluntarily" or "intentionally."

⁸V.26; cf. IV.104-108. The phrase ἐν τῇ πρὸ ταύτης βύβλῳ (which is taken by Pavano in his edition to be an error on the part of Dionysius), since it occurs in the context of the Melian dialogue, is cited by L. Canfora ("Tucidide Continuato," *Proagones* 10 [1970] 29-30) in support of his thesis that V.84-VII.18 comprised Book VI of Dionysius' text of Thucydides, and that V.26, accordingly, fell "in the preceding book." Cf. supra on chap. 16.8.

⁹Actually Thucydides says in Book V (26.5) that he was able to travel in enemy states once the armistice of 423 B.C. was concluded. See Pritchett, *Studies in Ancient Greek Topography* 2 (Berkeley 1969) 69. F.E. Adcock, *Thucydides and his History* (Cambridge 1963) 27-42, 120-122, observes that for all his speeches it was feasible for Thucydides to have obtained some sort of authentic information. See also K.J. Dover, "Thucydides," (*G&R*, Survey No. 7 [1973]) 23. – Wilamowitz-Möllendorff, "Die Thukydideslegende," *Hermes* 12 (1877) 326-367 shows that the most varying traditions became current about Thucydides' exile, death and burial. One account implies that he died in exile. He is said to have spent his banishment in Aegina, in Thrace, in Italy, to have died a natural death, to have been killed in Thrace or in Attica or in Italy.

¹⁰Dionysius seems to have read the form ἔγγιστα, whereas in 20.356.5, where he quotes the same phrase, the word ἐγγύτατα is found.

¹¹The verb βασανίζειν used in connection with style is employed by Dionysius only in *De Thuc.* (41.396.26, 42.398.10, and 55.417.23). 'Longinus' uses the word in 10.6. Literally, "to rub upon the touchstone" (βάσανος, on which pure gold leaves a yellow streak), the word was applied to inquiry by torture and in literary criticism signifies an artifical and affected way of speaking, "tortured, strained." See Geigenmüller, *Quaestiones* 26, and J. Martin, *Antike Rhetorik* (Munich 1974) 101. Roberts (*DS* 271) says that βάσανος, "torture," was a late word in the metaphorical sense. Grube (*GCDS* 145) suggests that the word implies both the pain of torture and the idea of testing the reader's ability.

¹² A quite different view of the Melian dialogue is given by B.E. Perry (*TAPA* 68 [1937] 427): "There can be no real appreciation of Thucydides and his type of mind, if, owing to your cordial disapproval of imperial ruthlessness, you fail to see that in the Melian dialogue, for instance, the folly of the Melians rather than the cruelty of the Athenians is the chief subject of contemplation. Thucydides has the strange faculty of seeing and telling the plain truth of a matter without trying in any way to bring it into line with the cherished beliefs of men. For that reason he has often escaped

comprehension."

[13] The verb is supplied by Usener where a hiatus exists in the text.

Commentary on Chapter 42

[1] As with the dialogues (chaps. 36-41), so with the harangues (chaps. 42-49) Dionysius first selects speeches which win his approval and then examines those which he considers deserving of censure. Six win high praise: a) I.140-144, Pericles on eve of war; b) VI.9-14, Nicias in favor of Sicilian expedition; c) VI.11-15, letter of Nicias; d) VII.61-64, address of Nicias before final sea-battle; e) VII.77, Nicias' exhortation before retreat; f) III.53-59, defence of Plataeans. The two speeches which he criticizes in some detail are: a) II.60-64, Pericles' final speech, and b) VI.71-80, Hermocrates. His criticisms are based on grounds of propriety and style.

[2] Pericles' speech, so admired by Dionysius, was used in great part as the model for the speech of Appius Claudius in *AR* 6.59.64: J. Flierle, *Ueber Nachahmungen des Demosthenes, Thucydides und Xenophon in den Reden der römischen Archaeologie des Dionysius von Halicarnass* (Progr. Munich 1890) 33-37.

[3] *Oxy. Pap.* 1245 (fourth century) agrees with Dionysius in inserting ἄνδρες, which the manuscripts, followed by all modern editors, omit.

[4] W. Lüdtke (*Untersuchungen zum Satzbau des Thukydides* [*Das sog. Anakoluth*] Diss Keil 1930) quotes this passage in the opening sentence of his study of anacoluthon. He records (pp. 86-91) relatively few examples from the speeches (cf. W. Keil, *PhW* 51 [1931] 835) and finds that the great majority occur in constructions with parallel members (τέ - καί, μέν - δέ, καί - καί).

[5] καθαρός, used especially of water in the sense "clear of admixture, clean, pure" (LSJ), was frequently applied by Dionysius to such words as λέξις, λόγος, ὄνομα (see Geigenmüller, *Quaestiones* 13-14), just as θολοῦσθαι "to be made turbid," properly used of water, was used by "Longinus" (3.1) of "turbid" diction or style. In *De Lys.* 2, Dionysius mentions καθαρός as a striking characteristic of Lysias' diction. In Hermogenes (Spengel, *Rhetores Graeci* 2.275), "purity" is an element of σαφήνεια, "lucidity, perspicuity." It may be noted that with the Greeks and Romans the concept of speech as a stream which flows from the mouth is common: see van Hook, *Terminology* 12-13. Cf. supra on chap. 5.26.

[6] For σαφήνεια as one of the "necessary virtues," see supra on chap. 22.8. Cf. also on chap. 5.25.

[7] Models for actual pleadings, or real contests (ἀληθινοὶ ἀγῶνες), is a recurring theme in Dionysius: *De Lys.* 6.14.5; *De Isoc.* 11.71.4; *Ep. ad Pomp.* 5.244.10; and *De Thuc.* 53.413.1, as well as the present passage.

[8] See supra on chap. 41.11.

⁹This is the only occurrence of the verb κατεπιτηδεύω in Greek, although the noun ἐπιτήδευσις is used in *De Lys.* 8 of a "studied" style. Cf. also Roberts, *DHLC* 299-300.

¹⁰For the word χρῶμα, "color, embellishments of speech," see supra on chap. 24.57.

¹¹For examples of the word εὐεπής in Dionysius, see Geigenmüller, *Quaestiones* 85. The noun εὐέπεια is applied to diction in Plato *Phaedr.* 267c. Roberts (*CR* 18 [1904] 19) states that the word is to be understood in a rhetorical sense in Sophocles *Oed. Tyr.* 928. – In *De Comp.* 7.31.12-17, Dionysius selects a sentence (III.57.4) from this speech of the Plataeans as an illustration of how the pathos in a passage would be lost if the word order were changed: ὑμεῖς τε, ὦ Λακεδαιμόνιοι, ἡ μόνη ἐλπίς, δέδιμεν μὴ οὐ βέβαιοι ἦτε.

¹²H. Steinberg (*Beiträge zur Würdigung der thukydideischen Reden* [Progr. Berlin 1870] 23) gives an interesting analysis of the figures in this speech in support of Heilmann's statement, "Diese Rede ist, nach meiner Einsicht, eins der grössten Meisterstücke in dem rührenden Vortrage."

¹³With regard to speeches, Dionysius' practice as an historian accords with his criticism of Thucydides here. In the *Roman Antiquities* the speeches are of set types suitable for typical situations. From Book III onwards, the speeches occupy nearly one third of his total text. It has been shown that Dionysius composed speeches by following certain stereotyped rhetorical rules, rarely revealing the character and motives of the speakers, but for the most part giving a succession of platitudes and rhetorical commonplaces. J. Flierle (*Ueber Nachahmungen des Demosthenes, Thucydides und Xenophon in den Reden der römischen Archaeologie des Dionysius von Halikarnass* [Leipzig 1890]) has collected phrases, sentences, and passages of the Greek authors which were imitated by Dionysius in his speeches. A similar study could be made of the narrative section.

Commentary on Chapter 44

¹For ἱστορικὸν σχῆμα "in narrative form," cf. *De Comp.* 19.87.8, where a contrast is made of narrative form, dialogue, and forensic oratory.

²Cicero wrote about Pericles as follows: "What of Pericles? as to whose rhetorical powers we are told that although he used to speak with some degree of sternness in opposition to the wishes of the Athenians when the national safety required, nevertheless the very fact that he spoke against the popular leaders appeared to be popular and acceptable to everyone" (*De Orat.* 3.34.138. Loeb tr.). See also *Brutus* 44.

³Dionysius' preoccupation concerning τὸ πρέπον is the direct result of his rhetorical training and leads to criticisms which are not convincing, such as his argument here that Thucydides should not have represented Pericles as defending his policy by reprimanding the citizens in so outspoken a man-

ner but as soothing the anger of the mob. The development of the criterion of τὸ πρέπον in ancient literary criticism is treated by M. Pohlenz in *Gött. Nachr.* 1933 53-92 and *Antikes Führertum* (Leipzig 1934) 58-63. Pohlenz shows (p. 80) that the word, which originally meant "clear to the eye," takes on the meaning of "normal," and, finally, "the fitting, propriety." Dionysius makes it the subject of chap. 20 of the *De Comp.* E.M. Cope's study of the word (*Introduction to Aristotle's Rhetoric* [London 1867] 297-303) is still useful. See also C. Neumeister, *Grundsätze der forensischen Rhetorik* (Munich 1964) 59-62; H.F. North, *CP* 43 (1948) 2.

[4] Similar sentiments were held by Aelius Aristides, who says (28.71-72 [Keil]) that Pericles ought to have offered his counsels as a suppliant (ἱκετη- ρίαν θεῖναι); but that on the contrary he spoke "in a boastful manner, affirming himself to be the best orator among them and that at the beginning of his speech."

Commentary on Chapter 45

[1] The sentiment in the passage which he had quoted in the previous section was such a commonplace that S.T. Bloomfield in his edition of Thucydides (London 1829) notes that Dionysius used it himself in the *AR*. The passage occurs in a speech given to Tullus Hostilius (3.29.4). Bloomfield cites similar sentiments from Solon, Herodotus, Democritus, Plutarch, and Thucydides himself (I.124.1).

[2] The order of the two words οἴομαι ἥσσων is reversed in some of the Thucydidean manuscripts and in a papyrus of the fourth century. See A. Kleinlogel, *Geschichte des Thukydidestextes im Mittelalter* (Berlin 1965) 160. Shilleto and Marchant follow Dionysius.

[3] The genitive (νικωμένου) of the manuscripts of Thucydides and Dionysius is emended by some editors to the nominative. The gender may be masculine, but Classen and others make it neuter with τοῦδε (i.e. patriotism) as the subject.

[4] For a study of τόπος as a rhetorical term, see W.M.A. Grimaldi, "Studies in the Philosophy of Aristotle's Rhetoric," (*Hermes Einzelschriften* 25 [1972]) 115-135 (with extensive bibliography).

Commentary on Chapter 46

[1] The word μειρακιώδης is applied to Gorgianic figures by Dionysius in *Ep. ad Pomp.* 2, where W.R. Roberts translates it as "juvenile." [Longinus] *On the Sublime* 3.4 describes τὸ μειρακιῶδες as the antithesis of the "sublime." D.A. Russell's commentary on this passage is, "μειρακιώδης is not always an uncomplimentary term but can take its colour from any common characteristic of youth." For studies of the word, see J.F. D'Alton, *Roman Literary Theory and Criticism* (London 1931) 48, and E.M. Cope on Aristotle's *Rhetoric* 3.11.1413a.16.

[2] For καλλωπίσματα, see supra on chap. 29.15.

[3] The words καὶ ἀμύνεσθαι are omitted in the Thucydidean manuscripts.

[4] Dionysius has φρόνημα and ὑπό where Thucydidean manuscripts have αὔχημα, "boasting," and ἀπό. The scholiast to Thucydides says (incorrectly) that αὔχημα is identical to φρόνημα.

[5] Steup, Marchant, and others argue that this phrase gives no sense as a modifier of τόλμαν and transpose it to the next sentence after ἐλπίδι.

[6] In this sentence, Dionysius has the forms σύνεσις and ὀχυρώτεραν, where Thucydides used the spellings ξύνεσις and ἐχυρώτεραν.

[7] Some editors, including Classen, understand τόλμα "courage" as the subject; others, including Gomme, ξύνεσις "intelligence."

[8] Gomme (*HCT* 2.172) says that this passage is "not so obscure as Dionysius thinks and as some modern editors have made it." Madame J. de Romilly (*Thucydide: Livre II* [Paris 1967] 99) comments, "Le jeu des oppositions entre mots de sens voisins (à la manière de Prodicos) est donc ici particulièrement subtil; et l'on comprend que la simplicité d'esprit de Denys d'Halicarnasse s'en soit alarmée, au point de qualifier ces recherches verbales de ὀχληρά et μειρακιώδη."

[9] Pavano wishes to emend the text to τά τε γὰρ <φρονήματα καὶ τὰ κατα>φρονήματα in order to bring out the paronomasia. Krüger conjectured νοήματα as a substitute for φρονήματα.

[10] Geigenmüller, *Quaestiones* 108, says that σοφιστικός is always a word of contempt in Dionysius. For a discussion of this passage, see C. Brandstaetter, "*De notionum πολιτικός et σοφιστής usu rhetorico.*" *Leip. St.* 15.1 (1893) 235.

[11] ἀπειροκαλία is "tastelessness," especially as shown in the misuse of ornament: Roberts, *DHTLL* 185 and E. Norden, *Antike Kunstprosa*[5] (Stuttgart 1958) 1.363 n. 2; 2.559. Geigenmüller (*Quaestiones* 108) translates the word as "geschmacklos."

[12] An allusion to Heraclitus' well-known sobriquet, ὁ σκοτεινός, "the Dark;" his "obscurity" was proverbial: Aristotle *Rhet.* 3.5.1407b.6; Theon (L. Spengel, *Rhet. Gr.* 2.82); Strabo 14.25; Cicero *Fin.* 2.5.15. In *De Dem.* 35.206.15, Aeschines is said to have blamed Demosthenes for τὸ σκοτεινόν.

Commentary on Chapter 47

[1] All the first part of Chapter 47 is nothing more than a parody of Thucydides' language in Pericles' last speech. Dionysius combines phrases of Thucydides into one long sentence. For the benefit of the reader who has the Greek text of Dionysius before him, I give in the notes the Greek text of Thucydides which is being imitated.

[2] Thuc. II.61.3: ἀπροσδόκητον καὶ τὸ πλείστῳ παραλόγῳ ξυμβαῖνον.

³ γενναίως may also mean "in a manner befitting their race."

⁴Thuc. II.61.4: ξυμφοραῖς ταῖς μεγίσταις ἐθέλειν ὑφίστασθαι καὶ τὴν ἀξίωσιν μὴ ἀφανίζειν.

⁵ Thuc. II.61.4: ἀπαλγήσαντας δὲ τὰ ἴδια τοῦ κοινοῦ τῆς σωτηρίας ἀντιλαμβάνεσθαι.

⁶II.62.2: καὶ οὐκ ἔστιν ὅστις τῇ ὑπαρξούσῃ παρασκευῇ τοῦ ναυτικοῦ πλέοντας ὑμᾶς οὔτε βασιλεὺς οὔτε ἄλλο οὐδὲν ἔθνος τῶν ἐν τῷ παρόντι κωλύσει.

⁷ II.62.5: ἐλπίδι τε ἧσσον πιστεύει ἧς ἐν τῷ ἀπόρῳ ἡ ἰσχύς.

⁸Dionysius alters the words in two clauses of Thuc. II.61.2: "because trouble already has possession of each man's feelings" (διότι τὸ μὲν λυποῦν ἔχει ἤδη τὴν αἴσθησιν ἑκάστῳ) and "the advantage is not yet manifest to all" (τῆς δὲ ὠφελίας ἄπεστιν ἔτι ἡ δήλωσις ἅπασι). In the final sentence εἰ γε δή may be translated "if indeed it is plain that" to bring out the ironical force.

⁹For περιττῶς, see infra on chap. 54.5.

¹⁰Dionysius adds an article omitted in the Thucydidean manuscripts.

¹¹The final sentence of II.61.3 seems to have dropped out.

¹² The text of Dionysius reads τὰς συμφορὰς where the Thucydidean manuscripts have ξυμφοραῖς ταῖς μεγίσταις. As T.R. Mills notes in his edition of Book II, "the accusative is the case which Thuc. elsewhere uses with this verb" (ὑφίστασθαι). Herwerden and Marchant retain the accusative. But see E. Schwyzer, *Gr. Gram.* 2.141; Kühner-Gerth, *Gr. Gram.*³ 1.408.

¹³ Dionysius reads ὅστις ἄν ... ἐλλείπῃ for ὅστις ... ἐλλείπει of the Thucydidean manuscripts.

¹⁴ Dionysius with one good manuscript reads ᾧ ὑπὲρ ἅπαντας "in which you above all <others>" for ᾧπερ ἅπαντες and ᾧ ὑπὲρ ἅπαντες of the Thucydidean manuscripts. Marchant follows Dionysius. But Pericles' point is that *all* Athenians take pride in the empire. J.E. Powell (*CQ* 32 [1938] 78) suggests that the υ was introduced by correction into the archetype of the Vatican family of Thucydidean manuscripts.

¹⁵ A.W. Gomme (*HCT* 2.181) makes the following observation about this last speech of Pericles: "Many modern criticisms of Thucydides' speeches have been in essentials based on Dionysios' criterion. Thucydides may have composed this speech freely, out of his own head; but he surely intended it to illustrate what Perikles, and not any other man, was like, and what he was like just on that occasion, in that situation, and not on other occasions, as in the autumn of 432 or the spring of 431, or the winter of 431-430; nor, as it seems to me, is the speech at all what he would have said had he been able to view the whole course of events till the defeat in 404."

¹⁶The word δυσπαρακολούθητος, "hard to follow, unintelligible, obscure,"

is used by Dionysius in reference to πραγματικὸς τόπος (*Ep. ad Pomp.* 3. 237.11) or to λεκτικὸς τόπος as here. The word (= Lat. *obscurum*) is also applied by rhetoricians (e.g. Cicero *De inv.* 1.15.20) to one of the five kinds of σχήματα ὑποθέσεων (*figurae materiarum*); see H. Caplan in the Loeb *Rhet. ad Her.* p. 10. The adjective περίεργος (from περιεργία, lit. "over-labour" [Roberts]) is properly used of one " 'who troubles himself over much' (περί), either about his own affairs, or those of others" (Cope *ad* Aristotle *Rhet.* 1.4.1360a.10). Hence, it acquires the general sense of "superfluous, over-wrought, elaborate, curious." Aeschines taunted Demosthenes with περιεργία and τὸ πικρόν: *De Dem.* 55.248.1. Examples of μέτριος in Dionysius are collected by Geigenmüller, *Quaestiones* 70. Aristotle (*Rhet.* 2.14.1390b.9) couples the word with τὸ ἅρμοττον, "that which fits."

Commentary on Chapter 48

[1] The word κατόρθωμα, from κάτορθος "straight," is found three times in "Longinus" (33.1, 34.1, 36.2) and "is applied to a style which hits the mark not by chance but by due observance of rule. The term is, in fact, borrowed from the realm of morals and transferred to literature in the same sense of a success following on right judgment": Roberts, *LS* 202.

[2] The reading of the MSS. of Dionysius (ἐκεῖ) is here preferred by editors to that of the Thucydidean manuscripts (ἐκεῖσε).

[3] Dionysius reads ταῦτα where the Thucydidean manuscripts have τάδε. For similar use of both words, see Kühner-Gerth, *Gr. Gram.*[3] 167 and Schwyzer, *Gr. Gram.* 2.44.

[4] For the tense, see Goodwin, *GMT* 32.

[5] τάχος, "rapidity, speed, swiftness," is a virtue which the author of *On the Sublime* (12.4) attributes to Demosthenes. Dionysius in chap. 53 says that Demosthenes imitated Thucydides in the use of this quality. On the other hand, in chap. 24, Dionysius warns that rapidity can make the diction obscure: rapidity must be combined with clearness.

[6] Dionysius states in *De Comp.* 16.63.9 that κάλλος ("beauty") of words is due to beautiful syllables and letters, that language is rendered charming by the things that charm the ear in virtue of affinities in words, syllables and letters. Cf. Geigenmüller, *Quaestiones* 52. For a general discussion of beauty of words, see Cope's commentary on Aristotle *Rhetoric* 3.2.1405b.13. For various devices which Hermogenes regarded as producing κάλλος, see Usher, *JHS* 88 (1968) 131; J. Martin, *Antike Rhetorik* (Munich 1974) 342.

[7] For τόνος, see supra on chap. 23.25. According to Dionysius, Thucydides and his imitator Demosthenes were superior to Lysias and Isocrates in this virtue: Geigenmüller, *Quaestiones* 64.

[8] For μεγαλοπρεπής, see supra on chap. 23.24.

[9] For δεινότης, see supra on chap. 27.4.

[10] Οἷς refers to ταῦτα = "the words of this passage."

[11] Dionysius reads οὖν for δέ of Thucydides manuscripts. The word ἅμα is omitted by Dionysius.

[12] The word ἥκουσι has dropped out of the text and νῦν has been substituted.

[13] The paronomasia in κατοικίσαι ... ἐξοικίσαι may be brought out by translating the final phrase as "as to unsettle us." Hobbes translates, "and to me they seem not to intend the replantation of the Leontines, but rather our supplantation." Others translate "establish ... disestablish;" "replant ... transplant."

[14] This is the only occurrence of ψυχρός, "cold, frigid, tasteless," in this treatise, although the word is as common in Dionysius (see Geigenmüller, *Quaestiones* 114) and Greek literary criticism in general as *frigidus* is in Cicero and Quintilian. The literary faults which cause frigidity are discussed in Aristotle *Rhet.* 3.3; [Longinus] chap. 3; and Demetrius *On Style* 114-127, who gives some interesting examples of τὸ ψυχρόν. It is defined by Theophrastus as that which transcends the expression appropriate to the thought. The import and origin of the word, as applied to style, are well illustrated in E.M. Cope, *Introduction to Aristotle's Rhetoric* (London 1867) 286-287. The fault is exhibited in the use of compound words, of words archaic and foreign or so obscure as to require interpretation, of epithets, and chiefly of metaphors. B.L. Gildersleeve (*AJP* 30 [1909] 231-232) has an entertaining discussion of this technical term of Greek aesthetics which defies translation. The most detailed study of the word is that of L. van Hook (*CP* 12 [1917] 68-76) who concludes that "fustian" is the best rendition of the term since the vice is due to literary faults of commission and not of omission, the result of excess or extravagance. The tragic poet Theognis was nicknamed "Snow" because of his habitual frigidity.

[15] The verb πλέκειν (lit. "to plait, weave") is used of "involved, tangled" composition. The involved style is well criticized by Ben Jonson, *Timber* 44-45 (ed. R.S. Walker [Syracuse 1953]), "Our style should be like a skein of silk, to be carried and found by the right thread, not ravelled and perplexed: then all is a knot, a heap" (quoted by van Hook, *Terminology* 36). – For the word ἕλιξ (lit. "coil, whirl, spiral"), used of complex figures, see Lockwood *CQ* 31 (1937) 197.

[16] Dionysius reads οἵδε where the Thucydidean manuscripts have οὗτοι, and in the next line περὶ δὲ τοῦ for περὶ δέ. For the position of the preposition, see Kühner-Gerth, *Gr. Gram.*[3] 1.553; Ros, *Metabole* 137-138. Reiske emends the τοῦ to τῆς.

[17] A translation preserving the word-order is "It was not for the freedom of the Greeks that these, nor for their own freedom that the Greeks, withstood the Mede, but the ones for the subjection of the Greeks to themselves and not to him <= the Mede>, and the others for a change of master,

not more unwise, but more wise for evil." — Hobbes brings out the paronomasia by translating "not for one less wise, but for one worse wise." Others:
"not less shrewd but more shrewish." The sentence is analyzed by K.J. Dover,
"Thucydides," (*G&R*, Survey No. 7 [1973]) 11.

[18] The adjective κατακορής, which Dionysius uses substantively, has
various meanings (LSJ), "satiated, violent, immoderate, wearisome." Roberts
in his edition of "On the Sublime" (p. 201) translates it as "insatiable." If
Dionysius has in mind the frequent use of singular for plural, one may note
that this practice was common in all writers from Herodotus to Demosthenes:
see Kühner-Gerth, *Gr. Gram.*[3] 1.14, where this example is cited. But in this
speech of Hermocrates, he changes not only from "the Syracusans" and "the
Athenians" to "the Syracusan" and "the Athenian," but also from ἡμεῖς
(76.2 and 77.2) to ἐμός. Dionysius himself lapses into the deplored Gorgianic
style: ἐκ τοῦ περὶ προσώπων λόγου εἰς τὸ τοῦ λέγοντος πρόσωπον.

[19] This same passage of Thucydides is quoted in *Ep. II ad Amm.* 9.428.
21, where the same objection is made to change of number.

[20] The Thucydidean manuscripts read "will be fighting."

[21] Dionysius does not complete the sentence.

[22] The obscurity of the sentence results in part from ὀλοφυρθείς which
is interpreted as middle (LSJ) or passive (Classen, Dover). See W. Veitch,
Greek Verbs (Oxford 1887) 486, for a discussion of the problem. The
thought seems to be that he would be willing to have his jealousy renewed
by the restoration of Syracuse's prosperity.

[23] For ἐπιφώνημα, see Roberts, *DS* 81. "An ἐπιφώνημα (Dion. Hal.
Thuc. 48 fin.; Theon, *progymnasmata*, Spengel ii.91) is especially a comment, summing up details in a single pithy phrase": D.A. Russell, *'Longinus'
On the Sublime* (Oxford 1964) 77. See also D.M. Schenkeveld, *Studies in
Demetrius on Style* (Amsterdam 1964) 127-128. Dionysius probably ob-
jected to the much-used λόγῳ μέν ... ἔργῳ δέ, as well as to the tautology
in σῴζοι ... σωτηρίαν. J.D. Denniston (*Greek Prose Style*[2] [Oxford 1960]
13) also complains that Thucydides "drags in the λόγος ἔργον contrast in
season and out of season." A.M. Parry in an unpublished doctoral dissertation, "Logos and Ergon in Thucydides" (Summary in *HSCP* 63 [1958] 522-
523) maintains that Thucydides operates with a fundamental antithesis
between the rational faculty λόγος and the external world of actuality ἔργον;
cf. supra on chap. 21.5.

[24] Dionysius reads ἑαυτοῦ where Hude reports that the Thucydidean
manuscripts have αὐτοῦ. The Oxford text reads αὐτοῦ.

Commentary on Chapter 49

[1] For the "necessary virtues," see supra on chap. 22.8.

[2] The word ἀνακολούθητος is found in Greek only here. Krüger emends

to ἀνακόλυθα; so also LSJ. G. Ottervik (*Koordination inkonzinner Glieder in der attischen Prosa* [Lund 1943] 238-239) concludes that Thucydides had the most numerous and harshest inconcinnities of all Attic prose writers. He finds four hundred examples, or more than one example for every two pages of text. Examples of unlike elements combined in the same relationship are πολλῷ θορύβῳ καὶ πεφοβημένοι ... παρεσκευάζοντο (III.77.1); οἱ ἵπποι ἀπεχωλοῦντο ἐν γῇ ἀποκρότῳ τε καὶ ξυνεχῶς ταλαιπωροῦντες (VII. 27.5).

[3] This sentence is cited by G.F. Abbott (*Thucydides* [London 1925] 225) as evidence that Dionysius thought that the language which Thucydides used, in the speeches at least, is such as no Greek could have spoken. He quotes from G.B. Grundy's *Thucydides and the History of his Age* (London 1911) 52, where a great scholar is reported to have said, "Thucydides' Greek is at best good Thracian." This statement drew sharp criticism from B.L. Gildersleeve in his review of Grundy's book (*AJP* 33 [1912] 238-240), from which I quote one sentence: "A trifle old-fashioned may have been the Greek spoken in the house of Oloros, but it was not Thracian; nay, rather than subscribe to the notion that Thucydides' style is due to the imperfect mastery of his instrument, I should accept the doctrine of that pedantic creature, Dionysios, and consider him perversely anti-grammatical." – The sentence is also quoted by P. Moraux ("Thucydide et la rhétorique," *LEC* 22 [1954] 23 n. 61) at the conclusion of an article in which he maintains that the exposition of the arguments in the speeches of Cleon and Diodotus (III.37-48) accords perfectly with the rhetorical structure elaborated in the Aristotelian school and presumably derived from Thucydides' contemporaries, but that in language the historian made no effort to imitate the contemporary speech of public assemblies ("L'Athénien moyen du cinquième siècle aurait sans doute souscrit au jugement de Denys d'Halicarnasse sur certain passages difficiles des discours"). See also supra on chap. 34.8.

Commentary on Chapter 50

[1] Since Dionysius usually combines words for deliberative and judicial contexts, Pavano (p. 226) suggests that the phrase ⟨οὔτ᾽ εἰς τοὺς δικανικοὺς⟩ has dropped out of the text. See, however, the lengthy study of C. Brandstaetter, "De notionum πολιτικὸς et σοφιστὴς usu rhetorico," *Leip. St.* 15.1 (1893) 131-274, where our passage is discussed on p. 166.

[2] A.D. Leeman (*Orationis Ratio* [Amsterdam 1963] 1.181) believes that Dionysius here alludes to Caecilius of Calacte, who is known to have written two works on historiography. See also Leeman's article, "Le genre et le style historique à Rome," *REL* 33 (1955) 198. The use of the word σοφιστὴς in Dionysius is discussed by C. Brandstaetter, *Leip. St.* 15.1 (1893) 233-235.

[3] For μεγαλοπρέπεια, see supra on chap. 23.24.

[4] For σεμνολογία, see supra on chap. 23.23.

⁵ The noun κατάπληξις does not seem to occur elsewhere in Dionysius, although the adjective καταπληκτικός is found in *De Lys.* 13.23.6, where the style of Lysias is said to lack grandeur and spirit. The adjective is paired with θαυμαστός. Normally, the noun means "stupor, amazement, astonishment," but it is found in Polybius 3.90.14 in the sense of *admiratio* (Stephanus), "Bewunderung" (Mauersberger), "awe" (Paton).

⁶For περιττός, see supra on chap. 28.1. This sentence is translated in A.D. Leeman, *Orationis Ratio* (Amsterdam 1963) 2.435 n. 75. Leeman (1.181) comments on the striking resemblance of this description to the characteristics of Sallust's style.

⁷ The same phrase in *De Comp.* 25.131.15 is translated by W.R. Roberts as "general culture." For recent studies of ἐγκύκλιος παιδεία, see L.M. de Rijk, " Ἐγκύκλιος παιδεία: A Study of its Original Meaning," *Vivarium* 3 (1965) 24-93; M.L. Clarke, *Higher Education in the Ancient World* (London 1971); and S.F. Bonner, *JRS* 63 (1973) 269. In his opening chapter, Clarke explains that after the age of fourteen the students underwent a general education of three years for which the Greeks used the term ἐγκύκλιος παιδεία and the Romans, who took over Greek ideas of education with very little change, *liberales artes*. The encyclic or liberal arts were seven in number: grammar, rhetoric, dialectic, arithmetic, music, geometry and astronomy. Schools such as the Academy refused to accept anyone who had not studied the ἐγκύκλια μαθήματα. U. von Wilamowitz-Möllendorff (*Greek Historical Writing* [Oxford 1908] 15) states, "At latest in the school of Posidonius— and I think a little earlier–the so-called ἐγκύκλιος παιδεία, or 'universal instruction,' was formed into a system which has continued to our own Universities in the form of 'the seven liberal arts.' The study of history has no place in it."

⁸In effect, Dionysius says that obscurity and eccentricity are not virtues except in the eyes of literary coteries.

⁹The lacuna in the text is unfortunate, for Dionysius presumably summarized here the position of those with whom he disagreed about Thucydides' language. This incomplete sentence is frequently cited by those, like Poppo, who believe that Dionysius was mistaken in regarding Thucydides' diction as being at variance with the speech of his day; see W. Schmid, *Geschichte der griechischen Literatur* 7.1.5 (Munich 1948) 190 n. 9.

¹⁰So Cicero says (*Or.* 30-31, *Brutus* 287) that Thucydides should be imitated only for the writing of history, not for oratory.

Commentary on Chapter 51

¹Or, "the world we live in," the translation of the phrase in LSJ.

²Or, treating ἔνια as adv. acc., the translation would be: "without occasional recourse to a grammatical commentary." This reference to a grammatical commentary is combined with the evidence of *Pap. Oxy.* 853

and *Pap. Rainer* 29247 (= R.A. Pack, *The Greek and Latin Literary Texts from Graeco-Roman Egypt*[2] [Ann Arbor 1965] nos. 1536 and 1535) by Luschnat (*Philol.* 98 [1954] 14-58, esp. 22-31) to show that there were in existence Alexandrian commentaries on Thucydides. Cf., more recently, Luschnat, *Thukydides* 1312. See also J.G.A. Ros, *Metabole* 66; and supra on chap. 17.1.

[3] Roberts (*DHTLL* 41 n. 2) comments on this passage, "how many out-of-the-way pieces of literary history we owe to Dionysius." R.C. Jebb in his study of the style of *The Attic Orators* 1 (London 1876) 88-89, states, "Dionysios mentions him (Andokides) only twice; once, where he remarks that Thucydides used a peculiar dialect, which is not employed by 'Andokides, Antiphon, or Lysias' (*De Thuc.* 51); again, when he says that Lysias is the standard for contemporary Attic, 'as may be judged from the speeches of Andokides, Kritias and many others' (*De Lys.* 2). Both these notices recognize Andokides as an authority for the idiom of his day; and it is evident that he had a philological interest for the critic." Similarly, a second notice in Jebb about Antiphon reads (28), "But in Antiphon, as in Thucydides, the haughty, careless freedom of the old style is shown oftener in the employment of the new or unusual words or phrases. The orator could not, indeed, go so far as the historian, who is expressly censured on this score by his Greek critic. Dionysios speaks of τὸ κατάγλωσσον τῆς λέξεως καὶ ξένον in Thucydides (*De Thuc.* c.53), and remarks (*ib.* 51) that it was not a general fashion of the time, but a characteristic distinctive of him." The similarities between Antiphon and Thucydides, both regarded as exponents of the austere style, and both remarkable for ἀκριβολογία ("accuracy of expression"), are studied in the Münden programm of A. Nieschke, *De Thucydide Antiphontis discipulo et Homeri imitatore* (1885) 25ff., and, more recently, by J.H. Finley, *HSCP* 50 (1939) 62-84. However, whereas Antiphon exhibits antithesis strongly reinforced by symmetry of structure (σύνθεσις ἐναρμόνιος), Thucydides often seems to go out of his way to avoid any such tendency.

[4] W.R. Roberts ("The Greek Words for Style," *CR* 15 [1901] 251) has collected the examples of ἑρμηνεία in Dionysius' works, showing that the term is applied to ὁ λεκτικὸς τόπος as opposed to ὁ πραγματικὸς τόπος. D. M. Schenkeveld (*Studies in Demetrius on Style* [Amsterdam 1964] 67) also discusses the meaning of the word.

[5] This conclusion of Dionysius that Thucydides invented his extraordinary language from an affected desire to differ from other writers will satisfy few today.

[6] The verb ταμιεύω (lit. "to act as treasurer," metaph.: "to manage, exercise control over") is used of discourse "to be sparing, restrained." See the examples in van Hook, *Terminology* 33.

[7] For ἀπειροκάλως, see supra on chap. 46.11.

[8] The words μέτρος and καιρός are also combined by Dionysius in *Ep. ad Pomp.* 228.13. I adopt the translation of Roberts (*DHTLL* 99).

⁹The adjective αὐχμηρός (lit. "dry, without rain") is used metaphorically in the sense "rough, unkempt, squalid" (esp. of hair). In the rhetorical writers, the meaning is "jejune, spare, meager" (Latin *horridus*). A synonym is ῥυπαρός "dirty, sordid": 'Longinus' 43.5. See Roberts, *DHTLL* 186; Geigenmüller, *Quaestiones* 112; van Hook, *Terminology* 20; Lockwood, *CQ* 31 (1937) 196.

¹⁰Ernesti (*Lexicon* 275) cites this passage as an example where ποιητικόν must be translated *elaboratum, arte factum*. Geigenmüller, who has collected all of the passages in Dionysius where this word is used, disagrees (*Quaestiones* 103), translating "dicterisch." Roberts' treatment of the word (*DHTLL* 202; *DS* 299; *DHLC* 318) is inconclusive. See also supra on chap. 24.7.

¹¹For the many examples of συμμετρία ("moderation, due proportion") and σύμμετρος in Dionysius, see Geigenmüller, *Quaestiones* 70. Of interest is *On the Sublime* 33.1, where the author contrasts τὸ σύμμετρον with μέγεθος, "grandeur," and speaks of the former almost with contempt, advocating grandeur at the cost of flaws. For συμμετρία, see also Roberts *DS* 302, *DHLC* 324.

Commentary on Chapter 52

¹H.M. Hubbell (*The Influence of Isocrates on Cicero, Dionysius, and Aristides* [New Haven 1913] 41) states that this chapter is aimed at the school of Atticists that Cicero attacked. Lysias and Thucydides were the authors whom this school proposed to imitate. A.D. Leeman (*Orationis Ratio* 1 [Amsterdam 1963] 159-163) concludes that the "Thucydideans," who imitated Thucydides excessively, included C. Asinius Pollio and C. Sallustius Crispus. A.E. Douglas (*CQ* 49 [1955] 241-247; *Cicero's Brutus* [Oxford 1966] xiii) maintains that the difference between rhetorical schools has been greatly exaggerated by modern scholarship.

²Dionysius throughout refers to himself in the plural as a modest form of statement. Cf. Smyth, *Greek Grammar* 1008, and Kühner-Gerth, *Gr. Gram.*³ 1.83. Roberts (*DHTLL* 39) comments that Dionysius is "in the habit of making use <of the first person pronoun> when he wishes to lay stress upon his own originality."

³LSJ translates συκοφαντεῖν "to criticize in a pettifogging way," a sense derived from its ordinary meaning of "to make a false, calumnious charge."

⁴Roberts (*DHTLL* 164), citing A. Kiessling, *RM* 23 (1868) 254, translates the similar phrase τῶν ἠθῶν ἕνεκα καὶ τῶν λόγων in *Ep. ad Amm.* 1.257.16 "on account of his high personal qualities and his literary merits."

⁵H. Richards (*CR* 19 [1905] 254) wishes to emend to the future tenses παράξομεν καὶ παρεξόμεθα.

⁶Servile imitations of the speeches of the great orators circulated all too freely in the Hellenistic world and brought no little profit to those who

compiled them: see S.F. Bonner, *LTDH* 10-11. Much of Dionysius' work was concerned with the establishment of lists of genuine and spurious speeches.

[7] Dionysius' conclusions here are the same as in *De Dem.* 10, namely, that Thucydides had a tendency to obscurity as contrasted with the intelligibility of Demosthenes. A translation of chapter 10 is published by D.A. Russell, *ALC* 313.

[8] In the *Ep. ad Pomp.* chap. 5, Dionysius compares the style of Philistus of Syracuse, who wrote a history of Sicily, with that of Thucydides. Cicero characterized Philistus as "almost a miniature Thucydides" (*Ep. ad Quint. Fr.* 2.13.4). The influence of Thucydides on Philistus is studied by R. Zoepffel, *Untersuchungen zum Geschichtswerk des Philistos von Syrakus* (Diss. Freiburg 1965), with relevant passages from Dionysius discussed on pp. 56-62. See the summary of Zoepffel's work by Luschnat, *Thukydides* 1289-1291. Dionysius referred to Philistus as "wanting in variety" (ὁμοειδής), and the impression from a large fragment of his περὶ Σικελίας (events of the year 426), found in a Florentine papyrus (G. Coppola, *RFIC* 58 [1930] 449-466), is that his style was uniform and monotonous.

[9] The same series of four adjectives is used in *Ep. II ad Amm.* 2, where the word γλωσσηματικήν is spelled in the manuscripts with double tau.

[10] For Dionysius' rare use of the word hyperbaton, see supra on chap. 31.9.

[11] I give the translation of LSJ for ἐξ ἀποκοπῆς in this passage. So also Roberts, *DS* 268. I suspect, however, that the meaning is rather "by the suppression <of words necessary to complete the meaning>."

[12] The word schematismos, "construction," is studied by Roberts, *DHTLL* 207, and W.G. Rutherford, *A Chapter in the History of Annotation* (London 1905) 192-193 (= "word-formation") and 311 n. 5 (= "construction").

[13] As Geigenmüller (*Quaestiones* 24-25) notes, everything which seems to Dionysius to be a defect in Thucydides, is comprehended by the word ἀσάφεια, "obscurity." Cf. supra on chap. 24.66.

Commentary on Chapter 53

[1] In the final three chapters of the treatise, Thucydides' influence on Demosthenes is illustrated by several passages of the orator's work. Dionysius' conclusions here are similar to those in the earlier *De Dem.* chap. 10. Both are trying to vary normal usage and achieve special effects. But there is a difference in Thucydides' frequent tendency to obscurity as contrasted with the intelligibility of Demosthenes which manages also to give the impression of vigor (δεινότης). The practical purpose of "imitation" (μίμησις) dominates the treatise, and Dionysius holds up Demosthenes as a model, pointing out that Demosthenes in his turn had imitated Thucydides. The

theory of Dionysius is that Demosthenes consciously combined all the per-
fections of his predecessors, choosing the terseness and "pathos" of Thucydides, the grace and "ethos" of Lysias, the harmony and skilful arrangement
of material of Isocrates, and working them up into a mixed style, which
embraced all these virtues.

[2] A.S. Anastassiou ("Eine σύγκρισις von Demosthenes und Thukydides,"
Charis K.I. Vourveris [Athens 1964] 303) believes that the comparison of
Thucydides and Demosthenes, found also in the *Vita* of Thucydides which
bears the name of Marcellinus (56), can be traced to Caecilius. On συγκρίσεις
in general, see the long article of F. Focke, *Hermes* 58 (1923) 327-368, 465.
Focke demonstrates that the σύγκρισις was a common rhetorical exercise
(just as it is today a regular form of examination question) and rules for it
are to be found in the *rhetores*, especially Theon and Hermogenes.

[3] For the word systrophe, see Roberts, *DS* 305, and D. Hagedorn, *Zur
Ideenlehre des Hermogenes* (Göttingen 1964) 55. It is used for the twisting
of yarn and in its literal meaning might be applied to any squeezing and
compacting process. On the term see J.E. Sandys' edition of Cicero *Or.* 20.
The quality of συστροφή, which Dionysius ascribes to Thucydides and
Demosthenes, is found to be lacking in Isocrates (*De Dem.* 18). For the
translation "concentration," see Roberts, *DS* 305. R.W. Emerson (in
"Eloquence," *Society and Solitude* [Boston 1884] 89) writes, "Put the argument into a concrete shape, into an image,—some hard phrase, *round and
solid* as a *ball*, which they can see and handle and carry home with them,—
and the cause is half won."

[4] Dionysius says that τόνος "intensity, energy" was a virtue in which
Thucydides and Demosthenes excelled Lysias and Isocrates: Geigenmüller,
Quaestiones 64. See supra on chap. 23.25. Russell (*ALC* 313) renders the
word as "tension."

[5] τὸ πικρόν (lit. "sharp, pungent" of taste) is frequent in Dionysius
for a style having "pungency, incisiveness, sting." See Geigenmüller, *Quaestiones* 64-65; van Hook, *Terminology* 28.

[6] The MSS. M and P read στριφνόν, which is adopted by Usener-Radermacher, whereas the *editio princeps* of F. Sylburg (1586), followed by
Rieske, shows στρυφνόν. The same variants are to be found in *De Comp.*
22.108.4. The adjective στριφνός (lit. "firm, hard, solid") may be taken to
refer "to the *close texture* of the language of Thucydides": Roberts, *DHTLL*
205. Στρυφνός (lit. "bitter, astringent" as used of sour fruit) is translated
by R.C. Jebb, *Att. Or.* 1.35 as "his biting flavour, his sting." The latter
form seems to be preferred for our passage by Roberts and van Hook, *Terminology* 28-29.

[7] For δεινότης, see supra on chap. 27.4.

[8] Adopting the translation of LSJ for τὸ κατάγλωσσον. J.D. Denniston
(*Greek Literary Criticism* [London 1924] 158) translates, "the recondite side
of Thucydides' style." To judge from Geigenmüller, *Quaestiones* 103, this is

the only occurrence of the word in Dionysius. It is not found in the glossaries of R. Roberts.

⁹The views of Greek and Roman rhetoricians on the nature and function of μεταβολή have been collected by J.G.A. Ros, *Die Metabole (Variatio) als Stilprinzip des Thukydides* (Paderborn 1938). Ros defines the term as a device to avoid repeating at short intervals the same word, expression, construction or form of sentence. His book is devoted to a detailed classification, with copious examples under seven main headings (changed forms of the same word; variations of similar words; variations of different types of words; the *constructio ad sententiam*; variation in gender, number and case of nouns; variation in person, voice, tense and mood of verbs; variation of construction), of the forms of variation found in Thucydides. Ros concludes that while the "Gorgianism" of Thucydides is only the style of his period, the wide use of μεταβολή is his own. He demonstrates by sheer wealth of examples that *variatio* "muss ihm vielmehr in Fleisch und Blut übergegangen und gewissermassen zur zweiten Natur geworden sein" (p. 457). J.H. Finley (*AJP* 61 [1940] 99-102, with references to his earlier studies) has criticized this contention, comparing variations in the style of the sophist Antiphon. But although they are found, one must hunt for them. Nowhere do they occur at the rate of almost one per line. P. Huart ("Le vocabulaire de l'analyse psychologique dans l'oeuvre de Thucydide" [*Études et Commentaires* 69 (1968)] 20 n. 2) questions Ros' premise that *variatio* was used "pour donner plus d'agrément au style" (pp.96-97), concluding rather, "ce n'est pas l'agrément du style, mais la rigueur."

¹⁰The noun ποικιλία and the verb ποικίλλειν (lit. "to embroider, to work in various colors") is used for "decoration, variety" of style. See van Hook, *Terminology* 36. A literary composition is like a woven cloth whose texture may be thin, fine and delicate, or tangled and intricate. The quest for ποικιλία among Greek authors is a neglected subject. Students of Roman literature observe that ποικιλία in Latin seems to be distinctly due to Cicero, or, in any case, common as an element of style from Cicero on: G.L. Hendrickson *AJP* 16 (1895) 92. A. Gudeman (*P. Cornelii Taciti Dialogus de Oratoribus* [Boston 1894] 48) says that the dread of repeating the same word "is a modern stylistic sentimentality, quite foreign to the ancients." B.L. Gildersleeve (*AJP* 29 [1908] 120) observes that Pindar "does not hesitate to repeat himself even within a small compass." Quintilian (10.1.13-15) is careful to warn the beginner against change for the sake of change. E. Drerup (*Isocratis Opera Omnia* 1 [Leipzig 1906] lxxvi-lxxx) lists examples of *verba brevi intervallo repetita* in Isocrates, of whom J.E. Sandys in his edition of the *Panegyricus* (81) earlier said, "Here, and occasionally elsewhere, he <Isocrates> has the good sense to allow a repetition to stand unaltered." L. Campbell (*Sophocles* 1² [Oxford 1879] 83-85) studies the phenomenon in Sophocles. Three of the commentators cited in this paragraph warn the modern writer, trained to seek ποικιλία, to follow the maxim of Pascal (*Pensées* 1.10): "Quand dans un discours on trouve des mots répétés, et qu'essayant de les corriger, on les trouve si propres qu'on gâterait le discours,

il les faut laisser." – The antithesis to ποικιλία is παλιλλογία. In the first
part of his *Metabole*, Ros uses ποικιλία as synonymous with μεταβολή.

[11]For νόημα, see supra on chap. 24.43.

[12] The Ancients "considered that in the Figures lay some magic power
to enhance the beauty and sublimity of either poetry or prose. The orator
in particular set great store by them, and no scheme of rhetorical training
was regarded as complete without an exhaustive survey of the many Figures
which the ingenuity of rhetoricians had discovered or devised": J.F. D'Alton,
Roman Literary Theory and Criticism (London 1931) 106. Quintilian
devoted book 4 to σχήματα. The best Greek writing on the subject is the
famous chapter (16) of "Longinus." In the *Rhetorica ad Herennium*,
4.13.18-34.46, the author treats Figures of Diction; in sections 35.47-55.69,
Figures of Thought. He presents an elaborate terminology with many terms
peculiar to himself. See also supra on chap. 37.13.

[13] For the meaning, see Roberts, *DHTLL* 135.

Commentary on Chapter 54

[1]The two types are δικανικοί (forensic speeches) and δημηγορικοί
(public speeches, parliamentary orations, or harangues). See supra on chap.
23.36. In *Ep. ad Amm.* 4.260.16, Dionysius says that this oration *On the
Navy Boards* (14) was Demosthenes' first public speech.

[2]Dionysius reads πράττητε, where the Demosthenic manuscripts have
πράττηται: "if what we expect comes to pass."

[3]For the perfect of ἐξαλλάττω, used in the sense of "uncommon,
artificial" (lit. "is removed from"), see Roberts *DHTLL* 191. The phrase
τὸ ἐξαλλάττειν ἐκ τοῦ συνήθους (*De Dem.* 10.148.18) is translated by D.A.
Russell (*ALC* 313) as "to vary normal usage."

[4]The words τὰ δέοντα, "what was required," are omitted in the Demosthenic manuscripts.

[5] In the lengthy exhibit of the uses of περιττός (lit. "beyond the regular number") in Dionysius, Geigenmüller (*Quaestiones* 100-101) notes
that, although the word is occasionally used in the sense of "far-fetched,"
generally it characterizes "grand diction:" *quod communem modum excedit
et admirationem efficit.* Cf. Roberts, *DHTLL* 201; *DHLC* 316 ("extraordinary, richly wrought, exceedingly good, unsurpassed;" Latin *excellens*). D.A.
Russell in his commentary on 'Longinus' 2.3 writes, "περιττός–which can
mean 'extraordinary' or 'unwonted' as well as 'odd' in the arithmetical sense–
is often coupled with a second adjective which determines its meaning."

[6]The reference is to the Peace of Philocrates in 346 B.C.

[7] Translating the text of Dionysius. Some Demosthenic manuscripts
and most editors add ᾖ at the end of the sentence. J.H. Vince in the Loeb
edition follows A. Spengel (*Sitzungsberichte der k.b. Akademie der Wissen-*

schaften zu München 2.2 [1887] 301) in making δέδοικα ... ἀληθές a parenthesis and treats the next sentence as an anacoluthon.

⁸The text of the Dionysian MSS. for this passage of Demosthenes (9. 13) is unintelligible. Dionysius quotes this particular sentence three times. The text in *De Dem.* 9 (146.10) is a paraphrase. In *De Isae.* 13 (110.14), the reading accords with the majority of the Demosthenic manuscripts, and it may be assumed that Dionysius had the latter text before him. However, the text adopted by most editors is that of S: it is defended by J.E. Sandys in his critical edition.

⁹μνησθείς is a participle of coincident action. Cf. B.L. Gildersleeve, *Syntax of Classical Greek* 1.140-144.

¹⁰Usener's reading of ἤ makes no sense to me. M reads εἰ; P εἰς. Editors of Demosthens read εἰ (Dindorf, Blass) or omit it (Butcher, Mathieu, Goodwin).

Commentary on Chapter 55

¹For δεινότης, see supra on chap. 27.4.

²ἰσχύς, originally "strength of body," seems to occur only here in the *De Thuc.* The stylistic quality (Latin *vires*) is attributed to Demosthenes (*De Dem.* 21.176.2); but in the summary of Platonic faults at the close of chap. 29 of the same treatise, it is found to be lacking in the philosopher.

³In the battleground of the rhetorical schools over what models were to be recommended to students of forensic oratory, Dionysius takes a middle view, refusing to join either those who have nothing but praise for Thucydides or those who find no place for him within their rhetorical scheme; see S.F. Bonner, *LTDH* 83. It is important to bear in mind that "imitation" was the regular part of training in the schools. The *Rhetorica ad Herennium* 1.2.3 says that oratorical excellence depends on three things, the study of rhetoric, imitation, and practice: see the lengthy note with bibliography in H. Caplan's Loeb edition on this line. Dionysius (*De Din.* 8) says that there were perverse imitators of Thucydides who aped his eccentricities rather than his true excellences. Such imitators are also attested in Cicero *Orat.* 9.32. Imitation in general was defined by Dionysius as a "copying of models with the help of certain principles": *De imit.* A.III.28 (= 200.21 [Us.-Rad.]). He continues by describing the process as an "activity of the soul inspired by the spectacle of the seemingly beautiful." Although Dionysius' full teaching on the subject of imitation has unhappily been lost, these two quotations combined with chapter 55 leave no doubt but that his basic and guiding principle was the copying of the merits and not the defects of the prose model. This idea is implicit in all his judgments, which are made with the object of distinguishing what should be imitated and what avoided in each writer. D.A. Russell (*Plutarch* [London 1972] 20-21) has expressed the matter well: "Dionysius rejected all post-Attic prose as bizarre, eccentric or

disorganized; his remedy was a better use of the resources of the Attic classics, and especially the orators. This was archaism, but a positive and constructive archaism, which sought to enrich rather than restrict by prescribing models to imitate. It is quite distinct from the later archaism of the second-century Atticists, who compiled lists of words authorized by classical usage, and tried to confine themselves within these limits. Dionysius' work on word arrangement makes it particularly clear what his essential aims were: he wanted to exploit the versatility and vigour he found in the classics, so as to accommodate the intellectual excitement of pathos and rhetoric, which sophisticated readers now needed, in a disciplined but varied prose."

APPENDIX

APPENDIX I

Oxyrhynchus Papyri 6 (London 1908) No. 853. Commentary on Thucydides II. Translation of Grenfell and Hunt.

Dionysius of Halicarnassus in his treatise on Thucydides blames Thucydides on a few grounds, and discusses three chief points, first that he has not fixed his dates by archons and Olympiads, like other historians, but according to a system of his own by summers and winters; secondly that he has disturbed and divided the narrative and breaks up the events, not completing his accounts of the several incidents, but turning from one subject to another before he has finished with it; and thirdly that although he declares, as the result of his own elaborate examination, the true cause of the war to be this, that it was precaution against the power of the Athenians which induced the Lacedaemonians to make war on them, not really the Corcyrean or Potidaean affairs or the causes generally alleged, nevertheless he does not begin at the point which he has chosen and start with the events which led to the growth of Athens after the Persian war, but reverts to the commonly accepted causes. Such is Dionysius' view; but in opposition to this rash criticism one might reasonably retort that ... For the system of dating by archons and Olympiads had not yet come into common use ... (it was impossible) to relate Plataean affairs from first to last, and then go back to describe all the invasions of the Peloponnesians one after the other, and Corcyrean affairs continuously, differing as they did in date; for he would have thrown everything into confusion, or turned back again to periods which he had treated, in a fashion both unsuitable and unreasonable. For he was not dealing with a single subject or events at one time or one place, but with many subjects in many places and at many periods. Moreover, even if he had dated by archons, he would still have been obliged to divide the events, for these occurred some under one archon, some under another; it is when a person is only writing about a single subject that his narrative is continuous throughout. Hence Dionysius contradicts himself; for even if Thucydides ought to have dated by the archons, as he asserts, he would have been equally obliged to divide events according to the archons. If, however, the events are connected and the chronology offers no obstacle, Thucydides' narrative is continuous, as for instance ... in the seventh book ... As for the charge that Thucydides has not made the beginning of his history start with the growth of the Athenians, which he asserts was the truer cause of the war, in the first place it must be remarked that it was not his intention, after setting out to write a history of the Peloponnesian war, to introduce by way of a supplement several other wars since the Persian war itself, which may almost be regarded as the origin of the growth of Athens; for that would have lain altogether outside his subject. Secondly it must be remembered that it is the duty of every historian to describe accurately first of all the obvious and commonly alleged causes of events, and if he suspects the existence of any more obscure reasons (to add these afterwards ...).

BIBLIOGRAPHY OF DIONYSIUS,
DE THUCYDIDE[1]

A.A. Anastassiou, "Eine synkrisis von Demosthenes und Thukydides bei Dionysios von Halikarnass," *Charis K.I. Vouveris* (Athens 1964) 297-304.

J.W.H. Atkins, *Literary Criticism in Antiquity* 2 (Cambridge 1934) 104-136.

F. Blass, *Attische Beredsamkeit* 1² (Leipzig 1887) 208-244.

S.F. Bonner, *The Literary Treatises of Dionysius of Halicarnassus* (Cambridge 1939), esp. chap. V.

J.F. D'Alton, *Roman Literary Theory and Criticism* (London 1931).

J.D. Denniston, *Greek Literary Criticism* (London 1924) 157-158 (trans. of chap. 53).

M. Egger, *Denys d'Halicarnasse* (Paris 1902).

J. Ehlert, *De verborum copia Thucydidea quaestiones selectae* (Diss. Berlin 1910).

A. Espinosa, "Algunos rasgos de estilo en Tucidides," *Boletin del Inst. de Estudios helenicos.* Barcelona, Fac. de Filosofia 2.1 (1968) 51-56.

K. Fuhr, "Duo bei Dionys von Halikarnass," *BPhW* 36 (1916) 1255-1256 (text of *De Thuc.* 3.328.23).

P. Geigenmüller, *Quaestiones Dionysianae de vocabulis artis criticae* (Diss. Leipzig 1908).

G.M.A. Grube, "Dionysius of Halicarnassus on Thucydides," *Phoenix* 4 (1950) 95-100.

G.M.A. Grube, *The Greek and Roman Critics* (London 1965) esp. 226-230.

G.M.A. Grube, "Greek Historians and Greek Critics," *Phoenix* 28 (1974) esp. 78-80.

F. Halbfas, *Theorie und Praxis in der Geschichtsschreibung bei Dionys von Halikarnass* (Diss. Münster 1910).

C.E. Hesse, *Dionysii Halicarnassensis de Thucydide judicia examinantur* (Progr. Leipzig 1877).

---

[1] For general bibliography of the *Scripta Rhetorica*, see W. Rhys Roberts, *The Three Literary Letters* (Cambridge 1901) 209-219.

H.M. Hubbell, *The Influence of Isocrates on Cicero, Dionysius and Aristides*
(Diss. Yale Univ. New Haven 1913) 41-53.

W. John, *De veterum rhetorum studiis Thucydideis quaestiones selectae*
(Diss. Griefswald 1922).

E. Kremer, *Über das rhetorische System des Dionys von Halikarnass* (Diss.
Strassburg 1907).

K.W. Krüger, *Dionysii Halicarnassensis Historiographica* (Halle 1823).

H. Liers, *Die Theorie der Geschichtsschreibung des Dionys von Halikarnass*
(Programm Waldenburg 1886).

J.F. Lockwood, "The Metaphorical Vocabulary of Dionysius of Halicarnassus,"
CQ 31 (1937) 192-203.

M.H. McCall, Jr., *Ancient Rhetorical Theories of Simile and Comparison*
(Cambridge, Mass. 1969) 155-156.

J.G. Meusel, in J.C. Gatterer's *Allgemeine Historische Bibliotheke* 6 (Halle
1768), German translation of *De Thucydide* (*non vidi*).

M. Mille, "Le jugement de Denys d'Halicarnasse sur Thucydide," *Annales de
la Faculté des Lettres de Bordeaux* 1889, 83-101.

G. Pavano, "Dionisio d'Alicarnasso critico di Tucidide," *Acc. della Scienze
di Torino* 68 (1936) 251-259. "Of no value" = H. Bloch, *HSCP* Suppl.
Vol. 1 (1940) 311 n.

G. Pavano, "De Dionysii Halicarnassensis Peri Thoukydidou ad Q. Aelius
Tuberonem epistula quaestiones criticae," *RAL* 13 (1958) 107-124.
This article is reprinted verbatim as an appendix to Pavano's edition
of the *De Thucydide*.

G. Pavano, "De Thucydide Gorgiae imitatore apud Dionysium Halicarnaseum
atque de quisdam Dionysii locis vel supplendis vel restituendis," *Alti.
Accad. di Scienze e Lett. di Palermo* 16 (1955-56) 177-184.

G. Pavano, *Dionisio d'Alicarnasso Saggio su Tucidide* (Palermo 1958).

M. Pehle, *Thucydidis exemplar Dionysianum cum nostrorum codicum memoria confertur* (Diss. Greifswald 1907).

E.F. Poppo, *Thucydidis de bello Peloponnesiaco libri octo*, Pars 1 Prolegomena, Vol. 1 *De Thucydidis historia judicum* (Leipzig 1821).

A.B. Poynton, "Oxford MSS of the 'Opuscula' of Dionysius of Halicarnassus,"
Journal of Philology 28 (1901) 161-185.

J.E. Powell, "The Archetype of Thucydides," *CQ* 32 (1938) 75-79.

L. Radermacher in *RE* s.v. Dionysios 113 (1905) 961-971.

J.J. Reiske, *Dionysii Halicarnassensis opera omnia Graece et Latine.* Vol. 6 (Leipzig 1777) contains the *De Thucydide.* This was the standard edition until that of Usener-Radermacher.

W.R. Roberts, "Dionysius as an Authority for the Text of Thucydides," *CR* 14 (1900) 244-246.

W.R. Roberts, *Dionysius of Halicarnassus: The Three Literary Letters* (Cambridge 1901).

W.R. Roberts, *Demetrius on Style* (Cambridge 1902).

W.R. Roberts, *Dionysius of Halicarnassus: On Literary Composition* (Cambridge 1910).

J.G.A. Ros, *Die Metabole (Variatio) als Stilprinzip des Thukydides* (Nijmegen 1938).

L. Sadée, *De Dionysii Halicarnassensis scriptis rhetoricis quaestiones criticae* (Diss. Strassburg 1878: Published in *Dissertationes philologicae argentoratenses* 2).

D.M. Schenkeveld, *Studies in Demetrius on Style* (Amsterdam 1964).

H.G. Strebel, *Wertung und Wirkung des Thukydideischen Geschichtswerkes in der griechisch-römischen Literatur* (Diss. Munich 1935), esp. 42-50.

H. Usener - L. Radermacher, *Dionysii Halicarnasei Opuscula* 1 (Leipzig 1899).

LaRue van Hook, *The Metaphorical Terminology of Greek Rhetoric and Literary Criticism* (Diss. Chicago 1905).

R. Volkmann, *Die Rhetorik der Griechen und Römer*[2] (Leipzig 1885).

W.Warren, "On Dionysii Halicarnasei de Thucydidis idiomatis epistula," *CR* 16 (1902) 120.

E. Wenzel, "Zur Echtheitsfrage von Thukydides III.84," *Wiener Studien* 81 (1968) 18-27.

J. Wichmann, *Dionysii Halicarnassensis de Thucydide iudicia componuntur et examinantur* (Diss. Halle Sax. 1878).

R. Zoepffel, *Untersuchungen zum Geschichtswerk des Philistos von Syrakus* (Diss. Freiburg 1965) 41-64.

There are occasional references to the following typewritten manuscript (*non vidi*): P. Costil, *L'esthétique littéraire de Denys d'Halicarnasse* (Thèse Paris 1951).

INDICES

PASSAGES FROM THUCYDIDES QUOTED IN *DE THUCYDIDE*

References for Dionysius are to the chapter, page and line numbers of the Usener-Radermacher edition.

I.1.1-3	20.354.23-355.12	III.82.5	30.376.2
I.1.3-2.2	25.364.19	III.82.6	31.376.22
I.6.5	19.354.10	III.82.7	31.377.19
I.21.1-23.5	20.355.12-357.20	III.82.8-83.4	31.379.19-381.1
I.22.1	41.395.20	III.83.1	31.380.11
I.22.4	7.334.6	IV.34.1	25.365.7
I.23.4-6	10.338.23	IV.38.5	13.344.15
I.24.1	10.339.8	IV.54.2	14.345.9
I.88.1	10.339.17	IV.57.3	14.345.14
I.97.2	11.341.15	V.26.3-6	12.342.12
I.100.1	13.343.17	V.32.1	15.348.5
I.114.3	15.348.9	V.85.1-86.1	37.388.20-389.7
I.118.1-2	10.340.6	V.86.1	37.389.4
I.140.1	42.397.13	V.87.1	37.390.5
II.22.1-2	18.350.25-351.13	V.88.1	38.390.11
II.27.1	15.348.12	V.89.1	38.390.18
II.59.1-2	14.346.7	V.91.1	39.391.21
II.60.1	44.399.9	V.94.1	39.392.9
II.60.2-3	44.400.3	V.95.1	39.392.12
II.60.5	45.400.18	V.102.1	40.392.21
II.60.6	45.401.10	V.103.1-2	40.393.2
II.61.1-2	47.403.21	V.105.1-2	40.394.2
II.61.3-4	47.404.3	V.111.2	41.394.20
II.62.3-5	46.402.7	VI.76.2	48.406.15
II.63.1-2	47.404.12	VI.76.4	48.406.21
II.71.1-4	36.384.7	VI.77.1-2	48.405.2
II.72.1-75.1	36.385.12-388.7	VI.78.1	48.407.5
II.73.1	36.386.18	VI.78.2	48.405.22
II.74.1	36.387.10	VI.78.3	48.407.15
II.75.1	36.388.6	VI.80.3-4	48.406.6
III.81.2-82.1	28.372.16-373.21	VII.69.4-72.1	26.366.12-370.24
III.82.1	28.373.17	VII.70.1	26.366.17
III.82.3	29.374.1	VII.71.1	26.369.3
III.82.4	29.375.8	VII.72.1	26.370.20
III.82.4-5	30.375.22		

REFERENCES TO THUCYDIDES IN *DE THUCYDIDE*

I.3.1	19.354.2	I.138.3	8.334.22
I.5.1	19.354.3	I.140.1-144.4	42.397.13
I.6.3	19.354.7	II.35.1-46.2	18.350.12
I.13.2-3	19.354.12	II.60.1-64.6	43.398.17
I.13.6	19.354.14	II.65.5-10	8.335.2
I.13.6sq	19.354.16	II.83.1-92.7	13.343.11
I.23.1-6	19.353.22	III.2.1-114.4	9.336.16

III.27.1sq	15.347.23	V.84.1-3	37.388.11
III.35.1-50.3	15.347.23	V.84.2-116.4	15.348.1
III.36.1-6	17.350.3	V.104.1	40.393.21
III.36.4-49.1	17.350.8	VI.9.1-14.1	42.397.22
III.37.1-48.2	43.398.20	VI.15.1-5	8.335.5
III.42.1-48.2	43.398.20	VI.20.1-23.3	42.397.22
III.52.3-68.5	15.347.22	VI.76.1-80.5	43.398.22
III.53.1-59.4	42.398.9	VI.82.1-87.5	43.398.23
IV.9.1-23.2	18.351.14	VII.11.1-15.2	42.397.24
IV.15.1-22.3	14.346.15	VII.61.1-64.2	42.398.2
IV.26.1-40.2	18.351.14	VII.69.3-72.1	26.366.10
IV.53.1	14.345.1	VII.77.1-7	42.398.4
IV.104.4-107.3	41.395.14	VII.86.3-5	8.335.4
V.26.1-6	41.395.14		

PASSAGES FROM THUCYDIDES QUOTED BY DIONYSIUS, EXCLUDING THOSE FOUND IN *DE THUCYDIDE*

References for Dionysius are to the volume, page and line numbers of the Usener-Radermacher two-volume edition of the *Opuscula.*

I.1.1-2.2	II.106.18	I.138.3	I.426.3
I.1.3	II.385.21	I.138.3	I.436.15
I.2.1	I.437.9	I.141.1	I.425.13
I.2.2	I.428.6	I.144.2	I.428.1
I.2.2	I.434.19	II.35.1	II.74.11
I.2.6	II.386.6	II.35.2	I.429.10
I.6.2	II.386.7	II.35.2	I.429.15
I.8.1	II.386.4	II.36.4	II.307.24
I.9.2	I.435.12	II.37.1	I.426.6
I.19.1	I.425.10	II.37.2	I.425.13
I.22.4	II.108.11	II.39.4	I.431.17
I.22.4	II.376.21	II.42.1	II.308.6
I.23.1-3	I.214.2	II.42.4	I.436.4
I.23.6	I.427.10	II.44.1	II.306.23
I.24.1	II.19.1	II.97.4	I.430.2
I.40.4	I.425.11	III.4.4	I.425.11
I.41.1	I.426.18	III.57.4	II.31.12
I.52.2	I.425.10	III.82.3-7	I.128.17
I.66.1	I.425.11	III.82.4	I.425.13
I.70.2-3	I.433.21	III.82.4	I.437.16
I.70.3	I.434.7	IV.10.2	I.431.10
I.70.3	I.437.10	IV.10.3	I.429.5
I.71.7	I.433.11	IV.10.3	I.432.3
I.73.1	I.425.13	IV.12.1	I.426.11
I.73.2	I.429.21	IV.27.3	I.425.12
I.90.2	I.430.1	IV.38.1	I.425.11
I.92.1	I.425.12	IV.40.2	I.425.13
I.120.2	I.428.13	IV.63.1	I.425.12
I.120.2	I.428.16	IV.78.3	I.430.6

I V.86.6	I.425.13	VI.35.1	I.432.17
IV.87.1	I.425.11	VI.78.1	I.428.21
IV.117.1	I.425.11	VII.49.1	I.430.1
V.4.2	I.432.21	VIII.64.5	I.430.15
V.17.2	I.425.13	VIII.66.2	I.425.13
V.25.3	I.425.11	VIII.85.2	I.425.13
V.26.3	I.425.11	VIII.87.3	I.425.13
V.32.7	I.425.11	VIII.87.4	I.425.11
VI.24.2	I.430.3		

REFERENCES IN DIONYSIUS TO PASSAGES IN THUCYDIDES, EXCLUDING THOSE FOUND IN THE *DE THUCYDIDE*

I.22.4	I.149.4	II.42.1-4	II.280.2
I.23.2s	II.233.13-18	II.44.4	II.280.14
I.79.2	II.304.9	II.51.5	I.427.3
I.80.1-85.2	II.304.12	II.65.8	I.148.22
I.80.1-85.2	II.343.19	II.97.1-6	II.237.4
I.143.5	I.427.3	VI.2.1-5.6	II.237.5
II.41.5	II.290.2		

INDEX OF GREEK WORDS

References are to the Commentary, save for a few items (indicated by a small p.) in the text of the Introduction.

INDEX OF AUTHORS REFERRED TO

References are by the number of the chapter and notes to each chapter in the Commentary; those in the Introduction are indicated by a small p. and Roman numerals. The names of editors of Thucydides and Dionysius are not included.

[160]

Lamb, W.R.M., 9.11, 16.7, 24.44, 37.2
Laqueur, R., 5.18, 9.25
Lebek, W.-D., 24.4
Leeman, A.D., p.xxix, 7.2, 22.6, 23.24, 50.2, 50.6, 52.1
Lehnert, G., 10.10
Lersch, L., 24.36, 29.3
Leske, P., 24.51
Liers, H., 5.35
Lilja, S., 5.8, 24.49
Linders, T., 23.2
Lindhamer, L., 31.9
Litchfield, H.W., 24.7
Lockwood, J.F., p.xv, 4.2, 23.13, 27.8, 29.15, 34.6, 36.3, 48.15, 51.9
Lossau, M.J., p.xx
Lucas, D.W., 3.5, 5.21, 24.6, 24.34, 24.55, 25.4
Lüdtke, W., 42.4
Luschnat, O., *passim*

MacKay, L.A., 37.13
Maloney, G., 24.32
Marchant, E.C., p.xxxiv, 31.9
Marrou, H.I., p.xxviii
Martin, J., *passim*
Matthes, D., 9.1, 34.3
Mayer, H., 10.1
McBurney, J.H., 24.42
McKeon, R., 25.4
Meiggs, R., 9.8
Meister, C., 24.43, 24.44
Mestwerdt, G., 23.34
Miller, C.W.E., 24.37
Momigliano, A., p.xxii
Moraux, P., 34.8, 49.3
Morris, C.D., p.xxxiv, 31.9
Müller, K.O., p.xxxi, xxxii
Mueri, W., 29.10
Mutschmann, H., 25.2

Neumeister, C., 19.5, 44.3
Nieschke, A., 24.51, 51.3
Nietzki, M., 24.32

Norden, E., p.xxxiv, 24.51, 33.1, 46.11
North, H.F., 24.9, 44.3

Oeltze, O., 24.37
Ottervik, G., 49.2

Paladini, V., p.xxix
Parry, A., p.xxiii, 21.5, 48.23
Pavano, G., p.xviii
Pearson, L., 5.1, 5.15, 9.8, 10.1
Pédech, P., 16.7, 19.2
Pehle, M., p.xvii, 15.9, 41.6
Perrochat, P., 28.5
Perry, B.E., 41.12
Pfeifauf, A., 24.37
Pfeiffer, R., p.xxii
Pisani, V., 24.51
Plöbst, W., 19.2
Pohlenz, M., 44.3
Poppo, E.F., p.xxxiii
Posner, E., 5.20
Powell, J.E., p.xvi, xviii, 26.5, 47.14
Poynton, A.B., 5.10
Prentice, W.K., 16.8
Pritchett, W.K., 5.20, 9.7, 15.6, 23.2, 24.7, 41.9

Quadlbauer, F., 27.5

Rabe, H., 1.8
Rackham, H., 4.2
Radermacher, L., p.xiv, xvii, 2.8, 24.51, 24.52
Radford, R.S., 24.41
Rauchenstein, R., 24.27
Reid, J.S., 23.18
Richards, H., 2.3, 9.6, 52.5
Ries, J., 24.19
Rittelmeyer, F., 24.3, 24.54, 24.56
Rivier, A., 20.9
Roberts, C.H., 10.5
Roberts, W.R., *passim*
Robertson, J.C., 24.47, 24.51
Robins, R.H., 24.24, 24.33
Rohde, E., 5.36